Manhattan

Gil Reavill and Jean Zimmerman
Photography by Kelly Guenther and Poul Hans Lange

COMPASS AMERICAN GUIDES
An imprint of Fodor's Travel Publications

Compass American Guides: Manhattan

Editor: Daniel Mangin
Photo Editor: Jolie Novak
Archival Research: Melanie Marin
Editorial Production: Stacey Kulig

Designer: Siobhan O'Hare
Map Design: David Lindroth, Mark Stroud

Production House: Tien Wah Press, Ltd., Singapore

Cover photo (Times Square): Poul Hans Lange

Fourth Edition
Copyright © 2003 Fodors LLC
Maps copyright © 2003 Fodors LLC

ISBN 0-676-90495-5
ISSN 1539-3267

The details in this book are based on information supplied to us at press time, but changes occur
all the time, and the publisher cannot accept responsibility for facts that become outdated or for
inadvertent errors or omissions.

Compass American Guides, 1745 Broadway, New York, NY 10019
PRINTED IN SINGAPORE
10 9 8 7 6 5 4 3 2 1

For Our Parents

C O N T E N T S

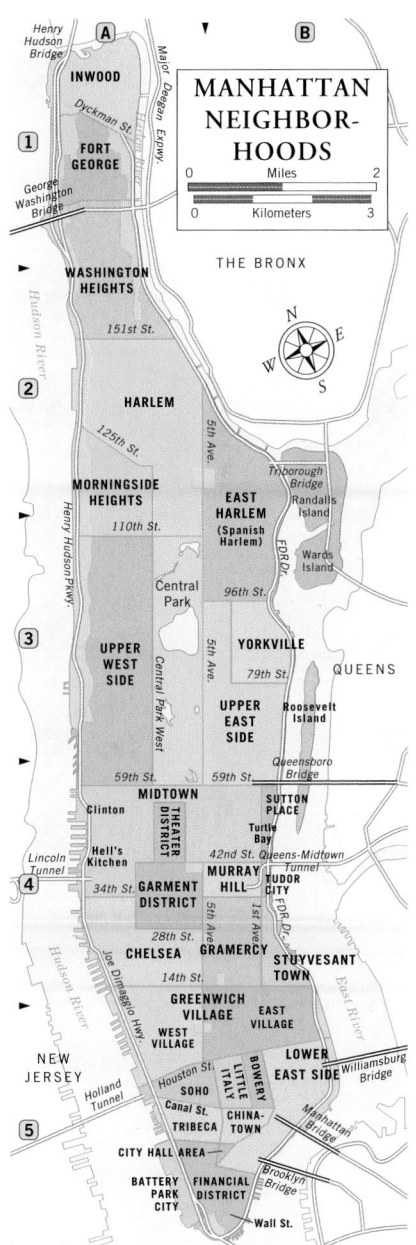

Maps

AUTHORS' ACKNOWLEDGMENTS

Every book is a collaboration, and this one owes a lot to the efforts of a host of people, among them Christopher Burt, Kit Duane, Julia Dillon, and Sarah Hollister, who worked on the original edition. Daniel Mangin helped guide us through an especially difficult revision process. Andy Zimmerman did research and footwork for the new edition and helped make this a better book. And the images of Kelly Guenther, Poul Hans Lange, Michael Yamashita, and other photographers provide a great counterpoint to the outpourings of a very wordy duo.

INTRODUCTION

The island of Manhattan is a little more than 22 square miles in area, narrow and irregular, posted at one of the greatest natural harbors on earth, and surrounded on all sides by great rivers and treacherous tidal straits.

The shape of it often reminds people of a fish. "New York City is made up of five boroughs," states a Depression-era guide, "four of which—Brooklyn, Queens, Richmond, the Bronx—compose like crinkled lily pads about the basking trout of Manhattan." The architect Le Corbusier called the island a "great unfilleted sole spread out on a rock." A more contemporary account suggests that Manhattan in the harbor is "like a smelt in a pan."

New York, New York, is famously uncontainable, a city with a surfeit of names, "so nice they had to name it twice." It has an impressive physical reality, at 41 degrees north latitude, 74 degrees west longitude. But more than any other city in the world—Paris may come close—New York has its own imaginative reality, its place in the collective dream of mankind.

At no time in New York's history did that imaginative reality establish itself more clearly than in the aftermath of the terrorist attack of September 11, 2001. The whole world mourned, and not only for the thousands who died and their grieving families, not only for the twisted hulk of the World Trade Center. It was as though the idea of New York had been assaulted, an idea that appeared, amid the outpouring of sorrow, rage, and pride, to be nearly synonymous with the idea of civilization itself.

And the dream proved stronger than the steel. The city's physical reality was battered, but the idea of New York City emerged from the crucible of those days stronger than ever.

"The only true metropolis" is what the novelist Thomas Mann called New York, but the city wears the mantle lightly. Ask a hundred New Yorkers if their city is "the capital of the world": fifty of them will walk right past you, one will try to talk you out of your wallet, and forty or so will deliver gesticulating, vituperative, arrogantly unassailable opinions, from "It's a Times Square boutique" and "Who cares?" to frothing rants against the United Nations. But at least one respondent will have the true answer: "Where else?"

Human and animal neighbors unwind at a dog run near the Flatiron Building.

New York City sprawls across five boroughs, each with a county-level government: Manhattan, Queens, Brooklyn, the Bronx, and Staten Island (Richmond County). More than eight million residents populate an area of a little more than 300 square miles, and additional millions of commuters flood in and out of the city each day.

Of the five boroughs, Manhattan is the jewel, the trump card, the first among equals. The name is Native American in origin, from the Algonquian word *Manahatn,* which means, depending on which authority you believe, either "the place of hills" or "the place where we all got drunk."

The area's original Algonquin inhabitants considered the ground serviceable but nothing special. They used the place chiefly as a summer resort, withdrawing inland when the winter winds whipped down the Hudson or off the ocean. Their mythology invoked a more particular idea of paradise, which they located somewhere near the modern-day environs of Trenton, New Jersey.

It has been less than four hundred years, really, since Manhattan grew from a windswept oystering station into the most densely populated place in America. On a purely physical level, the transformation has been extraordinary, a testament to the almost insane industry of Manhattanites. The "place of hills" was leveled, graded, plumbed, bricked over, bored into, and erected upon until it resembled the monstrous hive of a race of hyperactive worker bees.

Yet that's only half the story. There was another transformation afoot, one that is harder to place precisely in time and space. As it grew, Manhattan somehow managed to assemble itself from more than just paving stones and granite blocks and steel girders. Dreams, hopes, and ambitions seemed to mark the place.

Dreams of Manhattan have come not only from those who have lived here, but also from those who have only imagined the place. In the opening of his 1927 novel *Amerika,* Franz Kafka described the Statue of Liberty without ever having seen it. Manhattan Island has floated in the world's imagination like a golden fantasy, symbolizing all that is high and fine about the American experience, and much that is terrible.

This book covers the physical reality of Manhattan, the realm that can be reproduced on a map and talked about in terms of places to go and things to do. We also hope to communicate a little of the meta-Manhattan, both good and bad, the ectoplasmic island of people's dreams and the "terrible Jerusalem of the New World," as the journalist H. L. Mencken called it.

Children take a controlled stroll past Union Square diners.

As overpowering as brick-and-stone Manhattan can be, its mythology has the paradoxical effect of grounding it, keeping it human. "My city!" Walt Whitman apostrophized. For all its pomp and circumstance as a cultural capital, as a center for commerce, fashion, the arts, sports, and tourism, it is still possible for an individual to feel possessive toward it.

There is a secret to approaching the borough. Manhattan the Magnificent—the city of Broadway, Fifth Avenue, and the Financial District—is almost too large and overpowering to love. Admire, yes; respect, certainly, with perhaps an occasional shudder of outright astonishment. People can't live on the whole island at once, so they have broken it down into a series of villages, which are more manageable, more livable, and, yes, more lovable than the larger whole. Manhattan is the "global village," in Marshall McLuhan's original sense of a world brought close and made accessible. It is global in its cultural, commercial, and symbolic scope. It is global because of its collection of peoples, gathered from every nation on the globe.

(following pages) Central Park, an escape hatch in the middle of Gotham.

At the same time, Manhattan is a village, or rather, as Alistair Cooke called it, "the greatest collection of villages in the world." The way for a visitor to proceed, then—the way to proceed for anyone who wants to understand this amazing city—is to approach Manhattan the way people who live here do, neighborhood by neighborhood. "We'll have Manhattan," goes a Rodgers and Hart tune, and the way to have it is not all at once, but in small bites.

The great luxury Manhattan extends is its nearly inexhaustible choice. Most cities say, "Here's what we have." Manhattan asks, "What would you like?"

Architecture? The array here is staggering, and not only in terms of stylistic range. The density of the island's construction is such that the proud ship of Manhattan itself has become one great architectural artifact. "Just the fact of too many buildings in too small a space," says the master architect Philip Johnson, "makes it very exciting." As with a handful of other island cities around the world—most notably Hong Kong—watery boundaries prevented Manhattan from building outward. The only option for New Yorkers was to build vertically, and Manhattan soars.

The Greek word for human means "they who look up," and Manhattan rewards those who lift their eyes with inspiring, hubris-enhancing cityscapes—steel-and-stone extravaganzas like the Empire State Building, slick glass boxes like Lever House, hallucinatory terra-cotta confections like Alwyn Court. Throughout the city are marvelous architectural juxtapositions, such as the aristocratic Crown Building, across Fifth Avenue from the arriviste Trump Tower.

Not passionate about architecture? How about dance? For much of the 20th century, New York was the world's premier center for dance. The enthralling dramas of George Balanchine and Jerome Robbins, the boldly modern creations of Martha Graham and Merce Cunningham, and the great political-artistic jetés of Cold War–era Russian defectors such as Mikhail Baryshnikov all unfurled against a New York City backdrop. The parade of superb works continues from troupes like the Mark Morris Dance Group, Ballet Hispanico, the Alvin Ailey American Dance Theater, Dance Theater of Harlem, and the Bill T. Jones/Arnie Zane Dance Company; from offbeat outfits like Eliot Feld's Ballet Tech; and from major institutions like the New York City Ballet and the American Ballet Theatre.

Hungry? How about sausage and peppers in Little Italy, *chow fun* (flat noodles) in Chinatown, or curry in the East Village? Of course, you might choose to nosh on a bagel or a bialy, or you might prefer a power lunch at the Four Seasons.

On and on it goes, the dizzying spread that Manhattan lays out all year—painting and sculpture and photography and antiques, museums and events and historical sites, great restaurants and great shopping and great crowds. You can pick almost any discipline or art form, any pastime or hobby, any human endeavor at all: Manhattan, the gabby, assertive Walt Whitman of cities, will have something to say about it.

The place is so large and varied that the question for any writer approaching it becomes what to leave out. When Ralph Waldo Emerson said over a century ago that "New York is a sucked orange," he was talking about the fact that even back then, Manhattan had been pawed over pretty thoroughly by a long parade of writers and artists. All art is selection, and everyone who has written about the place—and there have been many—has faced some hard choices.

This book includes the essential stops on the tourist trail: museums, shopping districts, entertainment venues. Our impulse has been to slant the portrait toward the human side, the village side. We might give you an exhaustive tour of the Metropolitan Museum of Art (which gets two votes here for being the greatest art museum in the world), but we won't neglect to tell you about art in neighborhood parks and gardens.

To enjoy Manhattan you have to enjoy people of all kinds—people en masse, urban hermits, humans at their grandest, and humans at their weirdest. Here the tapestry is fully unrolled. "When you're tired of London, you're tired of life," said Samuel Johnson, and the same could be said of Manhattan. That brilliant phrasemaker, Anonymous, put it another way: "If you're bored in New York, you're boring."

E. B. White, the *New Yorker* writer and chronicler of New York, offered up this formulation of the three human elements that make up the city's life: There are the commuters—those millions of rushing workers who flood in and out of Manhattan every day—who give the city its velocity. There are the natives, the people who were born here and will die here. They give the city its solidity and permanence. And there are the transplants, the émigrés, the apprentice actors and writers and artists who come to Manhattan in pursuit of the ineffable. They give the city its dreams.

To White's formula we must, of late, add a fourth group—the marooned, the homeless souls who lend the city a tang of despair. They are the most distinctive and visible symbol of the failures of urban living in the United States at the start of a new millennium.

But the decay of the streets has at least stabilized, and New York seems in the throes of rebirth. Crime is at its lowest level since the 1960s; New York now claims to be the safest metropolis in the Western world. It remains at the heart of the global economy, a center of commerce unequaled anywhere, a matrix of international corporations, markets, and communications. The attack on the World Trade Center proved that centrality in a negative way—a blow to New York City was clearly a blow to the prosperity of the United States and the world as a whole.

Manhattan came to prominence on the global and national stage for many reasons. One is simply the location. It lies beside a harbor that seemed to have been designed by some patron saint of ship captains. Another is the good fortune that saw the skies over the city lit by the brilliant dynamo of America's century-long economic boom. Manhattan was simply the right place at the right time.

But today the harbor is less active, and busts are as much a part of the economic reality as booms. So why does Manhattan endure and prosper? We like to think the city's incredible resilience derives from its residents' devotion to a vision of life that is open, egalitarian, and expansive—their insistence on saying "Yes!" to whatever is handed them.

By 1650, when the population was only forty-five hundred, already eighteen languages were spoken in Manhattan. Today, in what sociologists call a "conurbation" of more than twenty million people—encompassing the entire metropolitan New York area, which includes parts of upstate New York, northern New Jersey, Long Island, southern Connecticut, and a sliver of Pennsylvania—more than 160 languages are spoken, with newspapers in two dozen of them. No other place on the planet bursts with such an amazing polyglot.

Though we can't say all 160 of those tongues are heard in this book, we try to emulate the open, expansive vision of Manhattan. "It's a nice place to visit but I wouldn't want to live there," is an oft-repeated formulation about the borough, but, in fact, the more your visit approximates what it's like to live here, the better it will be. This book attempts to give the visitor some sense of what it's like to exist as that anomalous creature, the Manhattanite.

What we want to leave readers with is some echo of Walt Whitman, so they can say along with him, about this place of boiling energy, superb paradox, and staggering hubris, "My city!"

Times Square regulars include the Naked Cowboy (top)
and music fans outside the MTV studios (bottom).

H I S T O R Y

"That's why they call it New York," the *New York Times* quoted a spectator witnessing the demolition of the old Pennsylvania Station in 1963. "Nothing's allowed to grow old here."

That's not entirely true, of course. There are glorious pockets of Manhattan where the past is remarkably well preserved. But to a startling degree, much of the industry that built Manhattan eradicated anything that came before. This was a city in which the mercantile urge was absolute, and all other values were required to genuflect before it. If there was a choice between history and commerce, commerce generally won.

The Europeans arrived, they conquered, they erased. The city's topography—its watercourses, hills, and shorelines, the products of eons of geologic activity—was leveled, drained, channeled, graded, and smoothed. A satisfactory tabula rasa was presented to the builder and the effects of millions of years of time were removed as if by scourge.

Equally extreme has been the obliteration of the island's aboriginal culture. In the face of the Europeans' windy ambitions, the native inhabitants of Manhattan vanished like smoke. Signs of their passing were discarded as worthless. But the good colonial burghers were equally cavalier about their own historical spoor. Thus we are left to reconstruct the early history of Manhattan from incomplete records and shreds of evidence.

■ MANHATTAN BEDROCK

In its original, unmodified state, the landscape of the island was rugged and relatively hilly, with low, abrupt slopes of 100 to 130 feet, higher at the northern end of the island. Geologists describe Manhattan as a gneissoid ridge, with underlying beds of schist.

The 450-million-year-old bedrock of schist and gneiss would eventually be pressed into service to support the foundations of the greatest collection of tall buildings the world has ever known. The immediately recognizable skyline of Manhattan—with an aggregation of skyscrapers in its midsection, and another, smaller concentration at its southern tip—is not an accident of urban design, but a function of geology.

Like a breaching whale, the Manhattan bedrock rises near the surface in Midtown (outcroppings can clearly be seen in Central Park). Then it dips back down below the accumulation of sediment, only to rise briefly again at the lower end of the island. Skyscrapers are most easily built where bedrock is close to the surface, so the Manhattan skyline follows this subterranean contour: the mini-Alps of Midtown, another range of towers around Wall Street, and a low-profile saddle of smaller buildings slung in between.

■ ALGONQUINS

At the end of the last Ice Age, around ten thousand years ago by the archaeological evidence, groups of Paleo-Indians, or Stone Age Indians, began arriving on the eastern seaboard and summering in Manhattan. The natives in the New York area

A painting by Frederic A. Chapman depicts the arrival of Henry Hudson's ship, the Half Moon, *in the bay of New York in September 1609. (Library of Congress)*

when the European explorers arrived were members of several of the hundreds of autonomous bands that hunted and fished the area. To the native peoples themselves, the only distinction worth noting was their specific clan or family. Anthropologists, however, have determined that these particular people were of the Algonquian linguistic family.

The Algonquins were a large and multifarious people, inhabiting territory that stretched from Montana and Alberta, Canada, in the west, south to northern Tennessee, and east to New England. In the northeast, their territory was encroached upon by the Iroquois, a fact that caused a great deal of warfare and scalp-taking. The Algonquins of the eastern woodlands, moreover, were no strangers to internecine battles, and one of their primary characteristics seems to have been that when they were not warring with their neighbors, they were fighting among themselves.

Along the Hudson and the Mohawk Rivers, there was constant pressure from the mighty Iroquois Confederacy of the northern interior. The Confederacy included the most well-organized and socially developed tribes in the East, highly efficient as fighting groups and adroit at maintaining a civilized peace when necessary. Later on, some of the governing principles of the Iroquois would find their way into the United States Constitution.

Among the people whom the Iroquois bedeviled were the Mahicans, including the Wappingers Confederacy. A small clan of this tribe, part of the Wickquaskeek band, moved away from the Iroquois threat to live in what is now Westchester County and the Bronx. They were known by the tongue-twisting name Reckgawawancs, after one of their sachems, or chieftains. They worshiped Kickeron as their supreme god, and feared Manitou, a horned snake, as their devil.

They were not much struck by the island of Manhattan. Its chilly rock shelves and open hillsides were too exposed to the elements, to the winds that blew off the sea or down Mahicanituck, the great river. For most of them, the island served simply as a summer resort. Great seafood eaters, they downed so many clams, mussels, and oysters that by each summer's end huge mounds of shells lay near their shoreline encampments, memories of feasts past. They fished with seine and gill nets, took deer and rabbit from the island's copious supply, and ate from small plots of corn, squash, and beans.

The distinct clans elsewhere in the area lived similarly close to the land, hunting, fishing, and farming. Brooklyn and Long Island were the territory of the Canarsee

An Indian Village of the Manhattans *(1858), by George Haywood. (Museum of the City of New York)*

tribe, and Staten Island was under the control of roving bands of the Lenape, or Delaware, tribe. Even though the coastal corridor from New York to Boston was the most densely populated area of eastern North America in aboriginal times, there were never more than five thousand Indians living in the New York City area, and usually far fewer. The names and sites of various towns on Manhattan have been recorded: Naigianac, between where the Manhattan and Brooklyn Bridges are now; Sapokanican, on the west side, near Gansevoort Market; and Shorakapok, "the resting place," on the northern tip of the island.

The Algonquins of Manhattan—the Wappingers and the other bands occasionally estivating here, including the Canarsees and the Delawares—were lumped together in early European literature as "devils," and perhaps to Western European eyes that is what they looked like. Tall, with black hair and black eyes, they sometimes stained their skin a saffron color and tattooed their faces with scenes from their dreams. The Algonquin men usually wore a scalplock, a single roach of stiffened hair, sometimes dyed red, with a lock trailing down as a goad to the enemy— as if to say, "take it if you can!" The men burned the rest of the hair off their heads with red-hot stones.

Algonquin women wore a single braid, sometimes with a square cap of beaded shells. Both sexes wore leggings, hemp or leather loincloths, and robes. The robes were sometimes marvelously worked, of wild turkey feathers for men, and of beaded shells for women. Algonquin houses, made of bark and resembling overturned bowls, were owned by, or identified with, specific women of the tribe. Men were associated with the houses only by marriage.

Given the unbroken expanse of concrete and asphalt that Manhattan has become, it is a fantastic game to imagine what the island was like before the Europeans arrived. The closest approximation in existence today might be certain rocky promontory islands off the Maine coast. Though covered with beech, locust, lime, and elm trees, Manhattan was known mostly for its many stands of birch, which must have whitened the light in the forest like so many daytime moons. A pure spring ran year-round from the bluff on the island's northern tip, making the area a favored resting spot for locals.

■ EUROPEAN EXPLORATION

The first transatlantic settlers to live among these aboriginal inhabitants may not have been Dutch. Basing their conclusions on no small amount of speculation and a little fanciful embroidering of old Norse sagas, some historians conclude that the Vikings preceded other Europeans to Manhattan by five hundred years.

In A.D. 1010, a Norseman from Greenland named Thorfinn Karlsefensi established a ragtag colony that he called Streamfjord on the coast of North America. By comparing landscapes and directions, scholars have identified the place as Manhattan.

About 130 people, including Karlsefensi's new bride, Gudrid, lived on the island for three years. The explorer himself continued down the eastern seaboard as far as Albemarle Sound in North Carolina, briefly setting up a colony at Powell Point. But Indians drove the colony away, and Karlsefensi returned to Streamfjord, where he found the disgruntled male population fighting over Gudrid and the few other women. Disgusted, Karlsefensi decamped for Greenland.

The Norse settlers left behind no artifacts, were reflected in no legends, and seem to have left no impression at all upon the island's original inhabitants. Indeed their presence is highly conjectural, and when they left, it was as though they had never been there. For half a millennium afterward, no other foreign intrusion disturbed the suzerainty of the local population.

That the official European "discoverer" of Manhattan was later eaten by cannibals may be considered simply the first note in a history of high irony that has kept New York entertained through much of its existence. Giovanni da Verrazano was a Florentine-born noble in the service of the French king and the silk merchants of Lyons, who were eager to find passage to the fabled riches of Asia. Or, as Verrazano put it, to "the happy shores of Cathay."

Here is how he describes his brief but memorable brush with the island of Manhattan in the 16th century:

> We found a very good piece of land situated within two small prominent hills, in the midst of which flowed to the sea a very great river which was deep at the mouth…. We went with the small boat, entering the said river to the land, which we found much peopled. The people…clothed with the feathers of various colors, came toward us joyfully, shouting with admiration, showing us where we could land the boat more safely. We entered the river, within the land, about half a league, where we saw it formed a very beautiful lake with a circuit of about three leagues. They [the native people] went across, going from one part to another, in as many as thirty of their little barges. Innumerable people passed from one shore to the other in order to see us. In an instant, as is wont to happen in navigation, a gale of unfavorable wind blew in from the sea. We were forced to return to the ship, and left the said land with much regret because of its commodiousness and beauty, thinking it was not without some properties of value, for all its hills showed indications of minerals.

And that was that. The river was the Hudson, the place "within two small prominent hills" was the Narrows, now named after Verrazano, and the "very beautiful lake" was Upper New York Bay. (A French nautical league equals about 2.2 miles, so Verrazano's calculation wasn't off by much: the Upper Bay is about 5 miles across.) The explorer christened the place Angoulême, after the given name of the French king, Henri Angoulême.

This fully documented European visit was a decided anticlimax, not only for Verrazano but for the inhabitants of the area, who no doubt would have wished for a closer commune with their visitors. *La Dauphine,* a 100-ton ship of the French navy, which Verrazano had borrowed courtesy of the French king, François I, was

the largest vessel that had ever sailed in those waters. It must have appeared to the natives as something from a dream.

That the *Dauphine* arrived at all was almost a miracle. Verrazano's 1524 voyage was not only a wonderful feat of seamanship, it was a marvel of good luck. Departing from Dieppe, France, on the English Channel, he crossed the Atlantic smoothly, heading as far north as he could to avoid France's enemy, the Spanish. He made landfall at Cape Fear, North Carolina, and sailed up the coast to Newfoundland in a little over three and a half months, with favorable winds and without serious bad weather.

The caution Verrazano displayed in New York, when he turned tail at the slightest hint of ill wind, continued to make his journey a catalog of missed opportunities. He missed the Chesapeake and Delaware Bays altogether. Samuel Eliot Morison, the Harvard historian of the European discovery of America, calls Verrazano's failure to explore the Hudson "the greatest opportunity missed by any North American explorer."

If Verrazano did not pursue his opportunity upon entering New York Harbor, his French patrons also squandered the chance for imperial expansion he presented them. François I was soon distracted by a disastrous war against Charles II in Italy, and the silk merchants of Lyons were not impressed by the samples of tobacco and other New World artifacts Verrazano brought back.

Four years later, in 1528, off the Caribbean island of Guadeloupe, Verrazano's caution deserted him, and he waded ashore into the arms of a tribe of ferocious Caribs. While his brother and partner Girolamo watched in horror from a longboat offshore, the Indians killed the European discoverer of Manhattan and allegedly ate him on the spot, "down to the tiniest bone."

New York Harbor did receive some desultory French visitors, including Jehan Cossin, notable for having first mapped Manhattan. But generally, the French allowed the legacy of Verrazano (whom the French called "Jean Verason") to lapse into obscurity. It took New York's large Italian-American community to resurrect this native son, put up a statue of him (in Battery Park, facing his eponymous Narrows) and celebrate his discoveries.

A year after Verrazano's brief visit, another European, Esteban Gomez, a Portuguese Moor sailing for Spain, also sighted the magnificent bay and the little island floating therein.

Modern Manhattan seen from Brooklyn, where the Canarsees once lived.

Then, for a long time, nothing.

Wars in Europe, the vagaries of navigation, and the immense logistical effort required for any colonial enterprise kept the Europeans from New York for most of the 16th century. Despite the scarcity of newcomers, the Algonquins at this time were like swimmers in a pool whose plug has been pulled. Some of them might even have felt the faint herald of the sea change coming. On September 2, 1609, the future arrived, in the form of a 74-foot sailing brig called the *Half Moon*. Its pilot was an Englishman, Henry Hudson, in service to a Dutch master.

As had Verrazano and other early explorers, Hudson came to the area looking for something else. (The similarities between Verrazano and Hudson are striking: they both sought passage to Asia, were employed by foreign governments, and came to violent ends—Hudson during his exploration of the bay later named in his honor, when he was set adrift by a mutinous crew.) The Dutch East India Company, chartered in 1602 by the Dutch government, had hired "Hendrick Hudson" to search for the Northwest Passage to the Spice Islands of the Orient.

According to a contemporary history, Hudson "entered into as fine a river as can be found, wide and deep, with good anchorages on both sides." He laid in on the west side of the harbor, in Hoboken Bay, amid marshes thick with waterfowl. There he was visited by friendly Raritan Indians. Looking through his spyglass across the expanse of river, he could see Mahicans standing in canoes among the reeds at the northern end of Manhattan Island. A few days later, in an encounter with this group, he kidnapped two Indians, intending to take them back to Holland for display.

The shallow-drafted *Half Moon* was no more than a yacht, and Hudson was able to use it to explore as far as Albany. On his way upriver, one of his Mahican captives drowned, and the other escaped and made his way back to Manhattan. When Hudson decided the river was not the fabled Northwest Passage after all, he turned back to the sea.

He found an unfriendly reception when he retraced his route. His former captive had raised the alarm about the aggressive tendencies of the visitors. On October 6, as the *Half Moon* hove into view above Manhattan, a half-dozen canoe-loads of Mahicans shot out from the reeds at Spuyten Duyvil Creek. Hudson had to use his cannon to fight them off. Thus was launched the battle that would be taken up intermittently over the next half-century. Indeed, the local Wappingers (of which the Mahicans were a tribe) still recalled Hudson and his perfidy fifteen years later, when they met with colonists who had come to settle New Amsterdam.

■ COLONIAL ERA

Unlike the French with Verrazano, the Dutch immediately followed up on the possibilities illuminated by Hudson's 1609 visit to New York. The next year and for almost every succeeding year until a permanent settlement was established, the New Netherlands Company sent vessels stocked with goods to trade with the Indians for furs. Adrian Block, the Dutch captain of the *Tyger,* navigated the East River—which he named "Hell Gate" for its treacherous currents—and was the first to chart Manhattan as a separate island. When the *Tyger* caught fire, Block spent the winter of 1613 on the island and built another ship with which to sail back to Holland.

In 1624, another government-chartered trading cartel, the Dutch West India Company, established the first permanent European presence on Manhattan. Yet the original settlers were not Dutch at all, but Belgians. Fleeing religious persecution, about a hundred French-speaking Protestant Walloons came to the New World and headed for Fort Orange, at the present-day site of Albany. Eight families stayed behind on Governors Island, off the southern tip of Manhattan, and over the next year, thirty Dutch families arrived. Subsequently they all moved to lower Manhattan, and the colonial experiment of New Amsterdam began in earnest.

The colony's Dutch director general, Peter Minuit ("Peter Midnight"), liked to do things by the book, so he formalized the settler's possession of Manhattan by purchasing it from the Canarsees. In trade he gave them knives, beads, ceramics, cloth, and tools—not the "trinkets" that are generally reported.

The transaction had other aspects enshrined in pseudo-history that bear reexamining. Take the oft-quoted price that Minuit paid for Manhattan, for example. The goods he gave the Canarsees were said to be worth sixty guilders, translated into the "$24" that endures to this day.

By what mysterious method of monetary conversion was this number calculated? It's hard to say. Yet the price has taken a solemn place in the annals of history, and is offered up as evidence of either aboriginal naiveté or imperialist exploitation. (In the 1970s, when New York City was on the verge of bankruptcy, representatives of the Algonquins wryly offered to buy Manhattan back—for $24. "Guilt feelings have plagued us all," the Algonquins professed. "We knew it was a bad investment when we sold it.")

To the original Indians, however, metal blades and tools and ceramic pots were priceless. Furthermore, to Indians, what could be traded was not the plot of earth, but temporary use of its resources. The Canarsees understood the deal as an agreement not to interfere with the Dutch colonials' fishing and hunting. The two peoples were trading apples and oranges.

At any rate, the joke was on the Dutch. The Indians they were dealing with, most likely Canarsees from Long Island, did not "own" Manhattan. The Wickquaskeek band had control of the northern two-thirds of the island, but Minuit was ignorant of such subtle gradations of Indian clan ties. Indeed, much to the consternation of the Europeans, the Native Americans of the area "sold" the same turf over and over again.

Land grab or no land grab, the little colony hung on. Its timber resources were prodigious, and Minuit built what was at the time the world's largest vessel, the 800-ton *New Netherland*. It evoked wonder when it sailed into European ports. Minuit, though, had a run-in with the home office and was fired, and like Henry Hudson before him, disappeared at sea.

A succession of incompetent or corrupt governors followed Minuit. One of them, the bellicose Willem Kieft, arranged for a massacre of Algonquins at

Peter Minuit Buying Manhattan from the Indians, May 4, 1626, *by Edwin Wilming Deming. (Museum of the City of New York)*

Corlear's Hook, touching off a five-year war. The superior firepower of the Dutch prevailed. Except for intermittent rebellions, such as the massacres of 1655 and the Peach Tree War (when a colonist killed an Algonquin he thought was stealing peaches), indigenous resistance to the colony ended by the close of the 17th century. Remnants of the clan that had held the island when the Europeans arrived eventually drifted north.

Under Willem Kieft, black slaves, first brought to the island in 1625, began to be manumitted in 1644. New Amsterdam had a generally enlightened policy toward slavery—"comparatively mild" was the gently ironic phrase that James Weldon Johnson used. One twisted example of the Dutch colony's relative kindness was the tradition of the Pinkster Fete, celebrated during the third week after Easter, when slaves were freed for the day.

Peter Stuyvesant arrived to take control of a shabby, struggling, miserable town in 1647. Irascible, authoritarian, and misanthropic, Stuyvesant hobbled about his domain on a wooden leg, organizing improvements such as a paid police force, a street plan, and a reorganized civic apparatus. The community thrived, but his iron hand was more a handicap than his wooden leg. When English warships appeared in the harbor in 1664, the colonists were so sick of the dictatorial Stuyvesant that they surrendered to the British without a fight.

Control of New Amsterdam seesawed back and forth between England and Holland during the Anglo-Dutch Sea Wars of the mid-17th century. The Dutch retook the colony in 1672 and renamed it New Orange, but in 1674 the British

(above) Peter Stuyvesant, the imperious governor of New Amsterdam. (Library of Congress)

traded their claim to Surinam in South America for Manhattan, one colony for another. The conventional wisdom of the time held that the Dutch got the better deal, because the rich forests of Surinam would be forever worth more than a hardscrabble colony numbering fewer than two thousand souls, whether it was called New Amsterdam or New Orange.

Charles II of England wanted to call the colony New York, after his brother the Duke of York (later King James II). As with the Dutch, under the English the citizenry became increasingly dissatisfied with the colonial yoke. An abortive move against British rule in 1691, called Leisler's Rebellion after its hapless ringleader, Captain Jacob Leisler, was one of several uprisings against the Crown. Leisler wound up hanged for his trouble.

The English governors were an uneven lot, some of them decidedly eccentric. Witness Lord Cornbury, who enjoyed riding his horse into taverns and ordering a drink for himself and water for his steed. At a party he extolled the virtues of his wife's earlobes, demanding that every man present feel them for himself. Legend has it he liked to dress in women's clothes, explaining that since he was the cousin and representative of Queen Anne, it was proper that he show the colonials what their sovereign might look like. All this might have been forgiven, had it not been for Lord Cornbury's proclivity for debt. He was eventually tossed into prison and shipped back to England.

■ INDEPENDENCE

Corrupt and despotic rulers like Lord Cornbury fed colonial unrest and contributed to a growing anti-British sentiment that swelled to a climax in the Revolutionary War. Although New York was the most pro-British of the thirteen colonies, rebellious fervor in Manhattan was potent, and when the Declaration of Independence was read on the steps of the old city hall (today the site of the Federal Hall National Memorial) on July 9, 1776, the crowd reacted violently, pulling down a statue of King George. The fledgling nation had declared itself, and the British were not about to wish it Godspeed. War began almost immediately, with Lord Cornwallis commanding British troops and a relatively unknown Virginia planter, George Washington, leading the Americans. Control of the Hudson River was deemed essential by the British, and England's General William Howe concentrated all his efforts on securing Manhattan, approaching the island via Brooklyn in the hot summer of 1776.

(top) Federal Hall, formerly city hall, as it appeared in 1797. (Library of Congress)
(bottom) An early engraving shows the Dutch colony of New Amsterdam. (Library of Congress)

The beleaguered position of the American forces can be deduced from the tone of a dispatch from General George Washington on the eve of the conflict:

> At the present time my forces consist entirely of Delaware militia and smallwoods Marylanders—a total of 5,000 troops to stand against 25,000 of the enemy, and I begin to notice that many of us are lads under 15 and old men, none of whom could truly be called soldiers.... As I write these words, the enemy is plainly in sight beyond the river. How it will end only Providence can direct, but dear God, what brave men I shall lose before this business ends.

The British landed at Kips Bay on September 15, and Washington's ragtag army ran like rabbits. Pursued westward across the island by the more formidable redcoats, they could do no more than fight courageous but doomed delaying actions, one of them at McGowan's Pass in what is today Central Park. By fall, Washington was in retreat, his army surviving only because of heroic measures taken in the Battle of Harlem Heights. The American army abandoned the island to the British, retreating north to West Point.

In New York, life during wartime took on an insular opulence in an otherwise threadbare world. As with many popular revolts, the empire held the cities, but the countryside was in the hands of the American irregulars—whom today we would call guerrillas. Manhattan became an island in more senses than one, a doomed outpost surrounded by a hostile sea of revolution. British officers could hold gala balls and great feasts, but nothing could entirely obscure the pervading siege mentality.

Manhattan—already more pro-British than not—became a haven for Tory Loyalists, mostly wealthy merchants and shippers, who prospered as suppliers to the British army. Those insurrectionists unable or unwilling to flee suffered the indignities of occupation, including the forced quartering of British troops in their homes. The occupiers put the torch to Manhattan anyway, burning a quarter of it, including Trinity Church. Meanwhile, the colonial forces stood their ground, defeating the enemy in battle and on the guerrilla front. With the help of the French, the Americans delivered the final blow at Yorktown in 1781.

By the time the Loyalists and British surrendered New York to the Americans on November 25, 1783—eight months after the war ended—the city was at half its prewar population of twenty-five thousand, ravaged and decimated, its economy

Detail from an engraving by Montbaron and Gautschi of George Washington's inauguration. (New-York Historical Society)

in ruins. From Trinity Church to the Battery, the city was nothing more than a charred swath. Its northern limit effectively ended at the old city hall at Nassau and Wall Streets, although there were a few scattered outposts farther up the island.

Two years later, New York City had recovered enough of its grandeur to become the capital of the United States. Meanwhile, New York delegates, led by Alexander Hamilton, participated vigorously in the Constitutional Convention of 1787, arguing for a stronger centralized government; Hamilton's Federalist views ultimately carried the day.

On April 23, 1789, George Washington returned in triumph to take an oath as the country's first president, but New York City would retain the title of capital only until 1790. Despite the ceremonial honor, there was a clear sense that New York's destiny lay elsewhere. The city began to grow, adding to itself as a magnet does when iron filings attach themselves to it. At the time of Washington's inauguration, 33,216 people lived in New York City (and thus in Manhattan, for until 1898 Manhattan and New York City were coterminous). Fifteen years later, the population would be twice that, with the old northern boundary line of City Hall long since surpassed.

■ COMMERCIAL IMPERATIVE

Growth begat more growth. The magnet was money. Manhattan's true ideal, tied to its great harbor, its trading history, and its flinty bedrock soul, would always be the commercial imperative.

In one sense business was a great leveler. In another it was social Darwinism at its worst. In post-Revolution New York City, many who were industrious or clever enough made great fortunes. Cornelius Vanderbilt began with a single ferryboat, transporting passengers from Staten Island to Manhattan for ten cents. By the time he was seventeen, he owned a fleet of ferryboats and was well on his way to being a millionaire. On the other side of the coin were the wretched of Manhattan, who lived miserable existences in the shadow of great wealth.

Devotion to trade determined how New York City would grow for the next hundred years. Here was a place where the urbanizing impulse could grow unchecked by any coherent program of restraint. The island was built close and narrow, its streets squeezed small to make more room for real estate. From its beginnings, New York was a utilitarian, no-nonsense commercial zone devoted to capitalist practice above all else. Comparable cities on the Continent might have broad

ALEXANDER HAMILTON

Alexander Hamilton may have been the quintessential 18th-century New Yorker, the kind of restless, questing man drawn to the energy and political excitement of Manhattan, elevated by the city, and elevating it in the process.

A brilliant orator and essayist, a ceaseless promulgator of a strong central government, he performed Herculean duties to assure the creation of the United States of America out of a coterie of territorial fiefdoms. When he was cut down in a duel at age forty-nine by his political rival Aaron Burr, New York was robbed of its first citizen, and the new country lost a founding father and perhaps a future president.

Hamilton typified the Manhattan experience in that he came here from somewhere else. He was born in the West Indies, on the island of Nevis, in 1755, an illegitimate son of a Scottish aristocrat. Hamilton hitched a ride on a Boston-bound boat, arriving in 1773.

New York was not a natural choice for a young man on the make—Boston and Philadelphia were much higher-profile cities then—but somehow Hamilton understood its fundamental importance to colonial America. Enrolled in King's College, he became a student leader, a veritable rabble-rouser for independence from England. One of Hamilton's fiery speeches to the student body forced the school's Tory dean to flee, fearing for his life.

During the Revolutionary War, Hamilton proved a brilliant military leader, contributing most notably to victories at Monmouth and Yorktown. As General George Washington's aide-de-camp and eventual amanuensis, Hamilton shaped the thinking (and many of the speeches) of the nation's first president.

His true métier was not guns but words and ideas. All his life, Hamilton would demonstrate the ability to sway people with oratory and carefully reasoned essays. His contribution to the *Federalist Papers* (written with James Madison and John Jay) was fundamental in changing the course of the young republic, unifying it into a more cohesive whole.

As secretary of the treasury, it was Hamilton who first put the fledgling country on a firm financial footing, chartering the Bank of New York on the model of the Bank of England. Even Thomas Jefferson, long Hamilton's political foe, characterized him as "really a colossus" of the opposition. Hamilton almost single-handedly carried the day on a number of important issues, from ratification of the U.S. Constitution to neutrality in the war between France and England.

Thus it was tantamount to a national tragedy when, on July 11, 1804, Hamilton met with Aaron Burr in Weehawken, New Jersey, for a duel that would cost him his life. Hamilton was opposed to dueling, partly because his son had been killed in a duel, and shot his pistol harmlessly into the air. Burr, however, demonstrated no such moral nicety, and Hamilton died the next day from a mortal wound.

The following are places associated with Hamilton's life:

Site of King's College. Hamilton graduated in 1778 from the college that evolved into Columbia University, now uptown in Morningside Heights. During his high-profile student career he joined several pro-independence groups. *Murray, Church, Barclay, and Greenwich Streets.*

Site of Hamilton's house. Hamilton lived on the south side of Wall Street in the post–Revolutionary War years. Aaron Burr lived a half-block away. *Wall Street at Broad Street.*

Museum of the City of New York. The museum's holdings include letters and other artifacts that reveal the father-and-son quality of the political relationship between Hamilton and George Washington. *1220 Fifth Avenue, at 104th Street.*

Statue of Hamilton. Carl Conrad's granite rendering is of a dynamic, youthful Hamilton. *Central Park, northwest of the Metropolitan Museum of Art.*

Bank of New York and Trust Company. With a graceful Georgian edifice (and superb interior), this was one of the many buildings erected over the years by the bank Hamilton chartered. *48 Wall Street.*

Site of the *New York Post*. The tabloid still makes much of its founding (as the *New York Evening Post*) by Hamilton in 1801, on occasion sporting a medallion-sized portrait of him in its logo. *210 South Street.*

Hamilton Square. The square marks the beginning of Hamilton Heights. The nomenclature of the "Heights" of Manhattan reflects a political reality, with Hamilton Heights just below Washington Heights. *Hamilton Place and West 140th Street.*

Hamilton Grange. Hamilton was living in his summer residence at the time of his duel with Burr. The National Park Service operates a small museum inside the home. A statue of Hamilton is in front. *287 Convent Avenue, at 141st Street.*

Trinity Churchyard. Hamilton's grave is in the southern sector, about 40 feet from Broadway and clearly visible through the iron railing along Rector Street. *Broadway and Rector Street.*

avenues or generous plazas, pleasant prospects giving out to wide, engaging vistas. None of that for Manhattan. Civic amenities were wrung from an obdurate ruling class, which viewed any departure from strict practicality—and any check on its commercial impulses—with almost hysterical suspicion.

Even New York's grid plan of 1811, its major claim to urban design, was adopted primarily as a way to render moneymaking more efficient. More east-west streets were included in the plan, for example, than north-south avenues, because the commercial traffic ran from river to river. The squares that punctuate Broadway today are not so much concessions to the public need for open space as design imperatives when one broad thoroughfare crosses another. Only Central Park can be seen as a major departure from the idea of Manhattan as a tool rather than an environment.

By the middle of the 19th century, many of the developments that were to make New York a world-class city were already in place. The New York Stock Exchange had been formed in 1792. In 1801, Alexander Hamilton founded the *New York Post*—not the city's first newspaper, but the oldest one still publishing. In the first decade of the 19th century, Robert Fulton successfully harnessed steam power, and, with the opening of the Erie Canal in 1825, New York became the nation's busiest seaport, eventually outstripping Philadelphia as a center of business.

Oddly enough, all this utilitarianism produced a city that had more romance, more dreams, more spirit attached to it than almost any other. Almost in spite of itself, Manhattan stumbled into a golden age.

■ NEW POLITICAL REALITIES

European immigrants continued to pour in: an average of four thousand a year during the 1820s, a total of fourteen thousand in 1830 alone. The German revolutions of the 1840s, the Irish potato famine of 1846 to 1851, and other political upheavals on the Continent spurred emigration. From 1840 to 1856, three million immigrants arrived in the United States, representing an extraordinary ratio of newcomers to the existing population.

With new political realities came grudging social reform and cultural opportunities. Full suffrage for white males was granted in 1826, and slavery in New York State was outlawed a year later. The New York Philharmonic was formed in 1842, and a nascent literary scene developed, spurred by Washington Irving, Edgar Allan Poe, Herman Melville, and James Fenimore Cooper.

It would be hard to underestimate the vitality of Manhattan as it prepared to enter its golden age, but it would be just as hard for modern sensibilities to comprehend the squalor that represented the flip side of growth. The Five Points area—the intersection of Baxter, Worth, and Mulberry Streets, near present-day Foley Square—developed into a morass of poverty, crime, and disease. Charles Dickens, a chronicler of the slums of London and the Continent, said on his visit to America that Five Points compared in misery to anything he had ever seen:

> What place is this, to which the squalid street conducts us? A kind of square of leprous houses, some of which are attainable only by crazy wooden steps without.... These narrow ways diverging right and left, and reeking everywhere with dirt and filth. Such lives as are led here, bear the same fruit here as elsewhere. The coarse and bloated faces at the doors have counterparts at home [in England] and all the world over. Debauchery has made the very houses prematurely old. See how the rotten beams are tumbling down, and the patched and broken windows seem to scowl dimly, like eyes that have been hurt in drunken frays. Many of these pigs live here. Do they ever wonder why their masters walk up right instead of going on all-fours, and why they talk instead of grunting?

Those pigs Dickens was talking about were the city's quasi-official street cleaners, and in 1817 there were twenty thousand roaming the city, scarfing down the litter and offal they found on the pavements. All this crowding and inattention to public hygiene unleashed a series of cholera and yellow fever epidemics that decimated the city. But it was not until 1896, largely due to the crusading efforts of the photographer and activist Jacob Riis, that Five Points was leveled.

As the mid-century rolled around, Manhattan's urban sprawl had reached 23rd Street, with farflung outposts to the north. Although high society in New York had started to solidify into the elaborate caste system portrayed in Edith Wharton's *The Age of Innocence,* New York was still comparatively a wide-open town. In 1854 a Rosa Parks–style civil suit, brought by Elizabeth Jennings against a streetcar company, opened public transportation to blacks.

The booming city attracted its share of predators. The most notorious one was born in 1823 on Cherry Street, rising through the ranks of the Democratic Party to head one of the most corrupt and long-running political machines of all time.

This was William Marcy "Boss" Tweed, the head of Tammany Hall. An erstwhile fraternal organization (devoted to "St. Tammany," a bogus Iroquois chieftain, in rude parody of upper-class organizations named after saints), Tammany Hall devolved into a graft-generating machine par excellence.

Tweed and his cronies looted the city of $160 million over the years, spending $10,000 on $75 worth of pencils, for example, and inflating the bill on the court-house north of City Hall (derisively known as "Tweed Courthouse" to this day) by millions. Tweed's reign did have some salutary side effects, perhaps unintended by him—and quite apart from his wide-ranging contributions to charities. Because its power base comprised the teeming wards of the Lower East Side, Tammany Hall busily registered to vote thousands of newly arrived immigrants, involving them, however shadily, in the political process.

Reformers repeatedly assailed Tammany Hall and Tweed, to which he would disdainfully sneer, "Well, what are you going to do about it?" Tweed's grip was finally broken by the combined efforts of reformers like Henry Ward Beecher, the

(above) Baxter Street North from Worth Street *(ca. 1873), by G.W. Pach. (Museum of the City of New York) (following pages) Ellis Island baggage exhibit. (National Park Service)*

A Jacob Riis photo shows immigrant children pledging allegiance to their new country. (Library of Congress)

political cartoonist Thomas Nast, and the *New York Times,* which was founded in 1851 and cut its teeth on the Tweed scandals. Boss Tweed fled the country to avoid prosecution, but was recognized by police in Spain from his portrayal in Thomas Nast's cartoons. He died in debtor's prison.

■ CIVIL WAR TO THE GAY NINETIES

In the years preceding the Civil War, New York City was a prime battleground for the Great Debate over slavery. From his pulpit at Plymouth Church in Brooklyn, Henry Ward Beecher led a fiery abolitionist charge. A tall, awkward political newcomer, Abraham Lincoln, wearing a tight black frock coat and a new pair of boots, made the speech of his political life at Manhattan's Cooper Union early in 1860. The words of his "right makes might" speech were printed by five newspapers the next day, sending Lincoln farther along the path to the presidency.

For all that, Tammany Hall and the Democratic leadership of New York City resisted Republican inroads. The shippers and exporters of Manhattan feared a war would disrupt the flow of cotton from the South. "The City of New York," read an editorial in the *Evening Post* the same month as Lincoln's Cooper Union speech, "belongs almost as much to the South as to the North."

New York is traditionally portrayed as a stronghold of "copperheads" (Confederate sympathizers) during the Civil War, and it is true that there was strong sentiment on both sides. The horrendous draft riots that gripped Manhattan during the conflict, however, were not so much pro-South as a reaction against the inequities of the conscription law. Poor Irish laborers, who could not afford the $300 to buy their way out of the draft, burned and looted for a four-day stretch.

Despite Tammany's plunderings and the disruptions of the Civil War, New York City continued to prosper and grow. The face of the city was changing quickly.

A Thomas Nast cartoon from Harper's Weekly *in 1871 depicts figures from the Tammany Hall scandal passing the blame. "Boss" Tweed is on the left. (New-York Historical Society)*

ABRAHAM LINCOLN AT COOPER UNION

In February 1860, Illinois representative and presidential candidate Abraham Lincoln was invited to speak at Cooper Union. Running against Stephen Douglas, Lincoln was the dark horse in the campaign, but his address, an analysis of the antislavery movement, was a staggering success. By the time Lincoln had delivered his concluding remarks (printed below) he had captivated his audience. Abraham Lincoln won New York and, nine months later, the presidency. Said Lincoln:

Neither let us be slandered from our duty by false accusations against us, nor frightened from it by menaces of destruction to the government, nor of dungeons to ourselves. Let us have faith that right makes might and in that faith let us, to the end, dare to do our duty, as we understand it.

The following day, Tribune *editor Horace Greeley printed his response to the event:*

The speech of Abraham Lincoln at the Cooper Institute last evening was one of the happiest and most convincing political arguments ever made in this City, and was addressed to a crowded and most appreciating audience. Since the days of Clay and Webster, no man has spoken to a larger assemblage of the intellect and mental culture of our City. Mr. Lincoln is one of Nature's orators, using his rare powers solely and effectively to elucidate and to convince, though their inevitable effect is to delight and electrify as well. We present herewith a very full and accurate report of this Speech; yet the tones, the gestures, the kindling eye and mirth-provoking look, defy the reporter's skill. The vast assemblage frequently rang with cheers and shouts of applause, which were prolonged and intensified at the close. No man ever before made such an impression on his first appeal to a New York audience. . . .

The firm of McKim, Mead & White, the greatest architectural concern in the country, formed in 1879 and would transform Manhattan with Beaux Arts masterpieces. Thomas Edison began supplying electricity to homes in 1882, and a decade later the first great blazing advertising displays of Times Square were erected. The Brooklyn Bridge connected New York State's most populous cities—Brooklyn and Manhattan—in 1883.

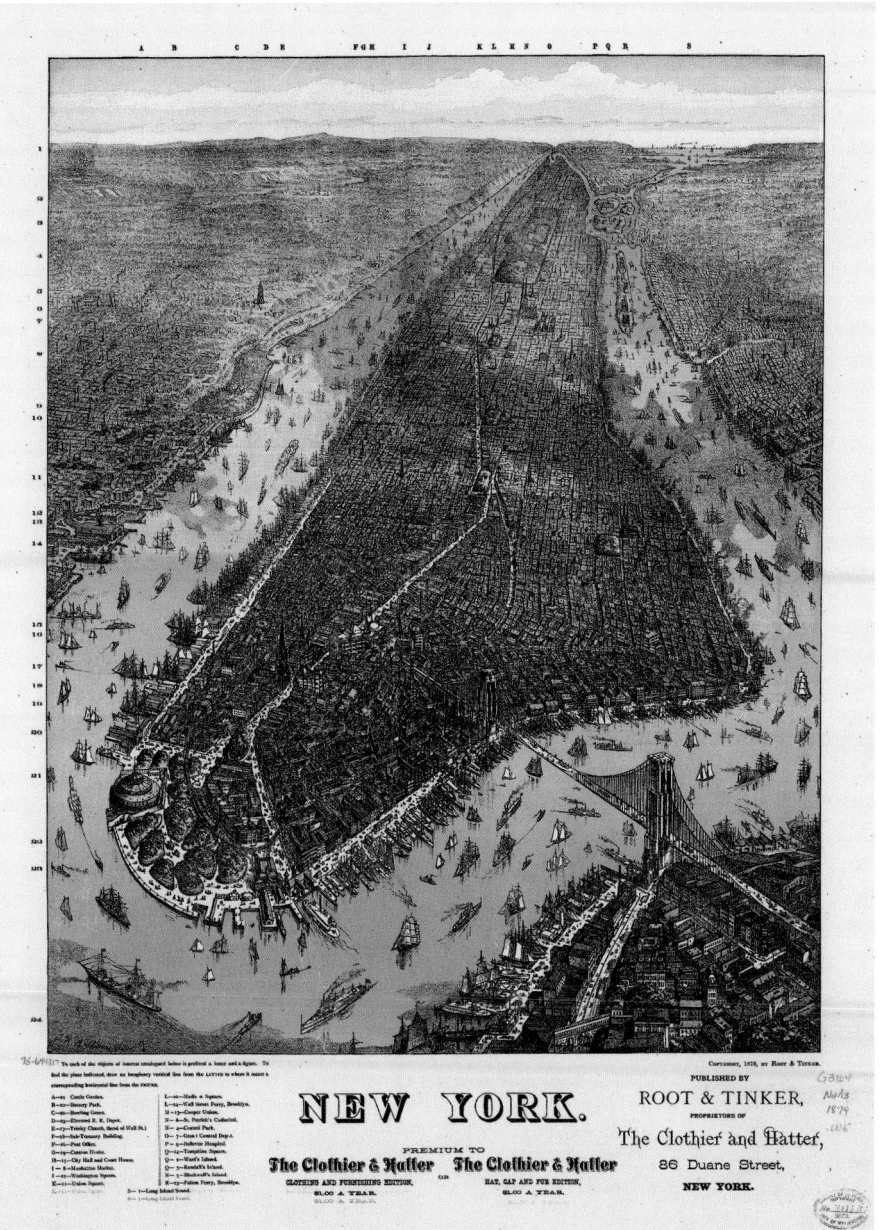

This map published for a Duane Street clothing concern shows how dense Manhattan had become during the 19th century. The patch of green at the northern part of the island is Central Park. (Library of Congress)

Two developments that made Manhattan what it is today occurred with relatively little fanfare. In 1857, Elisha Graves Otis installed the first elevator, or "vertical railroad" as he called it. And in 1888, architect Bradford Gilbert's Tower Building was erected on Exchange Place near Broadway. The world's first steel-framed skyscraper, it provided Otis's railroad with a "track" to run on. The elevator and skyscraper gave rise to the concentrations of offices in Midtown and the Financial District that transformed Manhattan into "headquarters city."

By the last quarter of the century, elevated trains were running on Third, Sixth, and Ninth Avenues, bringing the masses to the Financial District in the morning and carting them home again at night: the commuting society was born. Life in New York began to achieve some of the velocity for which it would become famous. As the transportation system reached into the surrounding cities, the map of New York City was summarily redrawn.

Many factors contributed to the formation of Greater New York City in 1898, but once again, the commercial imperative was overarching. The city's moneyed classes wanted the tax base that the densely populated cities of Brooklyn, Queens, the Bronx, and Staten Island could give them. They did not want workers taking their paychecks out of the city to pay taxes somewhere else. It was a case of unite and conquer.

For the upper classes, the last decade of the century was indeed the "Gay Nineties," a period of fancy-dress balls and social snobbery. The "400," defined by social sycophant Ward McAllister as the number of socially acceptable people who could fit into Caroline Webster Schermerhorn Astor's ballroom, were anointed as the new Manhattan royalty. The number was more symbolic than literal, because Mrs. Astor's ballroom could easily accommodate more than four hundred people.

Yet the world of the "400" was doomed even as it was celebrated. Vast socioeconomic changes were under way, fueled by one of the most astonishing population shifts the world has ever seen. Between 1900 and 1920, a third of Eastern Europe's Jews emigrated, most to New York City and its environs, more than a million and a half people in all. They joined peasants and laborers from southern Italy, and continuing influxes from Ireland, Germany, and Russia. In Ellis Island's peak year as an immigrant receiving station, 1,285,349 people passed through it, sometimes at the astonishing rate of five thousand a day. By sheer weight of numbers, the European immigrants tipped the political scales of New York to the left. Many of them, indeed, were socialists and communists fleeing from the oppressive regimes of Europe. They began to agitate for social and workplace reforms. At

Construction of Brooklyn Bridge, 1881. *(Museum of the City of New York)*

GOLDEN AGE SNOB

We here reach a period when New York society turned over a new leaf. Up to this time, for one to be worth $1 million was to be rated as a man of fortune, but now, bygones must be bygones. New York's ideas as to values, when fortune was named, leaped boldly up to $10 million, $50 million, $100 million, and the necessities and luxuries followed suit. One was no longer content with a dinner of a dozen or more to be served by a couple of servants. Fashion demanded that you be received in the hall of the house in which you were to dine by from five to six servants, who, with the butler, were to serve the repast. . . . Soft strains of music were introduced between the courses, and in some houses gold replaced silver in the way of plate, and everything that skill and art could suggest was added to make the dinners not a vulgar display but a great gastronomic effort, evidencing the possession by the host of both money and taste.

—Ward McAllister, *Society As I Have Found It*, 1890

first, these rumblings were dismissed or suppressed, but the 1911 Triangle Shirtwaist Fire, in which 146 sweatshop workers, mostly women, died, coalesced public opinion in favor of reform. Soon afterward the state legislature passed laws to protect workers from dangerous conditions and unreasonable hours and wages.

■ JAZZ AGE NEW YORK

The coming of Prohibition in 1920 transformed social habits in an odd and paradoxical way: by making alcohol forbidden, Prohibition managed to make it respectable. The impetus for Prohibition came largely from rural Protestants, perhaps one reason the measure was largely circumvented in urban and by then heavily Catholic Manhattan. The speakeasy became a new kind of social nexus. Often called the Jazz Age for the new music played in nightclubs, the 1920s were chronicled by writers as diverse as Langston Hughes, F. Scott Fitzgerald, Dorothy Parker, and Damon Runyon. The irrepressible Jimmy Walker, mayor of New York from 1925 to 1932, who used to arrive for work at one o'clock and leave by three, symbolized the hard-partying atmosphere of New York during this period.

The Jazz Age was a decade-long party from which the city awoke, depressed and chagrined, with the Wall Street Crash of 1929. Walker was turned out of office in a wave of scandals, and a Jewish-Italian bulldog named Fiorello La Guardia took over the mayor's office in 1934 and served through 1945. La Guardia was the living symbol of New York all through the hard times of the Depression. He was always perceived as taking the part of the little guy—perhaps because he was one himself. When thousands of unemployed workers camped out in Central Park, they joined their disgruntled counterparts across the country in calling their collection of shanties a "Hooverville," after the Republican president—but they never blamed their mayor.

One art that La Guardia perfected was going hat in hand to the Democratic president (and ex-governor of New York State) who replaced Hoover, Franklin Delano Roosevelt. Again and again, La Guardia would journey to Washington, D.C., coming back with a New Deal public works trophy that employed thousands of people. The impact on Manhattan's skyline was noticeable: the Triborough Bridge, the Henry Hudson Bridge, the Battery Park Tunnel, and numerous highways and other projects were constructed through this partnership of city and federal governments.

Overseeing much of the construction was Robert Moses, officially the parks commissioner but a holder of numerous other governmental titles as well. A master builder with a monstrous ego, Moses ruthlessly imposed his vision of New York City on Manhattan and the other boroughs. That vision was monumental in scope, and though the grand achievements of Moses are undeniable—and everywhere to be seen—they were gained at great cost to the community. His roads bisected whole neighborhoods with little regard for the social repercussions. Moses imagined a Manhattan ringed by superhighways and slashed through with a network of elevated thoroughfares. Perhaps blessedly, Moses's grand vision was only partially realized.

New York City entered World War II on the threshold of another population shift, one that would change its fortunes forever. Only dimly perceived in the tumult of the war years, suburbia was growing even during the Depression. But the burgeoning satellite communities of New Jersey, Connecticut, and upstate New York spelled doom for the urban way of life that Manhattan had symbolized for a century.

■ POST-WAR TO PRESENT

The pattern that developed in Manhattan during the 1950s was being duplicated in large urban centers throughout the country. The automobile and the superhighway were making commuting long distances cheap and easy, and suddenly America saw itself changing from an urban society to a suburban one. New York City's tax base began hemorrhaging at an alarming rate. In the two decades following World War II, more than one million families left New York. Corporations decamped to exurban ring cities, lured by lower taxes and rents.

Fiorello La Guardia. (The La Guardia and Wagner Archives)

In simple terms, everyone prosperous enough to leave the city seemed to be doing so, until Manhattan was left with a brutally segregated, two-tiered society: the rich, who could afford the high cost of living and the higher taxes, and the poor, who drained the coffers of social welfare funds.

By 1975, New York City teetered on the edge of bankruptcy. "Ford to City: Drop Dead," screamed a famous headline in the *New York Daily News,* referring to President Gerald R. Ford's refusal to back a federal bailout strategy. Only a vigorous state plan, engineered by the investment banker Felix Rohatyn, saved the city from defaulting on $13 billion in bonds. The Municipal Assistance Corporation was formed, to borrow money when the city's credit turned sour.

The state's investment in the city turned out to be sound. During the '80s, Manhattan in particular and New York City in general did well. Corporate takeovers and a surging bull market anchored a new prosperity that extended to the arts, to the rebuilding of the city's battered infrastructure, and to the spirit of New York as a whole. The propulsive mayoralty of Ed Koch, who served from 1978 through 1989, epitomized the street attitude of the time: New York City was reveling in the tough, exuberant pride of the survivor.

The go-go 1980s gave way to the go-go 1990s. The city's first African-American mayor, David Dinkins (1990–93), lost his reelection bid to a former federal prosecutor named Rudolph Giuliani, New York City's first Republican mayor in decades, a famed racketbuster voted in at a time when fear of crime—if not crime itself—was at an all-time high. Giuliani, who ran the city from 1994 through 2001, took it in hand with a style that recalled one of his heroes, the most famous other Republican mayor of New York, Fiorello La Guardia. Crime rates started a steep descent that finally upended New York's reputation as a dangerous place. Hotels were bursting, Broadway was on a roll, and unemployment and homelessness dropped. New York City was back with a vengeance.

The city's population swelled by almost ten percent from 1990 to 2000, to a record eight-million-plus inhabitants. Prosperity brought its own set of problems, among them spiraling rents that began to squeeze out the middle class. As the mayoralty of Rudolph Giuliani drew to a close, signs abounded that the boom of the 1990s had run its course and that huge cuts in city spending to reduce the city's deficit would be required.

September 11, 2001, marked the end of a golden era in Manhattan. On that morning, two airliners hijacked by terrorists and filled with passengers slammed one after another into the twin towers of the World Trade Center. Together with the attack on the Pentagon in Washington, the devastation of Manhattan's tallest landmarks seared horrific images upon the world's memory.

Yet as indelible as those pictures might be, what afterward seemed more significant were the tales of heroism by New York's firefighters and police, killed by the hundreds when the buildings collapsed. Memorable also was the drawing together of the city's famously disparate communities into a united whole. It was a fact that somehow spoke to what is most human in us, that the aftermath of the tragedy offered a greater truth, a more enduring truth, than the murderous event itself.

New York proved once again that it had a lesson in toughness to teach. The exhilarating highs and bruising lows of the modern era have established resiliency as chief among the city's protean qualities. Throughout its fractious history, New York has managed to emerge from its trials intact and more powerful than ever. If past is prologue, Manhattan will continue to do more than survive. It will endure as it always has—strong, brash, and triumphant.

Historical and Cultural Time Line

1524 Italian explorer Giovanni da Verrazano is the first European to make a documented journey to New York Harbor.

1609 Henry Hudson, sailing for the Dutch, enters what is now the Hudson River.

1624 Belgian and then Dutch settlers arrive in New York City.

1626 Peter Minuit, first director general of New Amsterdam, purchases Manhattan from a local Indian tribe for knives, tools, and cloth.

1647 Peter Stuyvesant becomes governor of the Dutch colony.

1654 First Jewish settlers arrive after being expelled from Portuguese Brazil.

1664 Dutch colonists surrender New Amsterdam to the British.

1674 England gives Holland the South American colony of Surinam in exchange for Manhattan and names the territory New York.

1732 First city theater opens. A sign posted prohibits spitting.

1754 King's College, now Columbia University, is founded.

1776 New York City falls to the British, who torch Manhattan.

1789 George Washington takes the presidential oath at Federal Hall.

1790 New York's five-year reign as America's capital city ends.

1792 Two dozen traders sitting beneath a buttonwood tree on Wall Street make a pact setting forth rules for trade in securities.

1801 Alexander Hamilton founds the *New York Post*.

1835 Great Fire: almost all of Lower Manhattan is destroyed.

1842 Charles Dickens visits New York City and finds the slums as bad as London's.

1849 British actor Charles Macready is accused of calling Americans vulgar. A mob storms the Astor Place Opera House during Macready's performance of *Macbeth*. More than two dozen people die in the Astor Place Riots.

1851 The *New York Times* publishes its first edition.

1857 The first elevator is installed. Work begins on Central Park.

1860 Presidential candidate Abraham Lincoln delivers a pivotal speech at Cooper Union, the country's first coeducational college, open to all races and creeds.

1863 In response to the Civil War draft, riots rage throughout the city.

1870 First subway is constructed by Alfred Ely Beach, inventor of the typewriter.

1873 Boss Tweed is convicted after years of corruption in Tammany Hall.

1877 Alexander Graham Bell demonstrates the telephone.

1880 Metropolitan Museum of Art opens.

1883 Metropolitan Opera debuts. The total wealth of the opening-night audience is estimated at $500 million; the Vanderbilts alone occupy five boxes.

Brooklyn Bridge opens, connecting Brooklyn to Manhattan.

1886 Statue of Liberty is erected in New York Harbor.

1891 Carnegie Hall opens with a performance by Pyotr Ilich Tchaikovsky.

1896 First bagel is sold in New York City.

1907 First *Ziegfeld Follies.*

1911 A fire at the Triangle Shirtwaist Company kills hundreds of workers, mostly young Jewish and Italian women. The tragedy sparks labor reform.

Along the Mall in Central Park. (Library of Congress)

1913 The Armory Show exhibition in Manhattan introduces Americans to Picasso, Duchamp, Matisse and other impressionist and modern artists.

The *New York World* prints the first crossword puzzle.

1919 F. Scott Fitzgerald moves to New York City, begins work in advertising, and writes a laundry detergent slogan, "We keep you clean in Muscatine."

1920 Babe Ruth joins the New York Yankees.

1925 Harold Ross founds the *New Yorker* magazine.

1927 Martha Graham performs *Revolt,* a dance about social protest.

Mae West is fined $500 for her performance in the racy Broadway show, *Sex.*

1929 Museum of Modern Art is founded by a trio of patrons, including Abby Aldrich Rockefeller, wife of John D. Rockefeller Jr.

Stock market crashes; Great Depression begins.

1930 Guggenheim Museum is established.

1931 Empire State Building is completed.

1932 Radio City Music Hall opens with Charlie Chaplin, Clark Gable, Amelia Earhart, and other celebrities in attendance.

1933 Prohibition ends.

1934 Reformer Fiorello La Guardia begins the first of three terms as mayor.

New owners take over Hurtig & Seamon's burlesque theater and end the whites-only door policy. The renamed Apollo Theatre becomes a huge hit.

1935 The first U.S. public housing project is erected on the Lower East Side.

1942 Frank Sinatra makes his solo debut in New York City.

Painter John Graham arranges a show at which the works of Jackson Pollock, Lee Krasner, and Willem de Kooning hang beside paintings by Matisse, Picasso, and Modigliani. New York is celebrated as the new art capital.

1943 *Oklahoma!* premieres, the first Broadway musical hit by Richard Rodgers and Oscar Hammerstein.

1945 The Tennessee Williams play *The Glass Menagerie* premieres.

1947 Jackie Robinson, the major leagues' first African-American baseball player, signs with the Brooklyn Dodgers.

1958 Leonard Bernstein joins the New York Philharmonic.

1964 The Beatles play at Shea Stadium during their first American concert tour.

1967 Hippie musical *Hair* opens Off-Broadway.

1969 Police raid the gay Stonewall Inn—and the patrons fight back.

The New York Mets win their first World Series.

1970 In first New York City Marathon, 127 runners circle Central Park four times.

The first tenants begin moving into the World Trade Center's north tower.

1971 The Whitney Museum of American Art hosts a major retrospective of pop artist Andy Warhol's works.

1974 Mikhail Baryshnikov debuts with the American Ballet Theatre.

1975 President Gerald R. Ford refuses to bail out bankrupt New York City; Felix Rohatyn's plan saves the city from defaulting on $13 billion in bonds.

1980 John Lennon is murdered outside the Dakota apartment building.

1981 The city's first AIDS cases are reported.

1987 The stock market drops 508 points on "Black Monday."

1991 Workers uncover the African Burial Ground in Lower Manhattan.

1992 Tony Kushner's *Angels in America,* an epic treatment of the AIDS era, debuts.

1993 Terrorists explode a bomb at the World Trade Center, killing six people.

1997 Disney reopens the New Amsterdam Theater, heralding a Times Square revival.

1998 Wall Street profits from investments in high-tech and other enterprises fuel a new wave of prosperity.

1999 Mayor Rudolph Giuliani attempts to slash the Brooklyn Museum of Art's city subsidy after an exhibit includes a picture of the Virgin Mary featuring elephant dung.

2001 *The Producers* smashes Broadway attendance records.

Terrorist attack destroys the World Trade Center, killing nearly three thousand people. City police and firefighters become international heroes for their efforts to save lives.

2002 Billionaire media mogul Michael R. Bloomberg is sworn in as mayor, having spent a record $75.5 million to win the post.

LOWER MANHATTAN

The chronology of Manhattan rolls out from south to north, making the island's southernmost neighborhood its oldest. It was here in the 17th century that the first settlers erected the primitive village of New Amsterdam. In the two centuries that followed, Lower Manhattan became a center of shipping and commerce, and in the 19th century the island's southern tip provided European immigrants with a first, throat-clutching view of their new home, as they cleared the Narrows and approached by sea.

Clustered in Lower Manhattan are the steel-and-concrete thickets of the **Financial District.** Flanking it on the southeastern shore of Manhattan are **South Street Seaport** and the clot of government bureaucracy known as the **Civic Center;** on the west are the suave, intricately planned precincts of **Battery Park City** and the **World Financial Center.** Also here is **Ground Zero,** the site of the former World Trade Center.

Chambers Street and the **Brooklyn Bridge** mark the area's northern border. As a vertical enclave of finance and government, Lower Manhattan is one of the island's least residential neighborhoods, although that is gradually changing. There's plenty to do in this highly walkable part of town, and you can easily take in the major attractions in a day.

Downtown is quiet at night and on weekends, and it's been that way at least since Herman Melville's time. Wall Street, he wrote in 1853, "of weekdays hums with industry and life, at nightfall echoes with sheer vacancy, and all through Sunday is forlorn." Things became somewhat livelier in recent decades, as developers converted vacant office space into condominiums. Downtown began to feel like a real neighborhood, though the World Trade Center attack slowed the residential momentum.

You can always tell when the financial markets are operating, simply from the increased swirl on the streets. Three million people invade Lower Manhattan each workday. They come by subway, commuter train, and taxi and car and bus, by helicopter and by ferry. At lunchtime, the streets bulge with humanity. Then, at around three o'clock, the exodus begins—to uptown neighborhoods, to the outer boroughs and elsewhere in New York State, and to New Jersey, Connecticut, and

The Woolworth Building was the world's tallest skyscraper for sixteen years.

LOWER MANHATTAN

E · F · G · H

CHINATOWN

Confucius Plaza
Museum of Chinese in the Americas
Bayard St.
Pell St.
Division St.
Doyers St.
"Tombs"
Criminal Courts
Hogan Pl.
Columbus Park
Mosco St.
Chatham Square
Catherine St.
Oliver St.
Market St.
Rutgers St.
Cherry St.
Rutgers Slip
Rutgers Houses
Pike St.
South St.
Pike Slip
Worth St.
Foley Square
Kent Pl.
Park Row
Pearl St.
Shearith Israel Cemetery
James St.
Knickerbocker Village
Monroe St.
Manhattan Bridge
Cherry St.
Catherine Slip
Water St.
Market Slip
African Burial Ground
Elk St.
Centre St.
Centre St.
Municipal Building
M J,M,Z
Police Headquarters
Pearl St.
Madison
St. James Pl.
Gov. Alfred E. Smith Houses
4,5,6 M
Spruce St.
Beekman St.
Southbridge Towers
Dover St.
Peck Slip
Front St.
Brooklyn Bridge
Park Row Building
Ann St.
M,Z M
M A,C
Pearl St.
Fulton St.
Fulton Market Building
M 1,2
Gold St.
John St.
Federal Reserve Bank
Platt St.
Schermerhorn Row
Burling Slip
South Street Seaport
Pier 17
Pier 16
Maiden La.
Fletcher St. La.
Cedar St.
William St.
Pine St.
M 1,2
Wall St.
Regent Wall Street Hotel
Morgan Guaranty
Water St.
Front St.
South St.
East River
Hanover St.
Gouverneur La.
Police Museum
Old Slip
Pier 11
Hanover Sq.
Stone St.
S. William St.
Coenties Slip
Stone St.
Bridge St.
Pearl
Fraunces Tavern
Vietnam Veterans Plaza
Water St.
Broad St.
M N,R
Shrine of Elizabeth Seton
Peter Minuit Plaza
Battery Maritime Building
Whitehall Ferry Terminal
STATEN ISLAND FERRY

FINANCIAL DISTRICT

1 · 2 · 3 · 4 · 5 · 6

LOWER MANHATTAN

0 — Miles — 0.25
0 — Kilometers — 0.3

even Pennsylvania and Delaware. By seven, the daytime scurry has diminished. This vast systolic movement, this ebb and flow of workers, lends Lower Manhattan its vitality. A few pockets of neighborhood life do exist, among them Battery Park City, but this section of the Hudson waterfront has an anomalous, almost suburban feel.

■ BATTERY PARK *map pages 58–59, D-6*

The original warehouses and mercantile buildings of Lower Manhattan were built right to the shoreline, but over the years the wonders of landfill have provided the Financial District with slivers of green. One such patch is Battery Park, the site of the Castle Clinton National Monument, the departure point for ferries to Ellis Island and the Statue of Liberty. The park is as fine a place to view New York Harbor as there is on the island. The lines of people waiting for the ferries draw pushcarts, acrobats, and street musicians to the Admiral George Dewey Promenade. The resulting mummery provides a great jolt of New York energy.

Battery Park has long been a place for New Yorkers to strut their stuff: in 1705, a constable here stopped Edward Hyde, Lord Cornbury, the transvestite Lord Governor who was cousin to Queen Anne, for parading in ladies' regalia. His defense was that he was emulating the queen, but given the crowd on the promenade today, the problem may just have been that he was marooned in the wrong century.

■ BATTERY PARK SIGHTS

Inside the landscaped confines of the park itself are several monuments, including, northwest of the Bowling Green subway kiosk, a memorial to explorer Giovanni da Verrazano, erected in 1909 as an Italian-American contribution to the hoopla surrounding the tercentennial of Henry Hudson's visit. Appropriately, Verrazano gazes out toward his eponymous Narrows and the bridge that spans it. A nearby memorial flagpole, given to the city by the Dutch government, commemorates Peter Minuit's 1626 "purchase" of Manhattan Island from the Canarsees.

Also in this quadrant of Battery Park is the Hope Garden, whose one hundred thousand roses memorialize those who have died of AIDS. The American Merchant Mariners Memorial, in the water west of the garden, depicts four shipwrecked sailors. The centerpiece of the World War II monument south along **Dewey Promenade** is a huge bronze sculpture of a fierce, soaring raptor, flanked by granite cenotaphs listing the names of soldiers and sailors who died in the Atlantic.

Battery Park, ca. 1935. (Library of Congress)

Castle Clinton sat 300 feet offshore when it was built in 1811. The Indians called the rocks on which the fort was built "Kapsee" when they came here from Brooklyn. Castle Clinton, originally called West Battery (its twin was East Battery, or Castle Williams, on Governors Island), was erected to defend New York against the British in anticipation of what evolved into the War of 1812. As it happened, no wartime shots were ever fired from the battery after which the park is named.

Over the years, Castle Clinton, which passed from federal to city control in 1824, has performed many functions. In 1826 it was turned into a theater, known as Castle Garden, and it was there that in 1850 huckster-showman P. T. Barnum presented his much-hyped discovery, the "Swedish Nightingale," the singer Jenny Lind. Reminisced one New Yorker years later, "So great was the desire to see her that parties who failed to obtain tickets for the Garden hired rowboats and rested in the river outside of the Garden during the performance." Later in the 19th century, the castle became a receiving hall for immigrants, and some contemporary New Yorkers remember it as the site (until 1941) of the New York Aquarium.

All this history is covered in a small, tidy museum near the castle's east gate. The museum's dioramas provide graphic representation of Manhattan's changing shoreline and the changing nature of the fort itself. Castle Clinton presently functions as the ticket booth for the ferry to Ellis Island.

A garland of superb architecture rings Battery Park. At its northwestern corner is **Pier A** (Battery Place and West Street), with its distinctive clock tower. Renovations that began in the late 1990s have restored some of the Beaux Arts trimmings of the pier, parts of which date to the mid-1880s. To the north is the neo-Renaissance **Whitehall Building** (17 Battery Place), whose shorter section (completed in 1902) was designed by Henry J. Hardenbergh, better known for New York's Plaza hotel and the Dakota apartment building. Also to the north are the Moorish-accented Art Deco masterpiece of the **Downtown Athletic Club** (19 West Street, near Morris Street), erected in 1926, and the 1905 entry kiosk for the **Bowling Green subway station** (State Street and Battery Place), one of the oldest in the system.

East of Battery Park is a 1793 Federal townhouse that is now the **Shrine of Saint Mother Elizabeth Ann Seton** (7 State Street). Mother Seton founded the Sisters of Charity, the nation's first order of nuns, in 1809. In 1975, she became the first native-born American to be canonized. Her shrine is inside the oldest residential building in Lower Manhattan, in what was originally a row of townhouses,

Castle Clinton was built to defend New York against the British.

Riders enjoy a sunny ride aboard the Staten Island Ferry.

built back in the days when harbor merchants lived right on the water. Nearby, at the back of the plaza, is the site of Herman Melville's birthplace, now the home of **New York Unearthed** (17 State Street), a wonderful archaeological museum administered by the South Street Seaport Museum.

At the southeastern corner of Battery Park, across State Street, is **Peter Minuit Plaza,** named after the Dutch director general of New Amsterdam. The plaza includes a memorial to New York's first Jewish immigrants, refugees expelled from Portugal's Brazilian colony, who arrived in 1654 in what was then New Amsterdam. Besieged by pirates and turned away from other ports, they found a home here in an early demonstration of the Dutch colony's attitude of tolerance and ecumenism. The twenty-three newcomers founded a synagogue (Shearith Israel, or "Remnant of Israel") and formed the core of New York's soon-to-burgeon Jewish community.

On the lower edge of Battery Park, the old Staten Island Ferry Building, damaged by fire in the early 1990s, should be replaced by the **Whitehall Ferry Terminal** by the end of 2003. Fiscal troubles, design squabbles, and political maneuvering have beset this project from the get-go, but with a rooftop deck and glass façades with New York Harbor panoramas, the building may become a destination in itself. Next door is the **Battery Maritime Building,** a 1908 Beaux Arts structure that is being restored. Ferries to Governors Island operate out of here.

The half-hour ride on the **Staten Island Ferry,** free for pedestrians, is still one of the best deals for natives and tourists alike. The view on the return from Staten

Island, as Lower Manhattan looms like a capitalist fairyland, is an awe-inspiring sight. "We were very tired, we were very merry," quoth Edna St. Vincent Millay, "We had gone back and forth all night on the ferry." Many people still take the ferry not for transport, but just for the joy of the ride.

■ BOWLING GREEN *map pages 58–59, D-5*

Bowling Green is northeast of Battery Park, where State Street debouches into Broadway. Yes, it originally was just that—a place for lawn bowling, rented by area property owners from the Crown at the rate of one peppercorn per annum.

This was the site of the famous statue of England's King George III, torn down on July 9, 1776, by a mob inspired by a reading of that rabble-rousing document, the Declaration of Independence. In a fine ironic turn, the lead in the gold-leaf, larger-than-life statue was melted down to make bullets—forty-two thousand of them—for use against the British (the final toll, according to legend, was four hundred redcoats killed). Only the tail of the statue's horse survives, in the collection of the New-York Historical Society.

Bowling Green is marked by glories of the past and present, including its colonial-era iron fence, likewise attacked by the 1776 mob and stripped of its royal golden finials. The ancient, tiny green seems somehow a fitting launching pad for Broadway, which bisects Manhattan to the north. Sea breezes gust around the landscaped fountain, and flocks of harbor gulls compete with city pigeons, as if this were the isobar of maritime and urban environments. *Broadway at State and Whitehall Streets.*

Facing Bowling Green on the south side and anchoring the whole space, is the architect Cass Gilbert's splendidly recherché **U.S. Custom House,** completed in 1907 and much more recently renamed the Alexander Hamilton U.S. Custom House. The statues on its façade—in keeping with the Beaux Arts style, there are a host of them—gaze up Broadway as if expecting something. But what? A blast of wind? Deliverance? A bus? Daniel Chester French's four large allegorical sculptures represent (from east to west) Asia, America, Europe, and Africa. The interior is worth a peek (admission is free), particularly the great rotunda murals by Reginald Marsh, which depict early American explorers. *1 Bowling Green.*

The **George Gustav Heye Center of the National Museum of the American Indian,** inside the Custom House, exhibits art and artifacts of native peoples of the Americas and presents dance, music, and other cultural programs. Admission to

Indian stands behind Liberty in Daniel Chester French's America, *at the U.S. Custom House.*

the museum, a branch of the Smithsonian Institution, is free. For an anachronistic commentary on the museum's subject matter, note the figure of the Indian in French's aforementioned *America* sculpture at the entrance to the Custom House. He stands in classic feather headdress, behind a torch-bearing figure of Liberty. *Alexander Hamilton U.S. Custom House, 1 Bowling Green; 212-514-3700.*

To the west of Bowling Green is the **Cunard Building** (25 Broadway), an elaborate throwback to the time when the firm's great liners traversed the Atlantic Ocean. It's now a U.S. post office. Opposite this is a quirky building that was the former headquarters of **Standard Oil** (26 Broadway). The humongous rooftop ornament is shaped like an oil lamp. Suitably enough, what was once the center of John D. Rockefeller Sr.'s empire now hosts the **Museum of American Financial History** (212-908-4519), "dedicated to the U.S. capital markets and the people who made them famous."

At the northern tip of Bowling Green, facing Wall Street, is Arturo DiModica's sculpture ***Charging Bull.*** DiModica had the chutzpah to erect his massive 3.5-ton bronze bull just after the October 1987 stock market crash, in the middle of the night, without permission from the city. In 1996, a car hit it and moved it 5 feet closer to Wall Street. The accident was considered a good omen by superstitious traders. The beast's testicles shine because they've been rubbed for good luck so many times.

■ STATUE OF LIBERTY AND ELLIS ISLAND

The irony is that in the beginning, the American people didn't even want the **Statue of Liberty;** they had to be goaded into accepting the statue as a gift from France. Eventually, though, they adopted her as their own, and *Liberty Enlightening the World* (as the statue is formally called) became a treasured symbol, perhaps the most celebrated public sculpture ever erected.

The Statue of Liberty under construction in the 1880s. (Library of Congress) (right) Miss Liberty touches up her makeup.

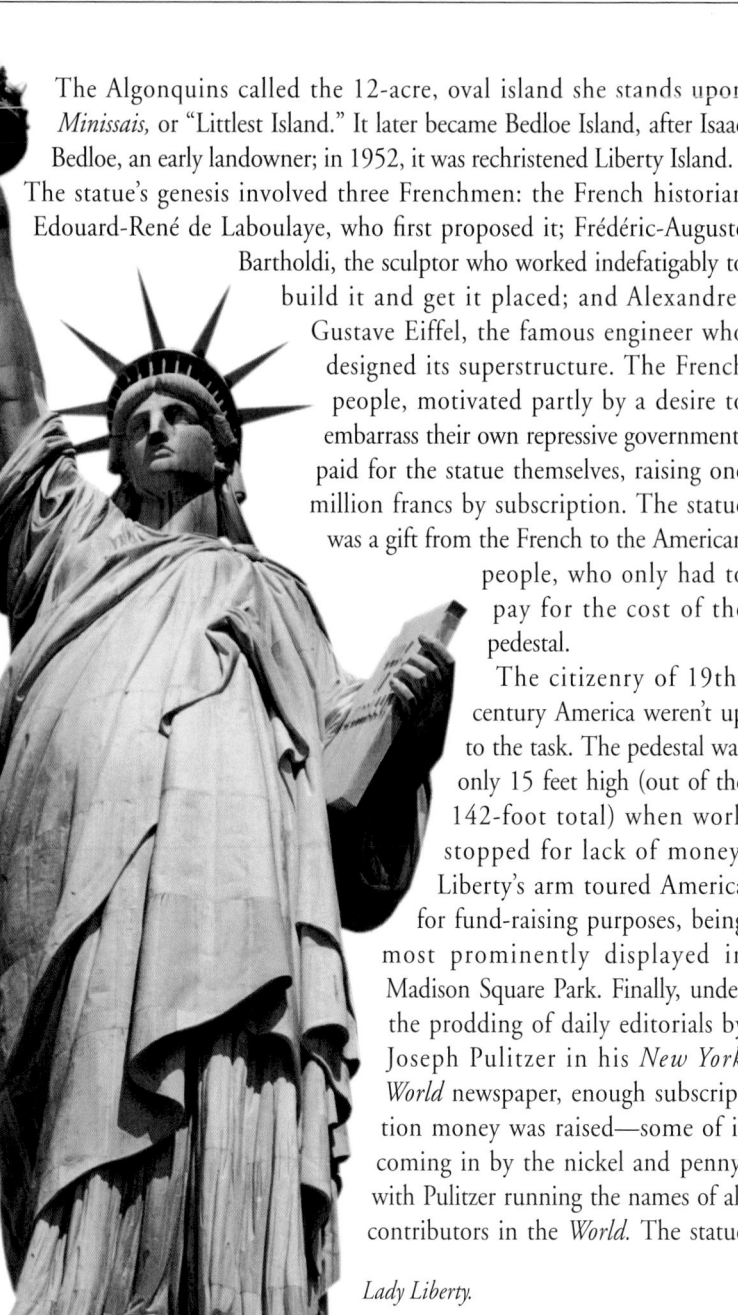

The Algonquins called the 12-acre, oval island she stands upon *Minissais,* or "Littlest Island." It later became Bedloe Island, after Isaac Bedloe, an early landowner; in 1952, it was rechristened Liberty Island. The statue's genesis involved three Frenchmen: the French historian Edouard-René de Laboulaye, who first proposed it; Frédéric-Auguste Bartholdi, the sculptor who worked indefatigably to build it and get it placed; and Alexandre-Gustave Eiffel, the famous engineer who designed its superstructure. The French people, motivated partly by a desire to embarrass their own repressive government, paid for the statue themselves, raising one million francs by subscription. The statue was a gift from the French to the American people, who only had to pay for the cost of the pedestal.

The citizenry of 19th-century America weren't up to the task. The pedestal was only 15 feet high (out of the 142-foot total) when work stopped for lack of money. Liberty's arm toured America for fund-raising purposes, being most prominently displayed in Madison Square Park. Finally, under the prodding of daily editorials by Joseph Pulitzer in his *New York World* newspaper, enough subscription money was raised—some of it coming in by the nickel and penny, with Pulitzer running the names of all contributors in the *World.* The statue

Lady Liberty.

was shipped over in crates from Bartholdi's workshop in Paris and dedicated on October 28, 1886.

Bartholdi's mother was the model for Liberty, who stands 151 feet tall, with a 42-foot arm and eyes that are 10 feet across. Even given the massive dimensions (30 feet taller than the Colossus of Rhodes, one of the Seven Wonders of the Ancient World), it is dwarfed in the expanse of New York Harbor. But to a generation of immigrants, the slowly shifting view of the Statue of Liberty as they steamed by it on the approach to nearby Ellis Island must have been overwhelming.

During a centennial refurbishing, Liberty's torch was retooled according to Bartholdi's original gold-leaf design (the old torch was removed to the museum lobby). The tablet she holds in her hands does not, as many people believe, contain lines from the famous Emma Lazarus poem, "The New Colossus":

> Give me your tired, your poor,
> Your huddled masses yearning to breathe free,
> The wretched refuse of your teeming shore.
> Send these, the homeless, tempest-tossed to me,
> I lift my lamp beside the golden door.

Instead, the tablet is meant to symbolize the American Declaration of Independence, and is inscribed with that document's date: July IV MDCCLXXVI. Lazarus's verse is engraved on the statue's base.

"The last time I was inside a woman was when I took a tour of the Statue of Liberty," cracks Woody Allen in his film *Crimes and Misdemeanors,* but the line to tour the statue is often no joke. On summer weekends, the only way to get into the statue for the elevator ride and the 171-step climb to the top is to go early in the day, because the National Park Service, which operates the Statue of Liberty, sometimes cuts the line off as early as two o'clock. For security reasons, the interior of the statue may be closed when you visit, and reservations may be required to tour the inside of the statue.

Another worthy experience is the **Ellis Island and the Museum of Immigration,** less monumental and more informational, yet just as impressive as the Statue of Liberty. The two-island trip requires a physical and emotional commitment but makes for an immensely satisfying day. The Park Service recommends Liberty Island first and then Ellis; but ferries run both ways, the New Jersey ferry going first to Ellis, and the Manhattan ferry going first to Liberty.

Ellis Island, which is actually two small islands joined and enlarged by landfill, is named after Samuel Ellis, the New Jersey farmer who owned it. The Indians called it Oyster Island, and the British, who used it for hangings, named it Gibbet Isle. The federal government turned it into a military outpost and munitions dump until the end of the 19th century. When Castle Clinton became overwhelmed as an immigrant-receiving station, operations were transferred here.

The first Ellis Island immigrant stepped ashore in 1892, and more than twelve million people followed, sometimes as many as five thousand a day. These were Emma Lazarus's poor, most of them traveling in steerage class. (First-class passengers were permitted to proceed directly to the Manhattan docks.) The immigrants were processed cattle-style, with medical checkups and legal tests designed to ferret out "any convict, lunatic, idiot or any person unable to take care of himself or herself without becoming a public charge." Only about two percent of applicants were turned away. Among those who came through Ellis Island as youths were songwriter Irving Berlin, film director Frank Capra, jurist Felix Frankfurter, poet Kahlil Gibran, and actors Claudette Colbert, Bela Lugosi, and Rudolph Valentino.

The Great Hall, where immigrants were processed upon arrival at Ellis Island.

Early-20th-century immigrants in line at Ellis Island. (National Park Service)

The present-day museum memorializing the immigrant experience was the work of a centennial committee headed by Lee Iacocca, the former Chrysler chairman and son of immigrants who came through Ellis Island. It is centered in the Byzantine-flavored Reception Hall, but there is also a Wall of Honor outside, inscribed with the names of 250,000 immigrants.

The experience of following the footsteps of immigrants can be extremely moving. On the first floor are rooms devoted to immigration in general, including a "Peopling of America" exhibit that shows just who came (and is coming) and from where. The second floor includes the Great Hall (officially called the Registry Room), which many immigrants later cited as their clearest memory of Ellis Island. Exhibit rooms off this impressive space lead the visitor through the check-in and vetting procedure that all new immigrants went through.

The third floor contains some dramatic exhibits: "Treasures from Home," which displays clothing, photographs, and artifacts the immigrants brought with them; "Silent Voices," a record of the spooky time that Ellis Island was abandoned; and a re-created dorm room that illustrates the quasi-military routine immigrants endured. The dioramas in "Ellis Island Chronicles" show how the island grew via landfill (much of it provided by subway excavation in Manhattan) and development.

When you visit Ellis Island, you are taking a trip not only into the past, but also into…New Jersey. In 1998 the U.S. Supreme Court ruled on a long-standing border dispute between New York and New Jersey, favoring the Garden State's claim to all but a small chunk of the island. The two states disagreed about which had sovereignty over the part of Ellis Island created by various landfill projects. An ancient deed ceding the island to New York, the Supreme Court ruled, applied only to the original acres. The interstate spat has little impact on the average tourist's visit to the island, and is more about boasting rights (and tax revenue) than anything else. Still, the phrase just doesn't ring true: Ellis Island, New Jersey.

With New Jersey's Liberty National Park just a stone's throw from Ellis Island, it might seem strange that visitors journey all the way from Battery Park to get there. So far, however, politics have circumvented plans for a footbridge linking the island to the New Jersey mainland. Which is probably a good thing, because the two-island ferry cruise represents a superb way to experience not only the monuments but New York Harbor itself.

A few pointers: to see both islands, the best thing to do is to make a day of it. A repast taken on the lawn of either island is a delightful way to break up the day, and the spellbinding views of Manhattan are thrown in for free. Although hordes of screeching schoolchildren might help you to imagine the clamor of immigration, perhaps the best time to hit Ellis Island is after 2:30 in the afternoon, when most of the school excursions have cleared out. The evening hours in summer can also be superbly meditative.

Tickets for the Liberty and Ellis Island ferryboats are purchased at Castle Clinton in Battery Park. Running usually on the half-hour, depending on the season, most boats go to each island in turn, and one ticket buys you passage to both. For security reasons, you cannot bring backpacks and large bags, though small purses are allowed. *Call 212-363-3200 for ferry and other information about the Statue of Liberty and Ellis Island Museum of Immigration.*

■ **WALL STREET**   *map pages 58–59, E-4*

Gothic, rose-hued **Trinity Church** stands at the west end of Wall Street like a Biblical admonition against the temptations of the materialist life. This is the third Trinity Church on the site—the first was built in 1698. Among the 1,186 New Yorkers interred in its pretty, moss-grown graveyard are founding fathers Alexander Hamilton and Francis Lewis, and Captain James "Don't Give Up the

J. P. Morgan in 1902. (Library of Congress)

Ship" Lawrence. A memorial to the steamship inventor Robert Fulton is outside; his remains are in the Livingston family crypt inside the church property. *Broadway and Wall Street.*

American capitalism's headquarters is the **New York Stock Exchange,** founded in 1792 under a buttonwood tree. The best way to catch a glimpse of the frenzied workings of the place is to show up at the visitors entrance at 20 Broad Street between 8:45 A.M. and 4:30 P.M. on weekdays (except trading holidays). Free tickets, passed out while the supply lasts, afford entry to the Interactive Educational Center. The exhibitions here and a short film on the exchange go a long way toward explaining what you are about to see. Then it's on to the gallery above the floor itself, where you can watch the hectic trading of billions of shares a day.

What you see below you is an array of "trading posts"—computerized command centers with video monitors and spindly brackets holding CRTs. Each stock is assigned to a specific section of the trading post, with a small army of clerks, runners, brokers, and pages assigned to each section. The frenetic action on the floor consists of buy and sell orders being funneled through this electronically sophisticated but still curiously anachronistic system of exchange.

In essence, the New York Stock Exchange is a raucous, roiling, free-running auction that sets the stock price for many of America's largest companies. The rule of the market is inexorable: if more people want to buy a stock than want to sell it, the price goes up; conversely, if more people want to sell than buy, the price goes down. Careers, fortunes, and lives have been made and wrecked as a result of this simple economic law. *Wall and Broad Streets; 212-656-5165.*

For an interesting counterpoint, check out the façade of the **Morgan Guaranty and Trust Company,** across Broad Street from the stock exchange. The building is still marked by the 1920 explosion of an anarchist's bomb, which took the lives of forty people—look under the second window from the east on the building's north side. This was long the headquarters of J. P. Morgan, financier extraordinaire and architect of the U.S. Steel conglomerate—and one of 19th-century New York's notorious robber barons. Morgan was the most respectable of these industrialists, whose motto was once pronounced by railroad buccaneer Jay Gould: "If it's not nailed down, it's mine. If I can pry it up, it's not nailed down." *23 Wall Street.*

Diagonally across from Morgan Guaranty stands the stolid Greek Revival **Federal Hall,** an 1842 Parthenon with a statue of George Washington out front. Washington was inaugurated on this site as the first president of the United States in 1789. The small museum inside is of marginal interest, though the interior is worth a quick peek (there's no admission charge). *Wall and Broad Streets.*

Federal Hall is a good place from which to follow one of four branches of the **Heritage Trail,** a self-guided walking tour of Lower Manhattan that is punctuated by informative markers.

(opposite) Soaking up sun on the steps of Federal Hall in view of the New York Stock Exchange. (above) The floor of the exchange buzzes with activity.

The oldest (lower) sections of the **Regent Wall Street Hotel** date from 1836, when this site was the Merchants' Exchange. Later in the 19th century the neoclassical structure was the U.S. Custom House, and for many years after that a bank. A look inside at the gorgeous marble rotunda will show you why the developers chose to adapt this building as a hotel. *55 Wall Street.*

The exhibits at the **Federal Reserve Bank of New York** include "The History of Money," which includes some interesting samples from the American Numismatic Society. The "Fed," as the bank is known, allows fewer than two hundred visitors per day and recommends that reservations be made at least a week ahead. The piece de resistance of a visit here is the trip five stories below street level to view the billions of dollars of gold stashed in a bedrock-level vault. *33 Liberty Street, at Nassau Street; 212-720-6130.*

A worthy side trip from Wall Street is to dip south on Broad Street to **Fraunces Tavern,** billed as the oldest tavern in New York City. The tavern's history is more complicated than that—most of the present building was erected in 1907—but the Fraunces Tavern Museum, inside the restaurant, effectively conveys the place's Colonial and early Federal history. The original tavern hosted George Washington as he bade farewell to his troops in 1783 and was noteworthy for being the hostelry of Samuel Fraunces, Washington's steward and one of the period's most prominent black New Yorkers. *54 Pearl Street, at Broad Street; 212-425-1778.*

■ SOUTH STREET SEAPORT *map pages 58–59, F-4*

Snobby Manhattanites decry the **South Street Seaport** (Fulton Street at the East River) complex of shops, museums, and markets as a playground for yuppies and tourists, but the district has a few things to recommend it. Yes, its bars and restaurants do get invaded after every workday by crowds of hungry and thirsty (mostly just thirsty) workers from Wall Street, but if this phenomenon bothers you, go before five o'clock.

The Seaport appears to be a worthy waterfront preservation effort, but the project's genesis reveals more complicated politics. A small group of preservationists began a campaign to save some of Manhattan's last 18th-century waterfront buildings. To their surprise, they received financial support from real estate interests seeking to limit the sprawl of the Financial District—and thus increase the value of existing downtown office space. The creation of South Street Seaport answered the needs of both the real estate moguls and the preservationists in one bold stroke.

For years, the Fulton Fish Market, at South and Fulton Streets, supplied the antidote to the cloying flavor of pre-packaged development (the Rouse Company, responsible for Faneuil Hall in Boston and Harbor Place in Baltimore, leases much of the Seaport). During its heyday the fish market, which is scheduled to relocate to the Bronx in 2003, was a sprawling, messy, smelly, old-fashioned ichthyic bazaar, thick with the polylglot cries of fishermongers and longshoremen.

These days, much of South Street Seaport is given over to stores and restaurants, its commerce anchored by a dollop of history. The *Titanic* Memorial, once located near Battery Park, was moved here in 1976. It was funded by subscription to commemorate the 1912 superliner disaster. The **South Street Seaport Museum** (212-748-8600) operates galleries in several buildings in the South Street Seaport Historic District and maintains several of the old vessels docked in the harbor. A row of galleries at **207–213 Water Street** includes a re-creation of a 19th-century printing enterprise and an exhibition of ocean-liner models and artifacts.

Until fall 2003 or so, the museum's visitor center will be at 209 Water Street. After that it will relocate to 12 Fulton Street, in **Schermerhorn Row,** a block of

South Street Seaport is part of an ongoing preservation effort.

Taking in the view from the South Street Seaport.

Federal-style red brick warehouses bordered by Fulton, Front, John, and South Streets. These buildings, originally erected on a wharf 600 feet from the shoreline, will also house *Worldport New York,* an expansive survey of the comings and goings in the city's ports from 1690 to the present.

Part of Schermerhorn Row faces the **Fulton Market Building** (11 Fulton Street), a scrupulous reconstruction of the 1883 original. Across South Street from the row stands the **Pier 17 Pavilion,** a massive assemblage of fast-food and other restaurants, T-shirt emporiums, and purveyors of tourist baubles that extends out over the East River. South of this, on Piers 15 and 16, are the Seaport's **floating exhibits.** Some of these ships are berthed here permanently: the *Peking,* the second-largest sailing ship in the world; the lighthouse ship the *Ambrose,* once anchored in the harbor; the three-masted *Wavertree;* and the century-old schooner *Pioneer.* Entry to all is included with museum admission (payable at the visitor center or any of the galleries).

From Pier 16, the **Circle Line** (212-563-3200) operates several harbor tours. A favorite with kids is *The Beast,* which travels so fast some passengers get splashed with water.

Bruce Weber wrote in the *New York Times* in June 1994 about a more mellow tour that left from these piers:

> On a sunny morning, with the wind spilling your hair in your eyes and the air as balmy as bath water, you look at the vertical spires of lower Manhattan, as tightly packed as porcupine quills, not to mention the Statue of Liberty, Ellis Island and the Verrazano-Narrows Bridge in the distance, and you understand why people want to come here and maybe even remember why you moved here yourself.

Several blocks south of South Street Seaport along the waterfront is the **New York City Police Museum,** which exhibits vintage uniforms, badges, equipment, and weapons. You can learn everything here from how to hold a gun correctly to why cops are called cops (the first badges police officers wore were made of copper). Don't be surprised to see raw recruits jog past you—the Police Academy occupies the same premises. *100 Old Slip, at Front Street; 212-480-3100.*

■ BROOKLYN BRIDGE *map pages 58–59, G-3*

One of the prime virtues of South Street Seaport is the view it affords of one of the architectural masterworks of all time, the **Brooklyn Bridge,** whose Manhattan terminus is at Park Row. The bridge was begun in 1869, overseen by John Roebling, who died before construction started: a ferry crushed his foot as he was surveying the site and the master engineer died of complications. His son Washington Roebling then took charge. After a construction-related incident left him paralyzed, his wife, Emily, supervised the project. By the time the bridge was completed in 1883, twenty people had died. Another dozen lost their lives in a stampede of panicked pedestrians a week after the span opened.

Originally called the New York and Brooklyn Bridge, the completed span linked what were then separate cities and was hailed as a modern miracle. The magnificent Gothic towers anchoring each end were meant to be gateways to their respective cities. Walt Whitman and Hart Crane memorialized it, Le Corbusier praised it as "full of native sap," and today architectural historians place it on par with the Eiffel Tower as one of the great engineering and aesthetic achievements of the 19th century. There were a few doubters: vaudeville comedian Eddie Foy was supposed to have cracked: "All that trouble just to get to Brooklyn."

Although a long central pedestrian ramp has replaced the graceful original walkways, crossing over the Brooklyn Bridge on foot remains one of the most exhilarating experiences the city offers, with great views of Lower Manhattan and access to attractive Brooklyn Heights at the other end.

■ CIVIC CENTER *map pages 58–59, D-2/3*

The Manhattan terminus of the Brooklyn Bridge is Park Row, a stretch of which was once nicknamed Newspaper Row because the *Sun, World,* and *Tribune,* among other papers, were headquartered here. In 1893, New York City had nineteen daily papers, and this street—now known mostly for computer and electronics stores—was the hub. When it was completed in 1899, the **Park Row Building** (15 Park Row) was the world's tallest building. Within sight of the Park Row Building is another titleholder, the Woolworth Building (more on that below).

North of Park Row is **City Hall Park,** a relatively quiet patch of green surrounded by a thick cluster of mostly government buildings. New York's famed ticker-tape parades for heroes and sports champions often end here. Diminutive **City Hall,** a hybrid of the French Renaissance and Federal styles, was completed in 1812. The front and sides were faced with marble, but cheap brownstone was deemed sufficient for the rear because the designers didn't expect the city to grow past the building. The entire façade was redone in limestone in the late 1950s. *Broadway and Park Row.*

The building within City Hall Park to the north of City Hall is familiarly known as the **Tweed Courthouse,** in recognition of the millions "Boss" Tweed skimmed off its construction budget. With so much money there for the taking, it's no wonder the courthouse took from 1861 to 1872 to finish. After an elaborate renovation project was completed in 2001, a tussle began over how to use the space, which in recent years had held city offices. Mayor Michael R. Bloomberg scuttled Rudolph Giuliani's plan to relocate the Museum of the City of New York here and announced that the Board of Education was to occupy the grand structure. *52 Chambers Street, east of Broadway.*

East of the courthouse is the **Municipal Building,** completed in 1914 and designed in the Beaux Arts style by the renowned McKim, Mead & White firm. The architects accounted for auto traffic, which nudges up against the structure. On the south side above the subway entrance you can view one of the city's several magnificent Guastavino tile installations (see sidebar on page 231). Behind the building is the plaza where artist Richard Serra installed his *Tilted Arc* sculpture, which gave rise to one of the more notorious confrontations over art in public spaces. The rusty metal monolith, 120 feet long and 12 feet high, bisected the plaza, forcing office workers to walk around it. Serra had wanted them to have an art experience each and every day. "Step by step the perception not only of the sculpture but of the entire environment changes," he asserted. But the workers rebelled, and after a lengthy court battle the sculpture was yanked in 1989—a victory for the practical-minded or the Philistines, depending on your point of view. *Centre and Chambers Streets.*

City, state, and government offices surround **Foley Square.** In the 19th century, this turf, known as Five Points (for the five streets that intersect here), had little to do with civic, or even civil, endeavors, as gangs with catchy names like the Plug Uglies and the Dead Rabbits haunted the slum-ridden sector. The area is the focal point of Martin Scorsese's film *Gangs of New York,* whose tag line, "America Was Born in the Streets," aptly conveys the ferocity of the rivalry between the native-born New Yorkers and recent immigrants who lived here. *Centre and Pearl Streets.*

North of Foley Square on Centre Street, you may recognize the **Criminal Courts Building** from television shows like *Law & Order, NYPD Blue,* and *100 Centre Street.* Harvey Wiley Corbett, who also had a hand in fashioning Rockefeller Center, designed this ziggurat-patterned Art Moderne rockpile. Since metal detectors were installed in the mid-1980s, cops routinely retrieve weapons from the bushes out front—ditched by people headed into court. *100 Centre Street, at White Street.*

In the same block as the Criminal Courts Building is the **Bernard B. Kerik Complex,** the detention center renamed in late 2001 for the former Department of Corrections commissioner who served as chief of police during the latter part of Mayor Rudolph Giuliani's term. As corrections chief he was credited with making New York's prisons safer and more humane. The jail more commonly goes by the name **the Tombs,** for two 19th-century buildings on the site, the first of which was modeled after an Egyptian mausoleum. *125 White Street.*

A sign on a fenced-in lawn west of Foley Square designates the **African Burial Ground,** an 18th-century cemetery that encompassed 5 or 6 acres. In 1991, human remains were discovered during excavation for a federal office building, and community outcry forced the abandonment of construction. In the coming years,

(following pages) The Brooklyn Bridge, one of the 19th century's engineering marvels, provides a spectacular point of entry into Lower Manhattan.

a permanent memorial to one of the oldest sites connected to New York City's African-American community will be erected, but already open is the African Burial Ground Interpretive Center (Federal Building, 290 Broadway), adjacent to the burial ground. *Duane Street between Broadway and Lafayette Street.*

Five blocks south of the burial ground, west of City Hall Park's southern tip, is the **Woolworth Building,** the work of Cass Gilbert, who also designed the U.S. Custom House. The giant Gothic confection was, from 1913 to 1929, the world's tallest building. For his ornate office, F. W. Woolworth, a farmer's son from upstate New York whose namesake department stores made him one of America's wealthiest men, replicated Napoleon's audience room at Compiègne. The equally ornate lobby contains a wry bas-relief of Woolworth counting nickels and dimes. An enduring mystery: why the building has no floors numbered 42, 48, or 52. Nicknamed "the Cathedral of Commerce," the Woolworth Building was long a goading vision that could be seen from all over Lower Manhattan—including the slums of the Lower East Side. Since the demise of the World Trade Center towers, the building has become more noticeable again. *233 Broadway.*

South on Broadway is **St. Paul's Chapel.** A delightful Georgian edifice built in 1766, the church is the oldest building in Manhattan. Wags say George Washington slept here, a reference to the dull Episcopalian sermons, but the Father of Our Country did come by to worship; a plaque marks his pew. The pink-and-green pastel interior, with Waterford chandeliers, is best enjoyed during the noonday chamber music concerts. *Broadway near Fulton Street.*

■ ALONG THE HUDSON *map pages 58–59, B/C-3/6*

Stretched along the Hudson River waterfront, resting on landfill partly made up of the earth cleared away to create the foundations of the World Trade Center, are the **World Financial Center** and **Battery Park City,** both of which present their arguments for urban design, end-of-the-millennium-style.

They are only partially successful. The World Financial Center is a complex of four office towers, ranging in height from thirty-four to fifty-one stories, each with a distinctive rooftop profile. The **Winter Garden** (2 World Financial Center), an airy and many-paned public space, had to be reconstructed after suffering grave damage when the World Trade Center towers collapsed. Expansive views of the harbor are the attraction, as are the concerts and other events held throughout the year. The center's shops are mostly high-end enterprises.

The World Financial Center: a so-so end-of-the-millennium statement in urban design.

The World Financial Center divides 92-acre Battery Park City, a well-intended but slightly flavorless mix of pricey condos and apartments, parks, and cultural institutions. The planned community's best features are not the antiseptic residential neighborhoods (there are four: Battery Place, Rector Place, Gateway Plaza, and the imaginatively named North Residential Neighborhood), but rather the river views and open spaces. **Hudson River Park,** which will eventually extend north into Chelsea, contains a fine playground at about Chambers Street and some great bronze sculptures by Tom Otterness.

The denizens of Battery Park City have embraced the **Esplanade,** a walkway along the Harbor with wonderful perspectives of the Statue of Liberty, Ellis Island, and the Narrows. Lower Manhattan in general is also the preferred venue for watching sunsets, because farther north the Palisades interfere. With New Jersey pollution creating a refracting haze, sunset can be a gorgeous, lingering light show.

The southern end of Battery Park City is increasingly becoming the turf of choice for cultural institutions and monuments. In different stages of planning and realization are large-scale public sculptures and artworks, as well as the New York City Police Memorial and the Museum of Women.

Skyscrapers tower over historic Battery Park.

By early 2003 the permanent home of the **Skyscraper Museum** should be up and running in the towering Ritz-Carlton New York, Battery Park. In its previous incarnations the museum mounted intriguing exhibitions about the Empire State Building and other skyscrapers. The smoothly curving ground-floor space at the Ritz-Carlton will celebrate "the world's first and foremost vertical metropolis," chronicling the skyscraper race from the late 19th century to current times, surveying buildings great and tall from aesthetic, engineering, and architectural perspectives. *2 West Street; 212-344-0800.*

New York–based artist Brian Tolle designed the **Irish Hunger Memorial,** which was dedicated in mid-2002. With an old fieldstone cottage brought over from Ireland, rows of potato furrows, and sixty-two species of native Irish plants and wildflowers, the memorial is a tribute to the millions who suffered or died in the *an Gorta Mor* (great hunger), a famine from 1845 to 1852 that prompted hundreds of thousands of Irish people to emigrate to the United States. The location of the memorial is fitting because Lower Manhattan was the point of arrival for many Irish. A small library on the site is devoted to the fight against starvation worldwide. *Vesey Green at North End Avenue.*

At the southern end of Battery Park City, just north of Battery Park on the shore of the Hudson, the **Museum of Jewish Heritage** is the graceful and well-designed end to a stormy half-century of wrangling over the form of a Holocaust memorial in New York City. The granite-clad, hexagonal main exhibition building represents the six-sided Star of David and the six million Jewish victims of Nazi genocide.

Each of the three floors is devoted to a different time period: before, during, and after World War II. The emphasis here is on personal artifacts—letters, snapshots, and other possessions—that mutely but eloquently convey the richness of Jewish life a century ago, the effects of the Holocaust on individuals and their communities, and the complex response since the Holocaust. Steven Spielberg's Shoah Foundation has donated documentaries recording the words and faces of Holocaust survivors, rescuers, and victims. The impressive main hall is joined by a larger, more recent, and architecturally more conventional east wing. *18 First Place, at Battery Place; 212-509-6130.*

Wedged between the museum and Battery Park is **Robert F. Wagner Jr. Park,** named for the son of a popular New York City mayor. A pavilion here has a roof deck that provides a bird's-eye view of the harbor and the Statue of Liberty.

The Statue of Liberty as seen from the Esplanade in Battery Park City.

IN MEMORIAM: The World Trade Center

Construction begun: 1966
Construction completed: 1976
Destroyed: 2001

We didn't know what we had until it was gone. Among some Manhattanites it was always fashionable to complain about the twin towers, to grouse about their chilly International style. Now that they have been demolished, they leave behind a massive absence, not only in the skyline but in our hearts.

"Politicians, ugly buildings, and whores," grumbles John Huston in a memorable line from *Chinatown*, "all get respectable if they last long enough." The World Trade Center was not permitted to last long enough. The hulking complex became respectable only in death.

What was destroyed on a sunny September morning in 2001 took an extraordinary engineering effort to erect, an accomplishment that was, without exaggeration, one of the modern wonders of the architectural world. A giant concrete "bathtub" first had to be created so that footings could be sunk below the waterline. About 1.2 million cubic yards of earth had to be excavated. Finally, upon a foundation of Manhattan mica schist bedrock, 100 million tons of steel (a dozen different grades), glass, concrete, and other materials had to be shaped into the massive, quarter-mile-tall twin towers.

The assault on the World Trade Center in 2001 wasn't the first on the complex. In 1993, six people died and more than a thousand were injured when a bomb was exploded in the underground garage of 1 World Trade Center. At the time, the novelist Robert Stone wrote a prescient piece for the *New York Times*, speculating on why these buildings in particular seemed the focus of fundamentalist ire. Why not the Empire State Building? Why not the Sears Tower? In Stone's analysis, the 1993 bombing was a lethal brand of architectural criticism. To be sure, attacking globalism, as embodied by the World Trade Center's very name, largely motivated the terrorists. But, Stone wrote, to a certain fervent mind-set the ultramodern towers, which soared so high, were also symbolic of man's hubris.

That the towers soared high, of course, is exactly the point. For a relatively short period, about three decades, the towers dominated Lower Manhattan, and for a few years they were the world's tallest buildings. (Though both buildings had 110 stories,

The twin towers dominated Lower Manhattan's skyline for nearly three decades.

the northern tower, 1 World Trade Center, rose 1,368 feet; 2 World Trade Center, whose observation deck millions of tourists and residents had enjoyed, was 1,362 feet tall.) The towers embodied the humanistic spirit of Manhattan that suggested that mankind should indeed soar high, build great, dream big.

On an average weekday, fifty-thousand people worked in the World Trade Center, and another eighty thousand visited. One of the horrors of September 11 is that we can say it is "lucky" that "only" about three thousand people died in the attack. Thousands in the buildings were saved by the heroic efforts of members of the New York Police Department, the New York Fire Department, and the Port Authority Police. Almost everyone from below the point of impact survived—except for the brave men and women who went in to make sure everyone got out alive.

It is easy to forget, caught up in the competing symbolisms of the atrocity, that if this was a wound to the world, it was also the ripping apart of a neighborhood. In the nights after the attack, huge banks of halogen floodlights, brought in to help the round-the-clock rescue and recovery effort, also spookily illuminated the entire radius of Lower Manhattan. The surreal glow turned night into day for thousands of New Yorkers who lived in what was, before September 11, a growing residential area. The whole of Lower Manhattan was immobilized.

Out of the billowing smoke and flames—the death of one symbol of New York— emerged what would become another, even more potent symbol: Ground Zero, an area bounded roughly by West, Liberty, Church, and Vesey Streets. It evolved from a jagged thirty-story-high pile of rubble into an eerie doomscape sanctified by the ongoing recovery effort. After that, Ground Zero changed again, its perimeter patrolled by hoarse-voiced street preachers and piled high with flowers, teddy bears, and scrawled prayers, with glimpses of the devastation. A viewing platform erected near St. Paul's Chapel became the focus of a pilgrimage for thousands of people, who lined up to witness the scene of the tragedy.

The site's metamorphosis continues. An interim memorial is planned, and afterward a permanent memorial park. The World Trade Center's developer, who bought the buildings only weeks before the attack, has formulated designs for a collection of smaller buildings where the twin towers once stood.

The broken gap in the skyline of Manhattan is devastating, visceral, insistent. There is no way New Yorkers can ever reconcile themselves to the loss. A shadow of sadness will always fall over that shred of sacred ground in Lower Manhattan. We can move on. But we can never forget.

(opposite) A damaged sculpture from the site of the towers became part of a memorial.

CHINATOWN TO SOHO

It is somehow fitting that sprawling north from the Civic Center is some of the most immigrant-hallowed turf in America. If Manhattan was made by "huddled masses yearning to be free," intensely parochial neighborhoods like Chinatown, Little Italy, and the Lower East Side are where they huddled.

And still huddle today. **Chinatown,** just northeast of the Civic Center, is an amorphous presence still chewing up blocks of **Little Italy** and other neighborhoods on its fringes—growing, absorbing, co-opting. Contrast the vibrancy of Chinatown with the static, museum-piece aura of Little Italy. Once home to a healthy chunk of New York's huge Italian immigrant population—most of whom have decamped for the boroughs, Long Island, or New Jersey—it now lives largely on its past reputation, although the dwindling core of a neighborhood, anchored by some gaudy restaurants, remains. Which is not to say that Little Italy doesn't have things to recommend it. A great cannoli is a great cannoli, after all.

Farther east in the **Lower East Side** are streets that once represented the center of Jewish life in New York, and some of the shops and eateries in this area are delightful throwbacks to that era. The teeming tenements and slums of the Lower East Side hosted a century-long ethnic jamboree that embraced not only Jewish but Italian, Irish, Eastern European, and Puerto Rican immigrants as well.

As has happened elsewhere in Manhattan, gentrification is transforming the Lower East Side. Evidence of this includes the increased presence of exhibition and performance spaces, hip boutiques, and au courant cafés and bars, some of them incongruously nudging up against purveyors of traditional ethnic goods and services. When a For Rent sign was slapped on Schapiro's kosher wine emporium, long a Rivington Street staple, it was clear the jig was nearly up. At the moment, though, the area is in the funky phase of renewal, especially on Ludlow Street just south of Houston Street.

"The role of the artist," said former mayor Ed Koch, indulging in some fine irony while simultaneously formulating a real estate aphorism, "is to make a neighborhood so desirable that artists can't afford to live there anymore." He was speaking of two neighborhoods in particular, **TriBeCa** and **SoHo,** which in the last few decades blossomed as residential and retail districts after being discovered and refurbished by artists in search of cheap studio space.

■ CHINATOWN *map pages 94–95, E-5*

What is said to be the largest community of Chinese in the Western Hemisphere is home to roughly two hundred thousand immigrants from all over Asia—ethnic Chinese from the mainland, Taiwan, Vietnam, Burma, and Singapore—plus a smattering of Chinese from places like Cuba and South America, mixed with a few other, primarily Asian, nationalities. A few hundred thousand more ethnic Chinese inhabit New York's other Chinatowns—Flushing in Queens, and Eighth Avenue in Brooklyn—but Manhattan's Chinatown is the central community.

The first immigrants to come here were primarily Cantonese railroad workers from the West, who during the 1870s settled in a proscribed area—the thirteen blocks bounded by Canal, Worth, and Baxter Streets, and the Bowery. The neighborhood endured for over a century without much change in its boundaries.

Not until 1965, when Congress increased Asian immigration quotas, did newcomers begin to flood in and Chinatown push north into Little Italy and the Lower East Side. Coincidentally, the 1970s witnessed an upsurge of interest in Chinese food, which all the newly arrived chefs were happy to provide.

More than 350 restaurants do business in Chinatown.

DOWNTOWN & THE VILLAGES

Chinatown is a noisy, garish, aromatic, jam-packed neighborhood with crinkum-crankum streets and some of the oldest tenements on the island. Living quarters are handed down over generations, and it is difficult for anyone outside the community to find a residence here. Many of the apartments are illegally subdivided into *gong si fong,* or "public rooms," crude flophouses that stack five, ten, sometimes fifteen people in what was originally a one-bedroom apartment.

For most *guey low faan*—"foreign devils"—Chinatown is primarily a place to eat and soak up atmosphere. But for the members of the hermetic Chinese community, some of whom might live here for years and never speak a word of English, Chinatown is a place of work. Hundreds of piecework garment factories are located here—some no better than sweatshops. There are more than 350 restaurants, and four dozen or so "spas," or *bagnios,* as well—combination health spas and massage parlors that employ hordes of young Asian women. The standard for all these places is a six-day, sixty- to eighty-hour week.

Chinatown has about two dozen banks, by far the highest bank-per-capita ratio in the city. Many immigrants working in the restaurants and sweatshops save for the "eight bigs" (a color television, a refrigerator, a washing machine, furniture, a camera, a VCR, a telephone, and a car), save to send money back to their place of origin (up to three-quarters of Chinatown residents are foreign born), or save to buy real estate or a small business.

Canal Street is Chinatown's traditional northern border, and the sidewalks are jammed with food shops of every flavor. The giant **Pearl River** (277 Canal Street) department store stocks a vast array of Asian consumer goods, and the neighborhood's many apothecaries offer ginseng and medicinal herbs.

Off Canal Street is the **Museum of Chinese in the Americas** (70 Mulberry Street, Second Floor; 212-619-4785), an archive of Sino-American culture that is worth a quick visit. Note the 4-inch slippers of mail-order bride Fokee Chan: her feet, unbound in her new land, later expanded to 8 inches.

Chinatown's classic thoroughfare is **Mott Street,** a kaleidoscope of sights, flavors, and odors. Restaurants and markets display racks of barbecued ducks in their windows, smoked in tea and glazed to caramel perfection. Head east off Mott on Pell Street to find tiny, crooked Doyers Street, its **"bloody angle"** notorious a century ago for battles between the Hip Sing and On Leong tongs (gangs). Though both tongs still exist, today Doyers is more famous for its restaurants.

A friendly (for money) game of pai gow.

Doyers Street leads out directly upon **Chatham Square,** the eastern locus of Chinatown. At its center stands a memorial to Chinese Americans killed in combat. Off the square is the **Shearith Israel Cemetery** (55 James Street), dating from 1683 and the oldest cemetery in Manhattan. Also nearby is **Knickerbocker Village** (Catherine and Monroe Streets), where in the summer of 1950 a squad of nine FBI men arrested Ethel Rosenberg (in apartment GE11) for the capital crime of treason. Three years later, Ethel and husband Julius were executed for selling nuclear secrets to the Soviet Union.

The bronze statue of Confucius by the sculptor Tiu Shih, in front of **Confucius Plaza,** the residential high-rise north of Chatham Square, was supported by traditionalists from Taiwan, but opposed by leftist mainland Chinese immigrants, who considered the sage a reactionary symbol of old China. That the statue is there tells you who won, and says something about the political makeup of Chinatown.

Confucius Plaza abuts the mangled terminus of the **Manhattan Bridge** (Bowery and Canal Streets), its once-grand triumphal arch modified beyond recognition over time by streetcar and subway approaches. The Daniel Chester French sculptures were transferred to the Brooklyn Museum of Art to make way for roadway modifications. One of the more bizarre sculptural touches to remain is the rendering of a buffalo hunt, right between the allegorical figures of Commerce and Industry. This 1905 bridge, designed for lighter traffic than today's auto, truck, and train onslaught, has suffered from its reconfiguring and pales in comparison with its mighty neighbor to the south, the Brooklyn Bridge.

■ LITTLE ITALY *map pages 94–95, E-4/5*

Little Italy is concentrated in the Mulberry-to-Mott corridor north of Canal Street, with most of the restaurants in the blocks around Grand and Hester Streets. Wander too far off this axis and you'll encounter signs written in Chinese—they'd be on Mulberry Street, too, if the local neighborhood association hadn't requested otherwise.

Even the **Festa di San Gennaro,** Little Italy's showcase street fair celebrated for the ten days around September 19, has become diluted with non-Italian influences—the vendors sell egg rolls and tacos alongside the traditional sausage and peppers. Named after the patron saint of Naples, the festival is either marvelously tacky, sentimentally moving, or obnoxiously raucous, depending on your mood. Still, to ride a miniature Ferris wheel among 19th-century tenements is a surreal enough experience to warrant a try.

Sidewalk scene, Little Italy, 1908. (Library of Congress)

A relic of another kind, of Little Italy's Mafia-connected notoriety, stood for years on the corner of Mulberry and Hester: **Umberto's Clam House,** where on April 7, 1972, "Crazy" Joey Gallo got his. Gallo was a mob rub-out guy with pretensions: he used to quote Sartre and dabble in oil painting. He also kept a lion chained in the basement of his social club in Brooklyn, in case he wanted to bring somebody down there and make him an offer he couldn't refuse.

Joey Gallo's assassination at Umberto's was payback for years of contract hits and high visibility. In 1997, Umberto's closed up the scene of the crime (twenty-five years after the murder) and reopened around the corner on Broome Street. Another legacy of the place's Mafia past has a certain delicious irony: for almost a decade, the federal government ran the place, taking it over after the arrest of Matthew (Matty the Horse) Ianniello and eight other owners. The proprietors had skimmed $2 million off the take at Umberto's, and the unlikely result of their convictions was the Feds "owning" a former mob hangout.

Little Italy's northern section has been transformed into **NoLIta** (for North of Little Italy), where milliners and glassblowers peddle their inventive handcrafts in jewel-box-like shops. The district centers on Elizabeth Street between Prince and Houston.

West of Little Italy, is the baroque **Old NYC Police Headquarters** (240 Centre Street), built in 1909 and converted to high-priced condos now occupied by celebrities. At Lafayette and East Houston Streets is the equally well-restored **Puck Building,** built by the founders of the fin-de-siècle humor magazine, *Puck,* and later home to *Spy,* the similarly catty satire magazine. The fictional Grace of the TV show *Will and Grace* has her office here.

■ LOWER EAST SIDE

map pages 94–95, F/G-3/4

"Everybody ought to have a Lower East Side in their life," said Irving Berlin, and it would take the composer of "God Bless America" to lay a sunny face on the conglomeration of slums, tenement dwellings, and historical misery to which the district played host.

In the 19th century, the miasmic living conditions in these tenement apartments—hovel-like structures illegally slapped onto the rear of the buildings (reformer-photographer Jacob Riis called them "caves")—meant that disease ran rampant. Families were packed in, and privacy was nonexistent. The whole seething mass of humanity was shorted on city services and quarantined from "respectable" people.

But Berlin had a point: hard times may take on a roseate glow in retrospect, especially when they are shared by as vibrant a community as the Jewish one that flourished here, a half-million strong, in the half-century or so after 1880. It's only part of the story on display at the **Lower East Side Tenement Museum,** which also tells the stories of other ethnic groups—most notably freed slaves and the Irish—that

(opposite) A gold-leaf statue of Puck adorns the Puck Building. (above) The structure is named for the satirical magazine Puck, *which had its offices here. (Library of Congress)*

are part of Lower East Side history. This is a "living history" museum, offering tours of one of the very tenements it seeks to memorialize as well as guided strolls through the neighborhood. Sights on the walks include the Jewish Daily Forward Building on East Broadway and the Hibernian Hook and Ladder Fire Company, now an apartment building. *97 Orchard Street; 212-431-0233.*

The neighborhood today is largely Puerto Rican, but Chinese and other Asian immigrants are settling the corridor of East Broadway. There are still remnants of the Yiddish Golden Age, like the **Eldridge Street Synagogue** (12 Eldridge Street), the first building in the New World erected by Eastern European Orthodox Jews. The vaudeville and movie comedian Eddie Cantor's boyhood home was across the street.

The shops of the neighborhood afford the clearest glimpse into the past. **Russ & Daughters** (179 East Houston Street) sells smoked fish, but is a purveyor of something far more ethereal—the authentic Lower East Side experience. **Economy Candy Market** (108 Rivington Street), where the halvah is made on the premises, has a colorful, mouth-watering inventory for the bargain-minded.

Orchard Street, south of Houston Street, is another cultural survivor masked as a retail bazaar. The street may no longer be dense with pushcarts, but the bargains live on in a riot of discount houses, cubbyhole shops, and spillover sidewalk sale racks. Name brands at a discount—the idea is commonplace today, but Orchard Street was the original. And even though the merchandise here may be infiltrated with cheap knock-offs, the sheer experience of retail frenzy (especially on Sunday, when the street is closed to cars) is hard to beat.

The **Williamsburg Bridge,** whose Manhattan terminus is on Delancey Street, was the second span to cross the East River to Brooklyn and is surely among the most uninspired bridges in the area. Homeless people lived in a shantytown beneath the bridge until bulldozers cleared it out. Nearby is the pioneering **Henry Street Settlement** (263–267 Henry Street), a social-service organization that was among the first to reach out to the vast population of the Lower East Side with medical, cultural, educational, and housing aid. Today its theaters and exhibit spaces host multicultural exhibits and performances.

East River Park, a green crescent beneath the Williamsburg Bridge north from Corlear's Hook, is an exuberant (if overgrown) "front yard" for the neighboring housing projects. Especially in summer, it is alive with the sounds of impromptu crap games, boom boxes, and softball. Vendors hawk tropical-hued cones shaved off

A Lower East Side apartment, ca. 1935. (Lower East Side Tenement Museum)

IMMIGRANT WORK

At eight in the morning I put my left arm through the strap of the basket, lifting it and adjusting it on my back, the other arm through the strap of the boiler, over my neck, keeping the boiler on my chest. All you could see of me from a distance was my troublesome straw hat! My instructions were to walk up Elizabeth Street four blocks, turn east and cross the Bowery, which already had the elevated, then walk two blocks more. When I reached the blocks of private houses, I was to walk up the stoops, pull the bell, and when the door opened, to say, "Buy tinware."

At my first port of call my heart was in my mouth. I hesitated. Taking a long breath, I climbed up a stoop and yanked the bell. I was in suspense. The door opened. A redheaded young giant appeared. He looked at me and my outfit without a word. He was not a bit rough. He merely laid his hand very gently on the boiler in front of me and gave me a good shove. I descended backwards rapidly, finally landing in a sitting position in the middle of the street, my stock strewn about me in all directions.... I turned back to Elizabeth Street. Entering a yard I saw an open door—a woman near it. I made my first sale—a cup for ten cents—the profit was not bad!

—Samuel Cohen, ca. 1900, as excerpted from *How We Lived: A Documentary History of Immigrant Jews in America 1880–1930,* 1979

Market at junction of Hester and Norfolk Streets, ca. 1898.
(New-York Historical Society)

Lower East Side signs reveal much about the neighborhood's history.

solid blocks of ice, or barbecued shish kebab with meat of unknown provenance. The bridge booms with traffic up above, while the East River tidal strait roils next door: one of the overlooked pleasures of Manhattan. *Along the East River from Jackson Street to East 14th Street.*

■ TRIBECA *map pages 94–95, C/D-5/6*

TriBeCa (try-beck-ah) was once known as the Lower West Side, but savvy realtors in the mid-1970s knew the power of a catchy name—they had just witnessed the wonders one had done for SoHo. Thus TriBeCa, an acronym of sorts for Triangle Below Canal Street, was born. Within the boundaries of Canal Street, West Broadway, and Hudson Street, there was much valuable turf waiting to be exploited. The makeover worked. TriBeCa is a thriving commercial, residential, and artistic community, and yet the area has retained—much more than SoHo—its urban-frontier feel. Despite the spiraling real estate prices, there is something provisional and sparse about TriBeCa as a neighborhood, which, given the overdeveloped and overpopulated character of other parts of Manhattan, is exactly how some residents like it.

The area first bloomed as a commercial center during the age of the steamship, when the deep-water wharves along the Hudson took away shipping business from the older, shallow-draft piers of the East River. The local Washington Market, the island's first major fruit and vegetable market—the nation's largest in the mid-19th century—became the impetus for much of the district's commercial development, as the Federal and Greek Revival residences in the area were converted to warehouses.

The eastern edge of the neighborhood is permeable, so we begin with an institution somewhat outside its purlieu, but fitting in with TriBeCa's overall mood: the **Clocktower Gallery,** a nonprofit arm of the Institute for Contemporary Art, with a magnificent Beaux Arts exterior. The gallery itself seeks to strop the cutting edge of the avant-garde, but the Clocktower's best feature has nothing to do with art: climb the stairs to see the escapement of the actual clock, fourteen stories above City Hall Park. *108 Leonard Street, at Broadway; 212-233-1096.*

Closer to West Broadway, which functions as TriBeCa's main stem, is **Franklin Furnace** (112 Franklin Street); part gallery, part theater, part "installation," it is all alternative. Nearby is **Let There Be Neon** (38 White Street), a riotous emporium offering small- and large-scale expressions of what began as an advertising gimmick and wound up as an art form.

Nearer the water is the **Tribeca Film Center** (375 Greenwich Street), a professional building located in an old coffee warehouse. Full of editing and screening rooms, production offices, and hot talent, the facility was developed by Robert De Niro as a kind of love letter to his profession and his hometown. De Niro keeps an office there, as do directors Steven Spielberg and Ron Howard and music producer Quincy Jones.

However, the most endearing aspects of trendy TriBeCa are those that reveal its historic origins. **Harrison Street** between Greenwich and Hudson Streets is a perfect museum of a block; its Federal row houses, some of them relocated here from Washington Street, stand in mute reproach to the massive **Independence Plaza** housing complex and the imposing **Borough of Manhattan Community College** campus nearby.

Duane Park, at Duane and Hudson Streets, is another neighborhood area with anachronistic appeal. Or try two-block-long **Staple Street,** a charming throwback to the days when this area supplied the island's "staples" of fruit, vegetables, dairy, and coffee. Nearby on Chambers Street between West and Greenwich Streets is **Washington Market Park,** one of the island's best-designed small parks, on the site of the original market.

A quiet street in TriBeCa.

At Pier 26 along the Hudson is the **River Project,** reaching even farther into the island's past to reclaim something that's almost totally disappeared: the littoral fringe of Manhattan. A park that restores this fragment of shoreline to its original state is proposed; for now, the River Project features an "estuarium," exhibits, and educational and other programs.

Canal Street, which forms TriBeCa's northern boundary and SoHo's southern one and runs east into Chinatown, has become a vast casbah of electronic shops, hardware stores, and bargain retail outlets of every kind. In New York's early days, there actually was a canal on Canal Street, 40 feet wide, with a promenade on either side. It drained the Collect, a freshwater pond that gradually became unusable from pollution. The canal—a public-works project meant to give employment to the restive unemployed—was covered over in the early 19th century.

Long known as a mecca for retail hardware, in the last two decades Canal Street has picked up a flea-market flavor. People knew something was up when East Village New Wavers began journeying downtown in the early 1980s to buy their fashion accessories at Canal Street plumbing- and electrical-supply establishments. **Pearl Paint** (308 Canal Street), the best-stocked, best-priced art supply store in town, helped to draw the bohemian crowd. Today, beginning with the flavor and funk of Chinatown, the thoroughfare is an island-wide celebration of bargain-bin retail.

■ SoHo *map pages 94–95, D-3/4*

SoHo was named not after the London district (confusingly known as "the Greenwich Village of London") but as an acronym formed from "South of Houston Street." Its development into one of Manhattan's priciest neighborhoods followed a process that has since become formula in other neighborhoods, most notably TriBeCa. It goes something like this: cheap commercial space attracts artists looking for studios, the artists exude a certain bohemian cachet, attracting trendoids with money but often little artistic cachet of their own, and the resulting competition for space forces out the artists, who move on to trigger the whole process elsewhere.

SoHo began as "Hell's Hundred Acres," so named because the crowded slums were repeatedly beset by inferno-like fires, but it boomed after the Civil War, when the neighborhood came to be known simply as the Eighth Ward. Whole blocks of cast-iron warehouse and factory buildings became the norm. The cast-iron façade, one of

SoHo is famous for cast-iron façades (above) and sidewalk wares (opposite).

BEFORE BIG ART

Up until a few years ago Soho was an obscure district of lofts used chiefly for storage and light manufacturing. It was, of course, a combination of many unattractive things that led to the Soho of today, but quite definitely the paramount factor was the advent of Big Art. Before Big Art came along, painters lived, as God undoubtedly intended them to, in garrets or remodeled carriage houses, and painted paintings of a reasonable size. A painting of a reasonable size is a painting that one can easily hang over a sofa. If a painting cannot be easily hung over a sofa it is obviously a painting painted by a painter who got too big for his brushes....

One day a Big Artist realized that if he took all of the sewing machines and bales of rags out of a three-thousand-square-foot loft and put in a bathroom and kitchen he would be able to live and make Big Art in the same place. He was quickly followed by other Big Artists and they by Big Lawyers, Big Boutique Owners, and Big Rich Kids. Soon there was a Soho and it was positively awash in hardwood floors, talked-to plants, indoor swings, enormous record collections, hiking boots, Conceptual Artists, video communes, Art book stores, Art grocery stores, Art restaurants, Art bars, Art galleries, and boutiques selling tie-dyed raincoats, macramé flower pots, and Art Deco salad plates.

—Fran Lebowitz, *Metropolitan Life,* 1974

New York's gifts to the world, was developed in the mid-19th century as a cheap way to mimic fancy architectural detailing. Cast-iron façades were bolted onto the brick or stone masonry of the building, sheathing it in elaborate, often lyrical ornamentation. SoHo's cast-iron buildings gradually outgrew their usefulness, as the light-industrial concerns that had operated here for decades moved to more modern facilities in the outer boroughs or beyond.

As late as the 1960s, SoHo was just one more fading Manhattan commercial district, filled with gorgeous but badly run-down architectural gems. The **SoHo Cast-Iron Historic District** (roughly bounded by West Broadway and Houston, Crosby, and Canal Streets) was created to preserve the exquisite façades, and the streets and curbs have been restored with their original "Belgian brick" cobblestones.

It is useful to remember, in order not to be taken for a total rube, that in Manhattan "Houston Street" is pronounced not like the city in Texas but as "HOUSE-ton." This is because the name came not from Sam Houston, nor yet from the Dutch words for "house" and "garden" (*huys* and *tuyn,* respectively), but from William Houstoun, a delegate to the Constitutional Convention from the state of Georgia. He married the daughter of the owner of the land tract that Houston Street originally cut through.

However you pronounce it, **Houston Street** is the northern boundary of a major gallery and retail district. Art transformed this whole neighborhood over the course of two decades. When the city legalized the previously commercially zoned loft spaces as residences in 1972, real estate values soared into the stratosphere and a star was born.

One of the great free shows in Manhattan is a leisurely tour of SoHo's art galleries, which offer a thick nest of color, lyricism, and pretension in a remarkably concentrated area. West Broadway (a few blocks west of Broadway) and Greene Street are SoHo's most prestigious addresses for galleries. Much of the art gallery action has moved to Chelsea, but there are still some impressive storefront exhibition spaces, and more dealers are warrened away on upper floors of old warehouse buildings. Most SoHo galleries maintain an open-door policy and welcome browsers. The atmosphere is similar to that of a small museum. For information about particular SoHo galleries, it's best to refer to the gallery guide available at most SoHo kiosks and galleries.

The **New Museum of Contemporary Art** (583 Broadway; 212-219-1355) exhibits cutting-edge contemporary works by artists most people haven't heard of—but may be hearing about. It's a worthy stop, as is its neighbor, the **Museum for African Art** (593 Broadway; 212-966-1313), which mounts superb shows and publishes books about African art and culture.

The live arts are equally well represented in SoHo, beginning with the **Performing Garage** (33 Wooster Street; 212-853-9623), one of the oldest alternative theaters in America and host to the resident **Wooster Group.** Monologist Spalding Gray got his start here; you can spot the theater in the film *Swimming to Cambodia.* On the western fringe of SoHo is the **Film Forum** (209 West Houston Street; 212-727-8110), a three-theater complex that supports an ambitious slate of art and revival films.

THE VILLAGES

"Greenwich Village has no boundaries," said Hippolyte Havel, anarchist, head-waiter, and longtime confrère to the crusading and equally anarchistic "Red Emma" Goldman. "It is a state of mind."

It is true that Greenwich Village and its fellow traveler, the East Village, have a combined reputation that far outstrips their geography—and habitually attract such lofty pronouncements as Havel's. But it is equally true that we can delineate the turf with some precision. The Villages girdle Manhattan from river to river, south of 14th Street and north of Houston Street. Broadway is the traditional boundary between the two, with the area between Hudson Street and the Hudson River informally known as the West Village.

Bleecker Street during the winter of 1896. (New-York Historical Society)

■ **GREENWICH VILLAGE**   *map pages 94–95, A/D-1/2*

"Greenwich Village" is redundant, since "Greenwich" itself means "green village." In the late 17th and early 18th centuries, the neighborhood was a sleepy farm-oriented suburb north of the clamorous urban mass of Lower Manhattan—a refuge of the wealthy, the Hamptons of its day. One of these arrivistes, Brooklyn farmer Yellis Mandeville, named the place "Greenwyck" after a village in Brooklyn.

Disease is what made the Village boom, what transformed it from a rich man's playground to an integral part of the urban metropolis. When a series of contagions hit Lower Manhattan, beginning with an epidemic of smallpox in 1739, western Greenwich Village was the refuge of choice for those rich enough to flee. (Disease did find some of these refugees, but the Village's sparser population seemed to promise less contact with the infected.) Subsequent scourges of cholera and yellow fever prompted new stampedes north, culminating in the great yellow fever plague of 1822. This last epidemic caused such a population shift that ferries from Brooklyn were rerouted to land at the Village instead of Wall Street.

When the fevers subsided, many of the displaced returned to Lower Manhattan, but others liked the pastoral precincts of the Village so much they stayed on. Its population quadrupled in the second quarter of the 19th century, but as Manhattan charged north, Greenwich Village remained a charming enclave, exempting itself from the grid plan that imposed utilitarian order upon the island. Greenwich Village's crazy-quilt lanes and streets, many of them following old Indian paths and colonial property lines, set it apart from newer neighborhoods.

The quirky nature of the surroundings attracted an equally quirky population. A burgeoning French presence in the Village, plus a subsequent influx of artists, political radicals, and bohemians, lent the place an air of the foreign, the free, and the licentious. In the years before and after World War I, the Village peaked as a hotbed of free love and socialism, free verse and abstract art. The 1950s and 1960s saw a renewal of the area's reputation for the unorthodox, with Abstract Expressionists, beatniks, and folkies taking up residence. Today, that reputation is only a faint ghost haunting a still picturesque, but determinedly upper-middle-class neighborhood.

Like a solar system with twin suns, Greenwich Village revolves around two squares: **Sheridan Square** and **Washington Square.** From Sheridan Square southwest to the Hudson River runs yet another important axis of Village life, **Christopher Street,** the historic center of gay and lesbian New York.

■ SHERIDAN SQUARE *map pages 94–95, B-2*

More a confluence of thoroughfares than a true square, Sheridan Square is a quadruple intersection where the automobile traffic runs in at crazy and sometimes terrifying angles. As a neighborhood, the Sheridan Square area is in many ways the heart of Greenwich Village, a heart that beats faster than a pedestrian's in a mad dash across Seventh Avenue.

Seventh Avenue is, indeed, the reason for the truncated nature of streets in the area. During World War I, the IRT subway, then operated by a private company, wanted to extend its line south, and it preferred to build under an established street. Such was the sway the IRT had with city government that a thoroughfare, Seventh Avenue South, was promptly cut through the Village.

Seen on a map, Seventh Avenue can be identified as the interloper it is. Long-time Villagers still refer to the swath it bulldozed as "the Cut." The Cut brought even more traffic and noise to the neighborhood once Seventh Avenue was connected to the Holland Tunnel.

Sheridan Square, bounded by West Fourth and Barrow Streets, Washington Place, and Seventh Avenue South, is sometimes confused with an adjacent space. The leafy park near Sheridan Square is actually **Christopher Park** (Grove and Christopher Streets, at Seventh Avenue South). One reason for the confusion just might be the statue of Civil War General Philip Sheridan, standing not in Sheridan Square but in Christopher Park.

Among other things, the Sheridan Square area is the "Times Square of Off-Broadway," with a concentration of popular, small, and experimental theaters. The Circle in the Square, the original Off-Broadway company, started out as the Loft Players at **5 Sheridan Square:** the fabled troupe's first hit, and the production that more or less created the phenomenon of Off-Broadway, was the Tennessee Williams play *Summer and Smoke,* which premiered in 1952. Circle in the Square moved to Bleecker Street in 1960, and then to Times Square in 1972.

At **One Sheridan Square,** the Axis Company, a theater group of relatively recent vintage, performs avant-garde and other productions in a space long occupied by Charles Ludlum's Ridiculous Theatrical Company, a neighborhood favorite for its outrageous (and stinging) parodies. Much further back in time the site was the home of Cafe Society, one of New York's first nonsegregated nightclubs. Jazz vocalist Billie Holiday made a major splash as a headliner at the venue in the late 1930s.

Grove Court is an idyllic cul-de-sac.

■ **CHRISTOPHER STREET** *map pages 94–95, B-2/3*

Matching the theater on the stage is the theater of the streets—especially Christopher Street. It was here that the first blow was struck for gay rights. On the night of June 28, 1969, police raided the **Stonewall Inn,** then located at 51 Christopher Street, for violating the state liquor law that forbade selling a homosexual a drink. The arrested patrons were at first docile, but the harsh police action created something previously unthinkable: a gay crowd, many of them drag queens, that fought back.

The Gay Pride movement dates from this event, with end-of-June marches all over the world celebrating the community and the victory over prejudice that the incident at the Stonewall signified. The bar next door that calls itself Stonewall is not the historic one, and the neighborhood itself has experienced a few transformations—much of the gay male scene has moved north to Chelsea—but the street is as gay as in the old days during the annual Halloween Parade.

Where Christopher Street hits Sixth Avenue, there is a small, crooked street that would seem to be an emblem of the homosexual community, but isn't.

(following pages) Chumley's is a great place to warm up on a cold day.

Gay Street is almost an alley, named after an early Greenwich Village farm family. From the mid-19th century to the 1920s, Gay Street was an incredibly overpopulated black ghetto. But in the 1950s it became famous as the site of the apartment (at 14 Gay Street) in Ruth McKenney's long-running Broadway play *My Sister Eileen*, starring Shirley Booth, and later made into the musical *Wonderful Town*, with Rosalind Russell.

Remnants of historical Greenwich Village are tucked away just off Christopher on its march west to the river. Bedford Street heads south from Christopher to Grove Street and **Grove Court** (entrance between 10 and 12 Grove Street), a cul-de-sac built for families of tradesmen, but now the domain of the wealthy.

Farther south on Bedford Street is the oldest house in the Village, **77 Bedford Street,** built in 1799. The 9$^1/_2$-foot-wide house next door, **75$^1/_2$ Bedford Street,** was home to Edna St. Vincent Millay and John Barrymore (at different times). During Prohibition days, **Chumley's** (86 Bedford Street) was a speakeasy frequented by literary lights such as F. Scott Fitzgerald. The place hasn't changed much since alcohol was legalized. On frosty afternoons when the wind's blowing hard off the Hudson, few refuges are cozier than Chumley's, with its fireplace ablaze and the smell of brews in the air.

West of Bedford Street on Commerce Street is the **Cherry Lane Theatre,** inside a building from 1817 that in 1923 Edna St. Vincent Millay and some friends turned into one of the first Off-Broadway theaters (though they weren't called that back then). Commerce runs into Barrow Street, which runs into Hudson after a few steps. On the west side of Hudson Street is **St. Luke's Chapel** (St. Luke's-in-the-Fields, 487 Hudson Street). The chapel had a complete square of rowhouses surrounding it when it was built, in 1822, the year of the yellow fever epidemic. Its parish house, still standing, was the boyhood home of the writer Bret Harte.

■ **JEFFERSON MARKET AREA** *map pages 94–95, C-1*

North on Sixth Avenue from the Christopher Street intersection is the **Jefferson Market Library,** a mock-Bavarian hallucination in orange brick. Built on the site of the old Jefferson produce market, the building was originally a district courthouse (the first night court in the country convened here). By 1945 it had fallen into disuse, its clock stalled at 3:20. Only a vigorous preservation effort prevented it from being replaced by an apartment building; it reopened as a public library in

The fanciful Jefferson Market Library.

1967. In 1995, a citizens' group reinstalled the clock and got its mammoth, two-ton bell to chime. *Sixth Avenue and West 10th Street.*

Near Jefferson Market are **Patchin Place** (West 10th Street across from Jefferson Market) and its twin around the corner, **Milligan Place** (off Sixth Avenue north of West 10th Street), hideaway residential courts that, like Grove Court, originally were working-class housing. The poet e.e. cummings was a longtime resident of Patchin Place, as was the novelist Djuna Barnes. Today, upscale groceries like the marvelously fragrant, jam-packed **Balducci's** (424 Sixth Avenue) and the **Jefferson Market** (450 Sixth Avenue) carry on the area's comestible tradition.

■ WASHINGTON SQUARE *map pages 94–95, D-2*

The area now called Washington Square, at the foot of Fifth Avenue, once drained a creek the Indians called *Manata*—"Devil Water." Minetta Creek, now channeled and controlled, still flows underneath the park. It's a reminder of the time when the area was a miasmic marsh, used as a communal burial plot. The bodies of cholera victims were dumped into the swamp, still wrapped in their yellow shrouds. Some were later moved, but an estimated ten to twenty thousand bodies remain buried beneath Washington Square—testimony to the lethal epidemics that hit Manhattan in the 18th and early 19th centuries.

From a cemetery and potter's field it was only a short leap to a hanging ground, which the site became in the 19th century. Like the subterranean Minetta Creek, there is a *memento mori* of this period, too: the celebrated "hanging tree," the large elm in the northwestern quadrant of the park. It is believed to be the oldest tree in Manhattan, and criminals were hung from its boughs as late as 1819. (Executions were popular public entertainment in old New York.)

It wasn't until July 4, 1828, that Washington Square opened as a public space—a military parade ground. The **Washington Arch,** the Square's most recognizable feature, had its first incarnation in 1889. The original arch was wooden, and commemorated the centennial of George Washington's inauguration as U.S. president. It proved so popular it was replaced by a permanent marble version in 1895, courtesy of funds raised from the public, partially through a benefit concert given by the Polish patriot and pianist Jan Paderewski.

In a stroke of performance art that claimed the arch for informed Village madness, a half-dozen co-conspirators—the artist Marcel Duchamp among them—

GENTEEL WASHINGTON SQUARE

The ideal of quiet and of genteel retirement, in 1835, was found in Washington Square, where the Doctor built himself a handsome, modern, wide-fronted house, with a big balcony before the drawing-room windows, and a flight of white marble steps ascending to a portal which was also faced with white marble. This structure, and many of its neighbors, which it exactly resembled, were supposed, forty years ago, to embody the last results of architectural science, and they remain to this day very solid and honorable dwellings. In front of them was the square, containing a considerable quantity of inexpensive vegetation, enclosed by a wooden paling, which increased its rural and accessible appearance; and round the corner was the more august precinct of the Fifth Avenue, taking its origin at this point with a spacious and confident air which already marked it for high destinies. I know not whether it is owing to the tenderness of early associations, but this portion of New York appears to many persons the most delectable. It has a kind of established repose which is not of frequent occurrence in other quarters of the long, shrill city; it has a riper, richer, more honorable look than any of the upper ramifications of the great longitudinal thoroughfare—the look of having had something of a social history. It was here, as you might have been informed on good authority, that you had come into a world which appeared to offer a variety of sources of interest; it was here that your grandmother lived, in venerable solitude, and dispensed a hospitality which commended itself alike to the infant imagination and the infant palate; it was here that you took your first walks abroad, following the nursery-maid with unequal step, and sniffing up the strange odor of the ailanthus-trees which at that time formed the principal umbrage of the Square, and diffused an aroma that you were not yet critical enough to dislike as it deserved; it was here, finally, that your first school, kept by a broad-bosomed, broad-based old lady with a ferule, who was always having tea in a blue cup, with a saucer that didn't match, enlarged the circle both of your observations and your sensations.

—Henry James, *Washington Square*, 1881

climbed to its top in January 1917 to declare "the Free and Independent Republic of Washington Square." They read a proclamation—consisting of the word "whereas," repeated ad infinitum—got drunk and toasted the New Bohemia. Later on, during World War II, the hollow interior of the arch was rumored to be the digs of an ingenious draft-dodger.

Washington Square today represents the benign tension between anarchy and order that continues to occur as the Village's old reputation for free-living clashes with its new reality as a solidly middle-class haven. The unruliness of the park crowd—which has at times included more than a few marijuana peddlers and pickpockets—occasionally upsets the upscale residents, but the police seem to have struck a compromise between carnival craziness and decorum. Much of the time, and particularly on summer weekends, Washington Square presents a superb *tableau vivant* of Village life, with street performers drawing huge crowds.

The institutional presence of **New York University** weighs rather heavily on the neighborhood surrounding Washington Square. **Bobst Library** (70 Washington Square South) is an especially oppressive presence, one of three "redskins" (buildings with red-stone façades) built when architect Philip Johnson proposed a comprehensive "look" for the whole university. Luckily, the plan was later abandoned. For a more graceful NYU presence, there's the **Judson Hall belltower** (51 Washington Square South), which now serves as a dormitory—although there's plumbing only on the lower floors.

Once a hanging ground, Washington Square Park typically swarms with activity. The Washington Arch frames the reveler above.

The townhouses that form "The Row" evoke the 19th century as depicted in the Henry James novel Washington Square.

Balancing out the institutional architecture on the south side of the square are the restored properties on Washington Square North. NYU owns or leases most of **"The Row"** of charming Federal and Greek Revival townhouses, some of them only the façades and shells of the originals. This is the Washington Square of the 19th century, when it was a residential haven for the wealthy, recognizable from the eponymous Henry James novel.

James's grandmother had a townhouse along the square on part of what is now the **2 Fifth Avenue** apartment building. In the lobby here is an odd little reminder of the area's swampy roots: a clear pipe, through which the waters of Minetta Brook may be seen bubbling from underground. From the southwest corner of the park—where fierce chess tournaments take place, similar to those portrayed in the movie *Searching for Bobby Fischer*—**MacDougal Street** provides an entry point into a "Positively Fourth Street" Dylanesque district of coffeehouses, jazz clubs, and restaurants. These narrow, busy streets were once one of Manhattan's many "Little Italy" neighborhoods, and trattorias are still here.

Off MacDougal, on tiny Minetta Lane, is the **Minetta Lane Theatre,** another Off-Broadway venue, and **Minetta Tavern,** where a locked door off the basement leads to another open channel of Minetta Creek. Another hidden treasure is the **MacDougal-Sullivan Gardens,** a private enclave mid-block, north of Houston Street. Also north of Houston one block over is the **Sullivan Street Playhouse** (181 Sullivan Street), where the longest-running show in American history, *The Fantasticks,* ended its marathon dance on the boards in 2002, after 17,162 performances. Dwight D. Eisenhower was still president when the show opened on May 3, 1960.

North of Washington Square, Fifth Avenue begins its long run on a graceful note at **Washington Mews.** Like most Manhattan residential courts (and like its sister mews, **MacDougal Alley,** one block west), this one became a prestige address only in the 20th century. It was originally a back street for tradespeople.

The long block of **Eighth Street** between Fifth and Sixth Avenues has become enshrined in the shoppers' Hall of Fame as a sort of wannabe jamboree. Shoe and accessory stores lining the street dispense an instant Village look that has itself

Greenwich Village is a magnet for music lovers.

Manhattan Jazz

New York City—and in this case we're talking Manhattan—remains the jazz mecca. In few other cities does such a confluence of resident masters, journeymen, and emerging jazz artists hold forth in so many nightclubs, restaurants, bistros, pubs, barrooms, and outright holes-in-the-wall dedicated to jazz performance.

These days the most vital jazz action takes place below 14th Street, but history-making haunts have included Midtown's famed 52nd Street strip and Uptown's Clark Monroe's Uptown House, Small's Paradise, Savoy Ballroom, the Cotton Club, and Minton's Playhouse. For the last forty years, though, Downtown, especially Greenwich Village, has been the place for jazz.

Below are a few venues worth checking out:

Village Vanguard. Descending this club's narrow flight of stairs to the small, unassuming basement, a newcomer gets few clues that this is the most historic of all current Manhattan jazz clubs. Stick around long enough and gaze at the posters of the giants who have made history here, and you'll be enchanted by the place's jazz truth. The sounds to be heard here range from the mainstream to the cutting edge. Come on Monday nights to hear the Vanguard Jazz Orchestra, now in its third swinging decade. *178 Seventh Avenue South, Greenwich Village; 212-255-4037.*

Blue Note. Some of the giants—especially the great singers—of jazz perform here. *131 West Third Street, Greenwich Village; 212-475-8592.*

Zinno. Head to Zinno for superb northern Italian cuisine and top-notch jazz/bass duos. *126 West 13th Street, Greenwich Village; 212-924-5182.*

Bradley's. One of the city's great jazz joints, Bradley's stays open later than most clubs. The music's fine, and it's often just as fascinating to see which jazz greats are checking out the sounds. *70 University Place, Greenwich Village; 212-228-6440.*

Iridium. Another Monday night classic takes place at Iridium, where the timeless guitarist Les Paul performs with his trio. During the rest of the week, you might catch Mose Allison or Ahmad Jamal performing. *1650 Broadway, Midtown; 212-582-2121.*

Knitting Factory. There's no drink minimum at this place for uncompromising music, jazz and otherwise. *74 Leonard Street, TriBeCa; 212-219-3006.*

Other options include snazzy **Birdland** (315 West 44th Street, Midtown; 212-581-3080), **Smalls** (183 West 10th Street, Greenwich Village; 212-929-7565), which stays open until the wee hours, and groovy **Smoke** (2751 Broadway, Upper West Side; 212-864-6662).

The *Village Voice* has complete jazz listings.

become a fashion, after a sort. At least one address here is the real thing: **Electric Lady Studios** (52 West Eighth Street) was founded by the late, great guitarist Jimi Hendrix in the 1960s.

To get a glimpse of what Fifth Avenue was like in its glory days of huge residential mansions, see the **Salmagundi Club.** Originally the Irad Hawley residence, after 1917 it became the new home to the oldest artists' club in the country, itself founded in 1870. The ground floor, maintained in its original 19th-century elegance, is sometimes open during exhibitions and is well worth a look. *47 Fifth Avenue, at East 11th Street.*

Also warranting a quick visit are the **Forbes Magazine Galleries,** interesting for their insight into what a millionaire does in his spare time. The late Malcolm Forbes, the flamboyant publisher of *Forbes* magazine, collected Fabergé eggs, toy soldiers, and yachts—all of which are represented here (the boats as models). Forbes enjoyed tweaking noses, and he located his headquarters not far from the offices of the American Communist Party. *60 Fifth Avenue, at West 12th Street; 212-206-5548.*

■ EAST VILLAGE *map pages 94–95, E/G-1/2*

When the Third Avenue El (elevated train) was pulled down in 1955, a longtime psychological boundary line went with it, allowing the Greenwich Village "state of mind" to migrate east. Today, the East Village is still something of a standard bearer for vanguard artistic movements and social advocacy. The name is of fairly recent vintage: the East Village was once only the northern part of the Lower East Side—and is still called "Loisaida" by its Latino inhabitants. In the 1950s, real estate developers borrowed the cachet of its western neighbor when they wanted to upgrade the area's image. They first tried "Village East," then, after 1961, the East Village. The results of all this image-buffing have been decidedly mixed. The East Village, populated by a mix of artists, students, and immigrants, among them many Arabs and Ukrainians, is one of the world's great street carnivals.

The eastern fringe of the East Village used to be called Alphabet City, after the neighborhood's Avenues A through D. That was when it was one of the louche

(opposite) The shops along St. Mark's Place reflect the East Village's colorful residents.
(following pages) Frivolity mixes with local politics at a parade to save the many community gardens that add a touch of green to the East Village.

parts of downtown, well known as a free-floating drug bazaar. Nowadays the areas to the east and south of Tompkins Square Park are among the city's liveliest, with new restaurants, galleries, and shops opening (and oftentimes closing) constantly.

The East Village began its life as part of the large estate of the Stuyvesant family, heirs to Director General Peter Stuyvesant's original land grant from the Dutch West India Company. The Bowery, the neighborhood's great historical thoroughfare and working-class answer to Broadway, was the road to Stuyvesant's farm, or "bouwerie." Stuyvesant is still there, his bones resting beneath a children's playground on the property of St. Mark's-in-the-Bouwerie church. But the East Village has undergone successive transformations from rich man's turf to immigrant haven to hipster's paradise. Its bohemian credentials have begun to fade, but it remains an animated neighborhood.

The best route to enter the neighborhood is via Eighth Street, which actually represents a little piece of the East Village that strayed west. East of Broadway, Eighth Street gives way to **Astor Place,** an abbreviated public space that sometimes serves as an informal flea market. **Astor Place Hair Designers** (2 Astor Place) is famed for its radical haircuts and for long lines that often spill out onto the sidewalk and add to the area's festival atmosphere. (A Super Kmart, a Gap store, several Starbucks, and other chain stores are indications that the neighborhood became too groovy for its own good, however.)

The Astor Place subway stop features a beaver motif on its decorative wall tiles, a reference to the fur-based fortune of John Jacob Astor, who lived on Lafayette Street south of Astor Place in the early 19th century. The stretch, known as **Colonnade Row** (428–434 Lafayette Street)—the name for the four of nine mansions here that survive—was once the fanciest address in town. The buildings are said to have been New York's first with indoor plumbing.

Across the street, what is now the **Joseph Papp Public Theater** was the original Astor Library, founded after John Jacob's death in 1854 and moved uptown in 1895. The Public Theater is the legacy of the late impresario Joseph Papp, who in the mid-1960s almost single-handedly saved the beautiful Romanesque Revival building from demolition and installed a theater complex that has proved ragingly successful. Underwritten in part by such Public-produced Broadway hits as *A Chorus Line* and *Bring in 'Da Noise, Bring in 'Da Funk,* the numerous stages here host a compelling lineup of drama and film. *425 Lafayette Street, at Astor Place; 212-260-2400.*

The Public, the avant-garde **La Mama E.T.C.** (74 East Fourth Street; 212-475-7710), and the **New York Theater Workshop** (79 East Fourth Street; 212-460-5475), where the musical *Rent* debuted, are the gems of East Village theater.

North and east of the Public, facing Astor Place and its huge, cubelike Tony Rosenthal sculpture *The Alamo* (push it—it weighs 3,000 pounds, but it turns!), is **Cooper Union** (7 East Seventh Street), one of the most remarkable colleges in the world. For one thing, in an age of spiraling educational costs, the school remains tuition-free, as intended by its idealistic founder, the remarkable inventor and self-made man, Peter Cooper.

Beginning with a grocery store, Cooper built a foundry and real estate empire that is the base of Cooper Union's extensive endowment (for example, Cooper Union owns the land on which the Chrysler Building stands). When Cooper Union opened in 1859, it was first in many areas: first coed, first nonsectarian, first nonsegregated, and first tuition-free college. All founded and funded by a man who could neither read nor write—but felt others should—and all across the street from his original grocery store.

The building is noteworthy for several reasons. A renovation in the mid-1970s confirmed that Cooper had used railroad rails as a structural device, making his school the first steel-frame building and a precursor to the modern skyscraper. The school's Great Hall hosted Susan B. Anthony, Mark Twain, and other luminaries. Abraham Lincoln gave a speech there that may have won him the presidency. A statue of Peter Cooper, by Augustus Saint-Gaudens (a Cooper Union graduate), sits in the square to the building's south.

North of Cooper Union, running diagonally off Third Avenue, is **Stuyvesant Street,** which follows an old colonial pathway to the site of Peter Stuyvesant's country farmhouse. Located there now is **St.-Mark's-in-the-Bouwerie** (131 East 10th Street), an Episcopal church that also serves the neighborhood as a community playhouse, public meeting hall, and cultural free-fire zone. The St. Mark's Poetry Project, founded by the late Allen Ginsberg, among others, is just one of the programs this remarkable landmark hosts and supports.

The area around East Ninth and Stuyvesant Streets is beginning to make a name for itself as a sort of Little Japan, hosting a collection of sake bars, restaurants, and Japanese-language video stores. Even more concentrated along East Sixth Street between First and Second Avenues is a **row of Indian restaurants** so chockablock that some diners speculate they share one giant kitchen. World-music aficionados

patronize **Tribal Soundz** (340 East Sixth Street), which hosts workshops by multi-cultural artists and sells digeridoos, Vietnamese silver flutes, talking drums, and other instruments. One of the immigrant cultures in this lively neighborhood is that of Eastern Europe: just step into one of the many sausage-festooned butcher shops here to be transported instantly to Ukraine.

St. Mark's Church also lent its name to **St. Mark's Place,** the three-block section of Eighth Street between Third Avenue and Avenue A. An essential stop for book-ish types whose taste runs to the literarily offbeat is **St. Mark's Bookshop**, where the best-sellers might include a work by Noam Chomsky. St. Mark's is anchored—if that's the word—by **Tompkins Square Park** (bordered by Avenues A and B and East Seventh and 10th Streets), the site of an infamous police riot in the summer of 1988, when real estate interests convinced the City Council to impose a curfew in the park and squatters and other demonstrators resisted.

The park has been completely refurbished, and signs of gentrification are every-where. One outpost of the alternative set is the **Nuyorican Poets Cafe** (236 East Third Street, near Avenue B), a bar and performance space that features "poetry slams," readings of unproduced screenplays, and other spoken-word performances. Alternative entertainment also thrives at the **Two Boots Pioneer Theater** (155 East Third Street, at Avenue A), a showplace for independent cinema that screens cutting-edge premieres and classic revivals and presents small film festivals.

(above and opposite) Over the years, Tompkins Square Park has been the scene of love-ins, shootings, stabbings, riots, poetry slams, wig festivals, and a million afternoons in the sun.

UNION SQUARE
TO MURRAY HILL

The area of Manhattan between the Villages and Midtown is something of a *quartier perdu*—a lost neighborhood—without the coherence of those districts above and below it. Within this sprawling heterogeneous belt, however, there are several celebrated neighborhoods that are among the most distinctive in New York. The area from 14th Street to 42nd Street could be characterized as the Balkans of Manhattan, but for its patchwork nature, not for ethnic rivalries.

The Balkans as if designed by a mathematician, that is. North of 14th Street, the city's grid system, implemented in 1811, kicked in with a vengeance. The plan lent the streets and neighborhoods a linear, calibrated atmosphere that seemed, in the eyes of early-19th-century Americans at least, ultimately modern.

This area became densely built at a rapid pace, during a time when Manhattan's settlement was quickly outstripping whatever boundaries were laid upon it. For a while, 14th Street was the town's northern limit, and whatever lay beyond was an ultima Thule. But the explosive population growth of the 19th century, fueled by an influx of immigrants, filled the Union Square area and neighborhoods to the north.

Chief among these is **Chelsea,** originally a stretch of farmland on the area bordered by West 14th Street, Eighth Avenue, West 29th Street, and 10th Avenue, which Captain Thomas Clarke named after the London neighborhood. A neighborhood that has consistently attracted Manhattan's elite is **Gramercy Park,** east of Chelsea and centered around the only private park in the city. Cheek by jowl with the aristocratic flavor of the park proper are the vast residential developments of **Stuyvesant Town** and **Peter Cooper Village**—vertical villages or human warehouses, depending on your point of view—but resolutely middle class.

North of Gramercy Park is a district which has recently been going by the name of **SoFi** (South of the Flatiron Building), a real estate developers' coinage with only mild currency. The **Garment District,** north of SoFi and Chelsea, has a much more secure identity, based in the area's design, manufacturing, and wholesaling of clothing. East of the Garment District is an area with an aristocratic past and fairly mundane present: **Murray Hill,** once the chosen turf of the city's upperclass "Knickerbocracy." On its western edge is the **Empire State Building.**

■ 14TH STREET *map pages 136–137, A/H-5/6*

Fourteenth Street is a slack wire strung through the gut of Manhattan, thrummed upon by a strange assortment of street singers, bargain-bin shills, trendoids, and meat-carcass teamsters. It's a place where dream books—those demotic pamphlets linking oneiric images with winning lottery numbers—are sold in vast quantities. When Tom Waits, that poet of the dispossessed, moved to Manhattan to oversee his Broadway show *Frank's Wild Years,* the place he chose to land was 14th Street. Say no more.

Stretching from river to river, the first great crosstown artery to announce the grid pattern to the north, 14th Street has for much of its existence served as a demarcation line. Even today, it is the traditional boundary that separates the leftish, arty districts of Greenwich Village, East Village, TriBeCa, and SoHo from the no-nonsense economic pursuits of Midtown.

But to walk along 14th Street from the East River to the Hudson River is like plunging into a living diorama of Manhattan, one that measures the rich diversity of the place. Begin in Project-Land, with the Jacob Riis Houses on your left as you

Workers lay the cable for the Broadway streetcar line at Union Square in the 1870s. (Library of Congress)

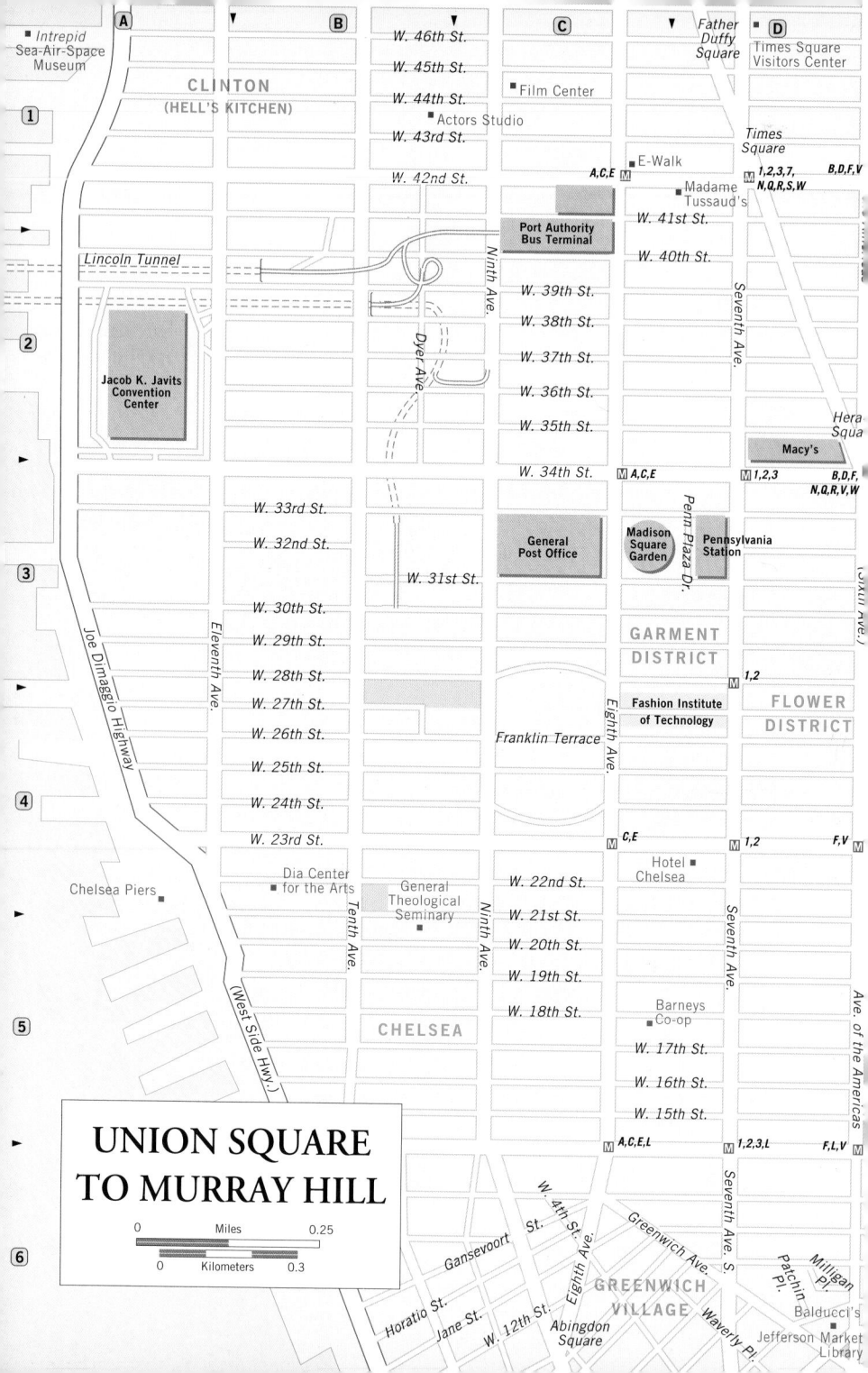

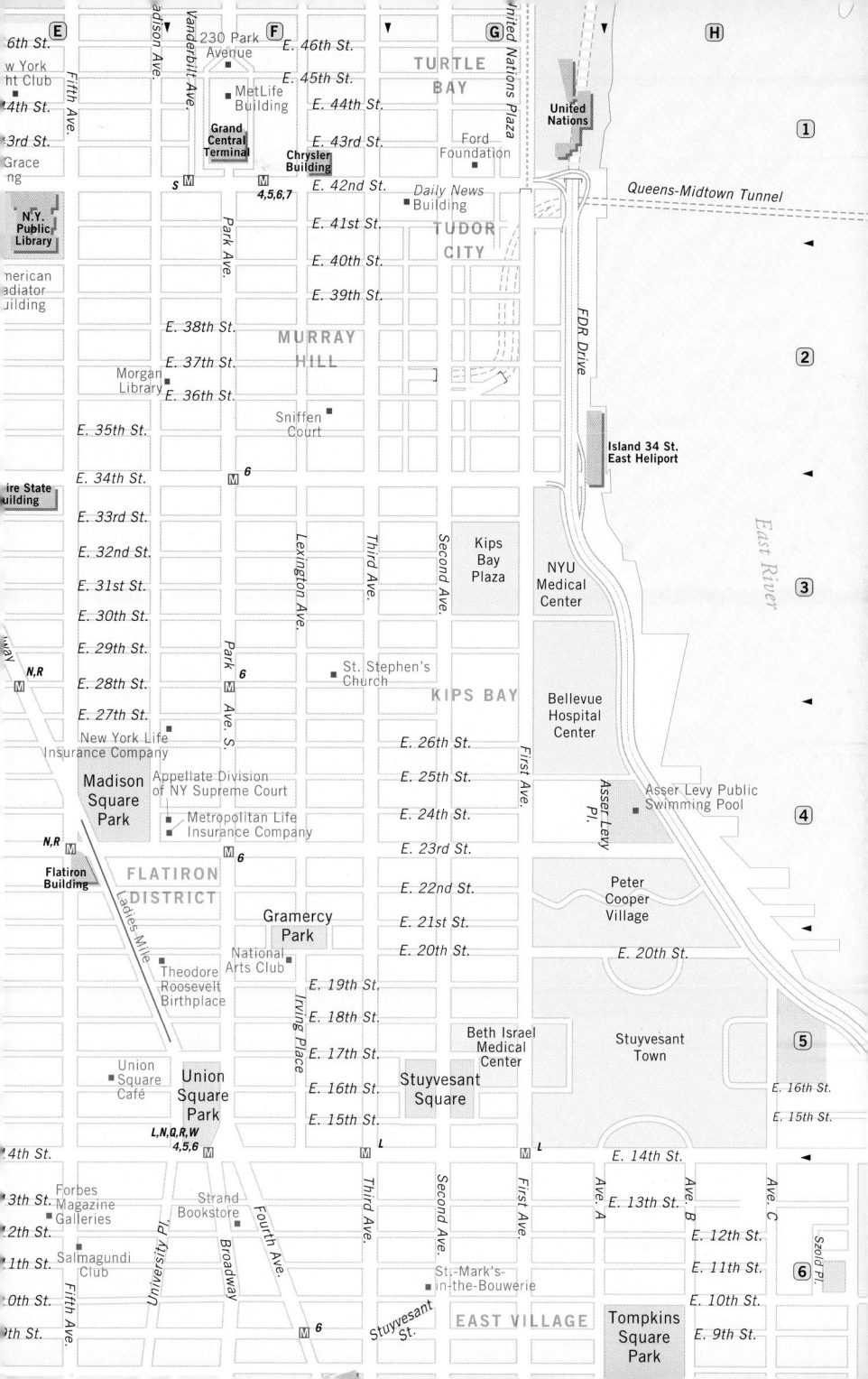

head west, and Stuyvesant Town looming on the right. You'll soon work into the nexus of history and present-day reality at Union Square. A short detour south leads to a proud vestige of Fourth Avenue's past as Manhattan's book-dealing district. The **Strand Bookstore** (828 Broadway, at East 12th Street), a New York institution that boasts of having "8 miles of books," sells both new and used books as well as collector's items. Back on 14th Street, you will immediately plunge into a three-block-long street bazaar that is a sort of third-world Kmart. "Inside! Inside! Sta-yep inside!" implore the street shills, an unnecessary invitation, since the wares are spilling out onto the sidewalk.

If you survive that gauntlet of nickel-and-dime capitalism, you'll wind up in what was once called Little Spain—the block of 14th Street between Seventh and Eighth Avenues—one of those Manhattan neighborhoods that host festivals for ethnic populations no longer living there. Then into the bizarre, lard-scummed streets of the Gansevoort wholesale meat market, an odoriferous place where packing crates are burned in 50-gallon drums all night long, and you're as likely to get knocked upside the head by a 100-pound slab of beef as to be propositioned by a transvestite streetwalker. Of late, the meat-packing district has been "discovered" by nightclubbers, artists, and fashionistas, lending a polished veneer to what was always a working-class hero of a place. It's a strange-flavored trip from river to river on 14th Street: imagine a J.R.R. Tolkien–William S. Burroughs collaboration with a dash of Mexican soap opera. This is the kind of journey that can be accomplished only in Manhattan.

■ **UNION SQUARE** *map pages 136–137, F-5*

Park Avenue South, Broadway, and Fourth Avenue all converge at **Union Square.** Although the square's name predates the Civil War and labor unions, many protests and rallies concerned with the war and unionism took place here. The labor leader Eugene Debs rallied the workers to the socialist cause in Union Square, and the offices of numerous unions still surround the park. On the south side stands a statue of Lafayette by Frédéric-Auguste Bartholdi, the sculptor of the Statue of Liberty. The Marquis de Lafayette, a French aristocrat who fought on the side of the American colonists against Britain, was a great hero to 18th- and 19th-century New Yorkers. The huge **Independence Flagpole** in the park's center was given to the city by the Tammany Hall political machine, whose headquarters was once nearby on East 14th Street.

Union Square Café

The hosannas that greeted Union Square Café's debut in 1985 are far in the past. The restaurant no longer qualifies as the latest rage. Instead, restaurateur Danny Meyer and chef Michael Romano have settled into providing something even more noteworthy than opening night splash: an everyday miracle. The result is an eatery consistently rated among the most popular in Manhattan.

The welcome that diners feel when they enter a Danny Meyer restaurant—he also owns several other venues, among them the also fine Gramercy Tavern—is achieved via the alchemy of graciousness, sophistication, and design. Years into Union Square Café's existence, reservations remain a must, but the long and commodious bar represents a fallback for walk-ins. An excellent wine-by-the-glass list, a raw bar, and a brace of lyrical appetizers complete the draw for the impulse visitor.

But the comfortable, low-ceiling main dining room can represent an experience that defines what dining out in New York City is all about. The menu has strong Italian inflections, but Romano pioneered the idea of New American cuisine—hearty fare that borrows a bit of its style from the more precious California cuisine. Somehow, with the staff's usually immaculate presentation, attacking dishes such as porcini gnocchi or chilled poached asparagus with chopped pistachios, mimosa, and sauternes vinaigrette can seem the most natural thing in the world. After a dinner like this, a fantasy dessert—a banana tart with honey-vanilla ice cream and macadamia-nut brittle, for example—seems only a further iteration of heaven.

Union Square manages the impossible, transforming refinement into something neither labored nor studied, but simply a whole lot of fun. *21 East 16th Street, between Fifth Avenue and Union Square West; 212-243-4020.*

On a different note, on the west side of Union Square, the denizens of pop icon Andy Warhol's **Factory** (33 Union Square West) cavorted from the late 1960s through the mid-1980s. It was here in 1968 that Warhol was shot and nearly killed by Valerie Solanis, an occasional Factory employee who told police Warhol "had too much control over my life."

Union Square is the site of a **Greenmarket,** which sprouts on its north side every Wednesday, Friday, and Saturday, a popular and crowded bazaar devoted to fruits, vegetables, and other comestibles. On the east side of the park, now obscured by the pyramid-topped Zeckendorf Towers apartment complex, is the clock tower of the **Consolidated Edison Company** (4 Irving Place) building. On the other hand, you won't be able to miss *Metronome* (1999), a several-stories-high sculptural meditation on infinity mounted on the façade of 1 Union Square South. The artwork's digital display counts the twenty-four hours of the day, simultaneously subtracting the day's remaining moments.

■ CHELSEA *map pages 136–137, B/C-4/5*

Always a bridesmaid, Chelsea never reached fully fashionable status in the 19th century, maintaining a slightly louche flavor that made it the natural landing place for Edith Wharton's Baroness Ellen Olenska in *The Age of Innocence*. It was not until well into the 1960s, however, that it recovered from its leapfrogged status to become a dynamic residential area with stores, theaters, and great restaurants. In the last few years, Chelsea has been the site of a burgeoning gallery scene, as art dealers are priced out of increasingly expensive and retail-oriented SoHo.

Chelsea flirted with greatness before, when in the late 19th century Sixth Avenue between West Eighth and West 23rd Streets contained such a concentration of clothiers and dry goods outlets that it was called **Ladies Mile.** It has also seen periods of notoriety. During the same period, and lasting until Prohibition, Sixth and Seventh Avenues north from West 23rd Street were part of the famed "Tenderloin," Manhattan's teeming, no-holds-barred vice district.

An apocryphal story tells us that the Tenderloin was so named by a corrupt police official, Alexander S. "Clubber" Williams, who earned his nickname from this famous quote: "There is more law in the end of a policeman's nightstick than in a decision of the Supreme Court." Williams was allegedly so gratified by the

(preceding pages) People from all over New York shop for flowers, fruits, and vegetables at the Union Square Greenmarket. (opposite) Lovey-dovey in the gay Chelsea district.

BOHO CENTRAL

One element that draws pilgrims to Manhattan is its great bohemian tradition, from the free-love heyday of early-20th-century Greenwich Village to the scruffy folk movement of the 1960s and the punk-rock upheavals of a decade later. Through it all, the headquarters and mecca of underground-beatnik-alternative New York has remained the Hotel Chelsea.

Thomas Wolfe worked on *Look Homeward, Angel* during his long residence at the Chelsea. The poet and playwright Dylan Thomas staggered out of the hotel one evening in 1953 and never staggered back in, dying in a Seventh Avenue snowbank after a drinking binge of epic proportions. His occupancy and demise are commemorated on one of many bronze plaques in front of the hotel: "Dylan Thomas lived and laboured here...and from here sailed out to die."

Singer-songwriter Bob Dylan followed in the footsteps of his namesake and wrote "Sad-Eyed Lady of the Lowlands" while in residence, and Andy Warhol's 1966 film *Chelsea Girls* immortalized the women of his circle who lived here. Punk rocker Sid Vicious allegedly stabbed and killed his girlfriend, Nancy Spungen, at the Chelsea, a dubious distinction deftly recorded in the movie *Sid and Nancy.*

The Chelsea's lobby reflects its eclectic clientele.

The Hotel Chelsea is a legendary haunt of artists, writers, and musicians.

On and on runs the list of Hotel Chelsea luminaries, from science-fiction guru Arthur C. Clarke to painter and sculptor Larry Rivers to playwright Sam Shepard. Left behind by artists who have lived and died here are innumerable artworks, some given to the Chelsea management in exchange for rent, which are displayed on a rotating basis on the walls of the lobby.

The hotel's rooms themselves can best be described as serviceable, and the building as a whole gives off a slightly seedy, residential flavor in perfect sync with its reputation. (The Chelsea started out as New York City's first cooperative apartment house, but when rich folk and the major theaters headed north at the beginning of the 20th century, 23rd Street lost its cachet. The cooperative went bankrupt in 1903, and the building was converted into a hotel in 1905.)

For those not willing to check themselves into Boho Central, a short-stay alternative is *Chelsea Walls*, the actor Ethan Hawke's directorial debut and a loving digital video valentine to the hotel, where Hawke keeps an office. *222 West 23rd Street, between Seventh and Eighth Avenues; 212-243-3700.*

possibilities for graft in his newly assigned beat that he commented to a reporter: "I was living on rump steak in the Fourth District, but I will be having some tenderloin now." Alas, the story does not survive careful etymological scrutiny, but the character of the neighborhood, called "Satan's Circus" by reformers, was real enough. Dope, gambling, and prostitution flourished, and was eventually ghettoized by street: 29th for whorehouses, 28th for high-stakes gambling, 27th for low-stakes games of chance.

Manhattan vice has since dispersed to points elsewhere, and Ladies Mile–style shopping is represented in Chelsea only by such meccas as **Barneys Co-op** (236 West 18th Street), the landmark men's and women's clothing outlet (a relative term at a place where a designer sweater "on sale" might set you back more than $200). And just north of Chelsea is **Macy's** (151 West 34th Street), long celebrated as "the largest store in the world."

Near Barneys, and an unavoidable dominating presence in lower Chelsea, is the gargantuan **Port Authority Building** (111 Eighth Avenue), whose elevators can fit full-size trucks. But the neighborhood's most famous landmark is the **Hotel Chelsea** (222 West 23rd Street), host to successive generations of bohemians and more famous for its guests than for its accommodations.

West of the Hotel Chelsea is the hulking **London Terrace,** a block-sized realm of 1,670 apartments on the site of the house of Clement Clarke Moore, the grandson of Captain Thomas Clarke. A classics professor, Moore founded the **General Theological Seminary** (175 Ninth Avenue), which survives today as a religious oasis; he also laid out many of the streets in the district. Moore is more famous for penning "A Visit from St. Nicholas," better known as "Twas the Night Before Christmas," though in 2000 his authorship of the beloved poem became a matter of dispute. In the book *Author Unknown: On the Trail of Anonymous,* the "literary detective" Don Foster presented fairly compelling evidence that a farmer from upstate New York, Major Henry J. Livingston Jr., wrote the verse.

Even farther west, at West 23rd Street and the Hudson River, the humongous sports complex of **Chelsea Piers** (Piers 59–62; 212-336-6800) proves that commercial development of Manhattan's shoreline is possible and profitable. It has the island's only golf driving range (four tiers), plus sand- and hard-court volleyball,

(above) Art lovers stroll through the Mary Boone Gallery. (below) At Dia Center for the Arts in Chelsea, a patron interacts with Gilberto Zorio's installation Reverb.

The one that got away: Pennsylvania Station before being replaced by one of the ugliest, most difficult to navigate rail terminals in America. (New-York Historical Society)

hockey and ice-skating, in-line skating, rock climbing, bowling, lacrosse, and more. A historical note: Pier 59 is where the ill-fated *Titanic* would have docked if it had managed to steer clear of killer icebergs.

West Chelsea's hopping gallery district is centered along and just off 10th Avenue in the neighborhood of West 23rd Street. Dozens of contemporary art dealers, such as Sonnabend, Paula Cooper, Max Protetch, and Barbara Gladstone, have joined the **Dia Center for the Arts** (548 West 22nd Street; 212-989-5566) to transform the whole area into an urban artscape. The **Empire Diner** (10th Avenue and West 22nd Street), once frequented heavily only in the wee hours, is these days filled to capacity at noon with the gallery crowd.

In recent years the center of gravity of gay male New York (as opposed to the lesbian center, which is in Brooklyn's Park Slope) has shifted uptown from the West Village to Chelsea, particularly along or right off Eighth Avenue. The shops, restaurants, and bars here turn over with some rapidity, but two stalwarts, and good places to check out the scene, are the amiably cruisy **Big Cup** (228 Eighth Avenue) coffee bar and the glib **Barracuda** (275 West 22nd Street), a bar daffily outfitted in 1960s-TV style.

If the somewhat embattled **Flower District,** centered at Sixth Avenue and West 27th Street, faces competition from out-of-town wholesalers, it nonetheless presents a superb middle-of-the-night tableau for the insomniac visitor: orchids from Colombia are hawked alongside tulips from Holland, and the scents, colors, and foliage overwhelm the senses.

North of Chelsea lies the entertainment and transportation locus of **Madison Square Garden** and **Pennsylvania Station,** which take up the blocks bounded by Seventh Avenue, West 31st Street, Eighth Avenue, and West 33rd Street. Penn Station, as it's usually called, represents one of the bitterest defeats for preservation forces in the history of Manhattan. In the 1960s, the soaring Beaux Arts majesty of McKim, Mead & White's original Pennsylvania Station was destroyed to erect the unabashedly ugly conglomeration that occupies the site today. Plans have been drawn up to transform the **General Post Office,** across Eighth Avenue from the Garden, into a new rail terminal. The post office was also designed by McKim, Mead & White, and its reconfiguration as the new Penn Station would do much to assuage an old wound.

■ GRAMERCY PARK *map pages 136–137, F-4*

Gramercy Park as a neighborhood is an amorphous thing, typical of Manhattan between 14th and 34th Streets. The Dutch word *Crommessie*, meaning "crooked dagger" (for the shape of an area brook), was close in pronunciation to the archaic English exclamation, "gramercy!"—so the two words were conflated. "Gramercy Park" as an address is a distinctive label claimed by far more area residents than perhaps warrant it, all wanting to cash in on its upscale cachet.

Gramercy Park itself is a charming quadrant at the southern end of Lexington Avenue from East 20th to East 21st Street. The park's loveliness is lessened only by the fact that it is closed to all but residents of the surrounding buildings—the locks to Gramercy Park are changed twice a year, and a key is a plum pluckable only by Manhattanites with luck or money. Occasionally, there are "Free Gramercy Park" rumblings, but the movement's momentum is diminished by fear of just what the city might do to a place that has remained so pristine under private ownership.

A stately home fronting Gramercy Park.

Surrounding the park's southern perimeter are elegant townhouses, some now turned into clubs or museums: the **Players Club** (16 Gramercy Park South), founded as a private club for theatrical types by Edwin Booth in 1888; the **National Arts Club** (15 Gramercy Park South), for artists; and the **Theodore Roosevelt Birthplace National Historic Site** (28 East 20th Street), a faithful reconstruction of the home where the twenty-sixth U.S. president was born. If you're interested in TR, the site is an engaging stopover. South of the park, on East 19th Street between Irving Place and Third Avenue, is the **"block beautiful"** row of restored townhouses.

Stuyvesant Town and **Peter Cooper Village** abut Gramercy Park to the east. Extending from East 14th to East 23rd Streets and East River Drive to First Avenue, they contain almost nine thousand apartments and house twenty-five thousand residents with an air of tidiness and middle-class quietude that remind one of Akron, not Manhattan. Both developments are owned by MetLife, the insurance company.

Stuyvesant Town (south of East 20th Street) and Peter Cooper Village (north of East 20th Street) are in the old Gashouse District, one of the most raucous and bloodthirsty neighborhoods of New York lore. The Gashouse District's historical juxtaposition with Stuyvesant Town is fraught with irony, given the development's leafy, kid-heavy, auto-free environment today. Just north of Peter Cooper Village is the **Asser Levy Public Swimming Pool** (East 23rd Street and Asser Levy Place), a throwback to the time when public works were erected in the hope of solving public problems. It has recently been restored to its original form. Stuyvesant Cove, a planned riverbank park between 18th and 24th Streets on the river, would allow the brave to wade in the East River, or walk along a pebbled beach.

■ SoFi and the Garment District *map pages 136–137, E-4*

Although the name "SoFi" is often derided, the area south of the Flatiron Building is booming, with publishing offices, shops, and cafés lending the area a vibrant street life. The **Flatiron Building** itself, of course, makes a superb centerpiece. Originally called the Fuller Building, the Flatiron was later nicknamed by New Yorkers for its skinny, triangular, ironlike shape. The Flatiron, which was completed in 1903, was not, as is widely believed, the world's first skyscraper or the world's tallest building, but it *is* an important example of its era's style of steel-frame building. Another stubborn myth swirling about the site is that the flapper phrase "23 skiddoo" was coined here, supposedly based on what cops said to male gawkers assembled to watch the winds around the building raise women's skirts. Interesting story, but ersatz etymology: the phrase was already popular in the 1890s. *175 Fifth Avenue, at West 23rd Street.*

North of the Flatiron (NoFi?) is **Madison Square Park,** a former potter's field and parade ground that by the mid-19th century was evolving into a fashionable patch of green. Stanford White designed the pedestal of Augustus Saint-Gaudens's elegant sculpture of Admiral David Farragut, a Civil War hero, in the park's northern section. White also designed the second incarnation of Madison Square Garden at the northeast corner of East 26th Street and Madison Avenue, now occupied by the New York Life Insurance complex. (Madison Square Garden has had a peripatetic history. The first Garden, on the same site as the second, evolved out of P.T. Barnum's Hippodrome, an open-air arena on land formerly used for stables. The Garden moved to Eighth Avenue and West 50th Street in 1925, before ending up at its present location above Pennsylvania Station in 1966.) *Bordered by West 23rd and West 26th Streets and Fifth and Madison Avenues.*

The Madison Square Park area is known for the wholesale Toy District, concentrated on its west side, and for the superb architecture of two insurance buildings and a courthouse on its eastern perimeter: the **Metropolitan Life Insurance Company** (1 Madison Avenue); the diminutive **Appellate Division of the New York State Supreme Court** (27 Madison Avenue), called the "busiest courthouse in the nation"; and the gilt-topped towers of the **New York Life Insurance Company** (51 Madison Avenue). At 24th Street west of the park, an obelisk marks the grave of the only man to be officially buried under a New York City street, the Mexican War hero William J. Worth, eponym of Fort Worth, Texas. The massive structure on the northwest corner of Fifth Avenue and West 23rd

Street was built on the site of the Fifth Avenue Hotel. In the late 19th century this was the city's swankest hostelry; it appears as itself or fictionalized in many novels. Edith Wharton was born in the much remodeled townhouse at 14 West 23rd Street.

The **Garment District,** which kicks in north of Madison Square Park and extends west to Seventh Avenue (renamed "Fashion Avenue"), is a dense hive of offices, showrooms, workshops, and factory lofts. Workers trundle huge racks of clothes on casters from one address to the other. This archaic form of transport helps set the tone

(above) The Flatiron Building on a Rainy Evening, with Horses and Carriages *(ca. 1906), photographed by Edward J. Steichen. (Library of Congress) (opposite) The Flatiron today.*

for the whole Garment District, whose obscure rules and narrow monopolies give it something of the air of a medieval guild. Within the district itself arcane subdivisions like the Fur District, the Fabric District, and the Millinery District prevail. Storefront wholesalers devote themselves solely to snaps or hook-and-eyes, and a jobber here might specialize in a single type of button.

If the Garment District has a central focus, it's at West 27th Street and Seventh Avenue, the campus of the **Fashion Institute of Technology** (FIT), the rag trade's flagship educational institution. The school often mounts shows and exhibits.

■ MURRAY HILL *map pages 136–137, F/G-2*

A residential area that used to contain estates of some of the wealthiest New Yorkers, Murray Hill has suffered from a lack of definition since the aristocrats moved up Fifth Avenue. No distinctive neighborhood characteristic rose to replace them. There are other historical resonances—the English landed at **Kips Bay** (East 34th Street and the East River) in the campaign against Washington in the Revolutionary War—but primarily the area has settled down into a comfortable, not-quite-Midtown blandness.

There are a few bright spots, though. The unassuming **St. Stephen's Church** (149 East 29th Street, at Lexington Avenue), contains a marvelous surprise—murals by the Italian-born artist Constantino Brumidi, famous for his frescoes in the U.S. Capitol, that transform a visit here into a museum-level experience.

J. P. Morgan was one of the world's foremost collectors of illuminated manuscripts and drawings, and as the financier's life drew to a close, he commissioned Charles McKim of McKim, Mead & White to design a building to house his holdings. Morgan chose a site adjacent to his Madison Avenue mansion and spared no expense on the construction of the tastefully ostentatious **Morgan Library.** Exhibitions here usually center on Morgan's glorious collection but also include works from other great archives from around the world. Another draw is the chance to see how the other half lived—the Morgan rivals the uptown Frick Collection in this regard.

The library is at 33 East 36th Street, but patrons enter through 29 East 36th Street, a 1920s reconstruction of Morgan's mansion. You can peek into his grand office, reassembled the way it looked in his time. (It was in the original office that Morgan is said to have held an arm-twisting meeting with other American financiers that saved the country's economy from collapsing in 1907.) Morgan's

Exterior of the Morgan Library, designed by Charles McKim. (Morgan Library)

library is also maintained just as he left it upon his death in 1913. The glass-enclosed Morgan Court, a fine place for lunch or a glass of wine—small musical ensembles often play here in the early evening on Fridays—separates Morgan's mansion from that of his son, J. P. Morgan Jr. The museum's gift shop is in Jr.'s house. *29 East 36th Street; 212-685-0610.*

Around the corner at **Sniffen Court** you can see how the horses of the other half lived—the lovely mews consists entirely of Romanesque Revival carriage houses from the mid-19th century. *150-158 East 36th Street.*

The area from **Beth Israel Medical Center** (East 16th Street and First Avenue) northward used to be called "Bedpan Alley," so great was its concentration of hospitals, and the **Veterans Administration Hospital, Bellevue Hospital Center,** and **New York University Medical Center** (First Avenue between East 23rd and East 34th Streets) still dominate the southeastern tier of Murray Hill. Bellevue, established in 1736, is one of the country's oldest hospitals, a municipal institution serving those with all illnesses but for many people synonymous with the nuthouse.

■ EMPIRE STATE BUILDING *map pages 136–137, E-3*

It's the nearest thing to heaven we have in New York.
—Deborah Kerr to Cary Grant in *An Affair to Remember*

Several buildings in the world are now "nearer to heaven" than the **Empire State Building,** but that's not the point. Even though it has been eclipsed as the world's tallest, the "ESB" (as it's known in real estate slang) remains in a league of its own. At the 102nd-floor observatory snow sometimes falls up (due to crossdrafts), rain appears pink (a trick of the city's light), and Manhattan resembles what the architect Philip Johnson called the giant "asparagus patch."

"Beauty killed the beast," said a policeman in the 1933 movie *King Kong* when the great ape toppled from the Empire State Building (or, to be precise, a Hollywood model of it), two years after the skyscraper was erected. Actually, it wasn't beauty but gravity that killed the beast, and in its elegant defiance of same the Empire State Building endures as the central beacon of Manhattan, part Midtown fertility symbol, part communal widow's walk.

The building's story begins with a black man named Francisco Bastian, who in 1638 took ownership of the site on which the structure would eventually rise. It was part swamp then, fed by Sunfish Creek, with a good fishing hole for eels. In 1799, a farmer named John Thomson bought the site, and then it changed hands several times in the go-go years of the mid-19th century, finally winding up the property of the first family of Manhattan, the Astors.

In the late 1800s, Caroline Webster Schermerhorn Astor ruled New York's social elite from her mansion here—the gorgeous ballroom scenes in Martin Scorsese's film *The Age of Innocence* re-create the look of Mrs. Astor's soirées. In part because Mrs. Astor's social standing eclipsed his wife's, William Waldorf Astor, Caroline's nephew, left for England and erected an elegant hotel, the Waldorf, on the site of his mansion, which was next door to his aunt's. When she headed uptown shortly thereafter, her son hired Henry J. Hardenbergh, who had designed the Waldorf, to replace his mother's mansion with the Astoria Hotel. The two structures were joined, though with connecting halls that could be easily walled off, should the family feud erupt again. Thus was born the Waldorf-Astoria, New York's most deluxe hotel from the end of the 19th century until the late 1920s.

Steel workers on top of the Empire State Building as it nears completion. (Library of Congress)

Until autumn, 1929 was a boom year, and America's commercial giants vied with each other to see who could erect the tallest skyscraper. Early in 1929, Walter P. Chrysler had topped off his landmark Art Deco shrine at seventy-seven stories, eclipsing the Bank of the Manhattan Company tower on Wall Street as the world's tallest building. But John Jacob Raskob, a vice-president of General Motors and the inventor of the installment plan, had no intention of taking Chrysler's aerial supremacy lying down. He joined with the recently defeated Democratic presidential candidate Alfred E. Smith to build a skyscraper to beat them all.

Raskob chose the site of the Waldorf-Astoria Hotel as the building's site, mainly because doing so would involve fewer land transactions—instead of having to buy up many property owners on a block, with one quick deal the developer acquired most of the lot he required. The Waldorf-Astoria was demolished and rebuilt at East 49th Street and Park Avenue, its present location.

Raskob hired William Lamb of Shreve, Lamb & Harmon to design the Empire State Building, and, on his sixteenth attempt, the architect came up with a beautifully pure single tower, with setbacks starting at the fifth floor, perfect Art Deco flavorings, and a crisp, simple dignity.

Two weeks after construction began, the stock market crash of October 1929 took the air out of the skyscraper race for a half-century, but Raskob was already committed. Work continued at a feverish pace (the *New York Times* called it a "chase up into the sky"), and the building was completed in a mere nineteen months.

Opening in the depths of the Depression, the building, as they say, laid an egg. Office space went unrented, so much so that the place was nicknamed the "Empty State Building." The observatories, though, were an immediate hit. The millions of visitors who paid admission to view the world from an impossible height saved the building from bankruptcy. Jan Morris captured the sentiment in *Manhattan '45*, her book about the city as the post–World War II era began:

> Everybody went up the Empire State Building, every visiting film star, everybody's aunt, every serviceman on leave, every child on a school outing…. Even Englishmen, in those days given to attitudes of general disdain, were impelled into admiration. "Gives quite an impression of height, doesn't it?" said one of them when asked for his reactions.

When it opened for business, the Empire State Building had so much unrented space it was dubbed the "Empty State Building."

The height of the 102nd-floor observation tower put Manhattan into comprehensible, if not sobering, perspective. "They look like ants!" was the cry, about the people below in the street. Actually, from that height, the human form appears to be less than a millimeter long. It's not ants they look like, but lice. Not everyone came just to gawk, though. The first suicide off the Empire State came eighteen months after opening day. The cruel-looking fingers of the suicide fence on the observatory terrace, put up in 1947 after a three-week period in which five people tried to jump, testifies to the building's attraction to the self-destructive. In 1979, a woman avoided the fence altogether by jumping from the eighty-sixth floor. Blown back onto an eighty-fifth-floor ledge, she survived.

But the most amazing catastrophe associated with the building occurred in 1945. On the morning of July 28, visibility was low and the air was foggy, but Lieutenant Colonel William Smith was scheduled to fly his B-25 bomber from Boston to Newark Airport. Instead, he wound up maneuvering his plane through the forest of skyscrapers in Midtown. "From where I'm sitting," Smith said, "I can't see the top of the Empire State Building." He barely missed the Salomon Tower before banking away, then climbed abruptly upward. Minutes later, he crashed his 12-ton bomber into the seventy-ninth floor of the Empire State Building.

One engine tore through the building and came out the other side. Another plummeted down an elevator shaft. Burning gasoline poured down the sides of the

---

EMPIRE STATE BUILDING FACTS

Site: 79,288 square feet

Interior: 37 million cubic feet

Steel: 60,000 tons

Bricks: 10 million

Stone: 200,000 cubic feet

Height: 1,224 feet to 102nd floor; 1,454 feet to top of lightning rod

Floors: 102

Radiators: 6,700

Steps: 1,860

Tenants: 25,000

Visitors: 40,000 visitors daily

Elevator shafts:
73, almost 7 miles total

Lightning strikes:
About 100 per year

Lives lost during construction: 14

Weight: 730 million pounds (365,000 tons)

View from atop the Empire State Building.

skyscraper to the seventy-fifth floor. The three men in the plane and eleven people in the building died. The number of fatalities was low because it was Saturday morning and the building was almost empty. An elevator operator survived a free fall from the eightieth floor; emergency brakes saved her. The building survived as well and remains a symbol of America's commercial ambition. It had a forty-year run as the world's tallest building, and fascination with it continues to this day.

A visit to the observatory begins at the ticket office in the basement concourse, snakes in a line through a two-phased elevator ride, and finally winds up inside the glass-enclosed eighty-sixth floor. There are sidewalk-size open walkways to the north and south, and more generous terraces on the east and west, with spectacular views all around. The view from the enclosed 102nd floor is not sufficiently different to warrant the wait for the elevator.

One of the most romantic things about the Empire State Building is that it is open until midnight. On a warm spring night, when static electricity gives each kiss a literal spark, Manhattan rolls out below like a romantic invitation. There might indeed be places around that are nearer to heaven, but none that are closer to it. *350 Fifth Avenue; 212-736-3100.*

MIDTOWN
AND TIMES SQUARE

If, for a lot of people, Manhattan is New York City, then for an equal number Midtown is Manhattan. This dense commercial quadrant has attracted the moth-like attentions of countless impresarios, restaurateurs, and other attendants, so bright is the flame of its money. The resulting matrix of watering holes, clubs, galleries, hostelries, boutiques, clothiers, and specialty shops is among the greatest in the world, thus drawing even more wealth and perpetuating the area's status as a sort of Meta-Manhattan.

Times Square is too integral to the neighborhood (although to call Midtown a neighborhood is a bit like calling New York a village) to be relegated to the rank of a support system for Midtown's wealth and prestige, but the Crossroads of the World, as its boosters have called it for decades, is still a place to spend money as well as to earn it. If you envision Midtown as a giant engine for creating wealth, then Times Square's theater, restaurant, and entertainment district is perfectly poised to siphon off a share.

The two districts create a glorious dipole crackling with excitement and energy. **Times Square** forms a huge booming canyon of light and neon at the confluence of 42nd Street, Seventh Avenue, and Broadway, while the heart of **Midtown** represents a picket line of tall buildings stretching almost across the width of Manhattan. The metaphor does not extend farther west, to **Clinton,** a former slum neighborhood that for much of its life was known as Hell's Kitchen, nor quite to **Turtle Bay** and **Sutton Place,** upscale residential areas near the United Nations, along the East River.

■ UNITED NATIONS *map pages 164–165, H-4*

The ghost of Woodrow Wilson hovered over San Francisco in May 1945, when the founding conference of the United Nations was convened. The U.S. president had labored to bring his League of Nations into being after World War I, only to have it rejected in the isolationist atmosphere of his own country. It took another brutal war and millions more dead before the spirit of cooperation between countries became a sufficiently recognized ideal to spur some sort of action.

What was given theoretical form in San Francisco would by the early 1950s become part of the Manhattan psyche and landscape as the **United Nations**—a wildly optimistic appellation, given the squabbling to which its participants have frequently descended. Politics was present at the creation of the United Nations, especially in the formation of the veto-empowered Security Council, whose permanent seatholders were the victors of World War II—France, Great Britain, the United States, and the Soviet Union (now the Russian Federation)—along with China, then ruled by Chiang Kai-shek.

Squabbling continued in succeeding decades. When Ed Koch was New York's mayor, he became so enraged by what he perceived as the U.N.'s anti-Israel bias that he threatened to boot the organization out of the city. He suggested that the "swords into plowshares" Biblical motto might, in the U.N.'s case, be reversed, with its members found guilty of beating plowshares into swords.

When the United Nations began casting about for a suitable site for a headquarters, Nelson Rockefeller, heir to a sizable portion of the Standard Oil fortune of his

An international team of architects designed the modernist U.N. complex.

grandfather, John D. Rockefeller Sr., was still years away from becoming governor of New York State. He was then serving as the point man for Rockefeller Center, the family's sprawling Midtown office project.

Nelson realized he could increase the value of Rockefeller Center and at the same time remove a potential competitor to it in one bold stroke. The last parcel of available Midtown real estate large enough for a U.N. site was called "X City." Encompassing the original Turtle Bay, where a creek the Dutch called Saw Kill debouched into the East River, the area had become a stench-ridden sector of slaughterhouses spread along the East River north of 42nd Street.

The developer William Zeckendorf owned the land, and if he raised office buildings on the site, as he planned, the value of Rockefeller Center would be severely diluted. But if the U.N. located there, it would have the opposite effect of raising Midtown property values immensely, making Rockefeller Center all the more valuable.

With typical drive, Nelson plunged into the negotiations to lure the U.N. to New York. As the deadline for site selection approached in late 1946, Nelson was overjoyed when his father, John D. Rockefeller Jr., announced he would donate the entire $8.5 million Zeckendorf demanded for the X City property ("Why, Pa, that's most generous!" Nelson is supposed to have gushed). Thus, because of a depressed Midtown real estate market and the irrepressible energy of Nelson Rockefeller (as well as his father's deep pockets), the United Nations became headquartered in New York.

It was a good choice. Manhattan may well be the place in the world that best suggests both the possibilities and limitations of cooperation among radically different cultures and people. Geneva, perhaps, might have a more ancient tradition of negotiation and diplomacy, but Manhattan has the bumptious, strident, unnerving challenge of its streets. It is somehow fitting that an organization embracing cooperation among all of humankind be located on an island that is home to so many peoples.

A visit to the stately precincts of the United Nations is a good place to kick off a tour of the East Side. And while you're removed from the immediate cacophony of Manhattan, you might also want to meditate on the foibles of the human character and the possibilities of peace.

Architecturally speaking, the tall International-style **Secretariat Building** plays nicely off the parabolic roofline of the **General Assembly,** and the whole complex

ELEANOR ROOSEVELT ON THE UNITED NATIONS

I know that a great many people in the United States and other nations today wonder what is the use of having a United Nations. "It is just a debating society. It doesn't do anything." Those are criticisms one can hear almost anywhere, though to my mind they are quite unjustified.

■ ■ ■

I would like to ask everyone who has made or been tempted to make some such criticism of the United Nations to remember just one fact: When the United Nations was set up in the spring of '45 we thought that as soon as the war came to an end we would make the peace. And the organization that was set up was to function in a peaceful world, maintaining the new peace and creating an atmosphere in which lasting peace could grow and develop.

■ ■ ■

The people who wrote the Charter did not assume that peace was going to drop down on us like a beneficent blanket from heaven and be with us forever. They were quite realistic about it. They knew that, even though we made a peace, we would have to work year in and year out, day in and day out, to keep that peace, and to see that the atmosphere of the world was conducive to its growth. They knew that throughout the world there were tremendous difficulties, that it would take a long while, for instance, to make it possible for the people of our country to understand what was happening to someone in South Africa or in India or in Siam.

■ ■ ■

Finally, if democracy—and the blessings of it both as a way of government and a way of life—are going to win this contest for the support of the peoples of the world, we must have moral conviction and spiritual leadership…. That is the challenge that we face in strengthening and making the United Nations work as a whole. Those are the standards that we set ourselves and, in the interest of the future, those are the standards by which we must live.

—Eleanor Roosevelt, "What I Think of the United Nations,"
United Nations World, 1949

The Rose Garden frames the Secretariat Building at the United Nations.

renders a distinct and graceful impression. The first four U.N. buildings, the Secretariat, the General Assembly, the Library, and the Conference Building, were erected between 1947 and 1953, their design created by a committee of leading architects from thirteen countries. Wallace K. Harrison, related to the Rockefellers by marriage and later the overseer of Lincoln Center's design, chaired the committee. Though some critics feel that the original concept by the modernist great Le Corbusier was watered down, the complex stands as a mid-century icon.

The **U.N. Rose Garden,** behind the General Assembly along the East River, is a glorious, gentle-scented enclave with blooms donated from all over the world. All in all, a stunning setting for a world peace organization.

The visitors' entrance is opposite East 46th Street. Almost every nation in the world has donated art for the building, and there are various exhibits inside the lobby—a Foucault pendulum, a replica of the Soviet-era *Sputnik* satellite, a moon rock, displays on the history of the organization itself—to enjoy while you await one of the hour-long tours, which leave every half-hour. *United Nations Plaza (First Avenue), between East 42nd and East 48th Streets; 212-963-7713.*

■ Near the United Nations

The neighborhoods immediately surrounding the United Nations have a largely staid and moneyed residential atmosphere, with many consulates and international offices located here as well. To the west of the United Nations, 42nd Street passes under **Tudor City,** a hideaway of three thousand apartments built in the 1920s and nearly self-contained, with stores, parks, and restaurants. Tudor City used to be even more self-sufficient when its grounds included a miniature golf course, a blandishment its residents must now seek elsewhere.

Nearby is the **Ford Foundation** (320 East 43rd Street), a good place to visit even if you don't have your hand out for a grant, just to experience the amazing twelve-story jungle atrium in one of the finest modern buildings in New York, designed by Kevin Roche John Dinkeloo & Associates. What Henry Ford would have thought of this elegant but progressive design is not known, but he once voiced his concern that excavation of the Empire State Building might affect the rotation of the Earth, so perhaps it's best he didn't live to see what his money had wrought.

Stop for a moment at Third Avenue and East 46th Street to imagine an uprising that almost tore apart the city during the Civil War. At this corner was the site of the draft office that was the target of anticonscription gangs, angered at a draft law that allowed rich citizens to buy their way out of the Union army for $300. The infamous Draft Riot, one of the worst civil disturbances in Manhattan history, started here on July 13, 1863. It eventually swelled to include the whole city, resulting in an estimated two thousand people dead, many of them of African descent. (The reasons the rioters, most of them Caucasian, opposed conscription included their unwillingness to risk their lives to end slavery.)

Just down the block, at 210 East 46th Street, is another notorious site, this one **Sparks Steak House,** where Mafia boss Paul Castellano and chauffeur Tommy Bilotti were gunned down on December 16, 1985. The triggermen were widely believed to be messengers of John Gotti, impatient to take command of the Gambino crime family. The rub-out increased the eatery's popularity exponentially, and it eventually expanded to meet the demand.

North of the U.N., the area changes into a residential neighborhood called Turtle Bay, named after the long-gone East River marsh that was, indeed, full of turtles—at least until the colonial New Yorkers hunted them down for soup. The district is typified by the quiet gentility of **Turtle Bay Gardens,** on the interior of the block between East 48th and East 49th Streets and Second and Third

Avenues. Not open to the public, the gardens are enjoyed by the residents—including the composer and lyricist Stephen Sondheim—whose elegant town-houses border them.

Farther north, between First Avenue and the river, are two neighborhoods that exhibit the same air of exclusivity and privilege as Turtle Bay. These are **Beekman Place,** running north from East 49th Street, and **Sutton Place,** north from East 53rd Street. Both are residential enclaves within easy walking distance of the United Nations. At 23 Beekman Place is the **Paul Rudolph house,** a showcase residence built by a leading light of modern architecture.

Sutton Place is an especially fine spot from which to view the **Queensboro Bridge;** you may remember the terrace at East 57th Street from Woody Allen's film *Manhattan.* Sutton Place is better known from another film, *Dead End,* based on the same-named play that commemorated the anomalous historical juxtaposition of slum and townhouse when the neighborhood was in transition.

Near Sutton Place, at East 58th Street, is **Riverview Terrace,** a rare private street in Manhattan, with the official residence of the Secretary General of the U.N. at the south end, off **Sutton Terrace Square.**

■ GRAND CENTRAL AREA *map pages 164–165, F-4*

From the United Nations, the logical approach to the more bustling center of town is to head east along that celebrated artery, **42nd Street,** toward the landmark Grand Central Terminal. The thoroughfare, which marks the southern border of Midtown, strings several architectural and cultural pearls along its length. At Second Avenue is the great Art Deco **Daily News Building** (220 East 42nd Street), worth a step inside for the huge spinning globe, bronze geography inlays on the floor, and various meteorological instruments in the lobby. The *Daily News* has since decamped, but the building's interior still effectively recalls the architectural mood of 1930, when the place was built.

For the most glorious incarnation of the Art Deco style, however, there is nothing in the world like the **Chrysler Building** (405 Lexington Avenue), built by auto magnate Walter P. Chrysler so his sons would have something to manage if they stayed on in New York. It was designed to be the tallest structure in the world—"Make this building higher than the Eiffel Tower," said Walter to architect William

The Chrysler Building's ornamentation includes large-scale re-creations of hubcaps, radiator grills, and other parts from 1929 Chrysler models.

Van Alen. The Chrysler Building's exact height (1,048 feet) was kept a secret during its construction to foil competitors in the skyscraper race. At the last moment, its 27-ton crown was hoisted to the top in one piece, and the Chrysler was finally unveiled as (briefly) the tallest building in the world.

Van Alen achieved some sort of aesthetic apogee with the Chrysler's exterior, with its stainless-steel-clad façade and lancet crown. Every decorative touch is

"Grand Central Station! Crossroads of a million private lives!" —opening words of the *1937 NBC radio drama* Grand Central Station.

The soaring vault of Grand Central Station is decorated with glittering constellations.

meant to signify "automobile," from gargoyles resembling 1929 radiator caps to abstract roadster graphics. In 1981, Van Alen's original lighting plans were rediscovered and implemented, resulting in a nightly Art Deco splash of fluorescence.

The Chrysler Building is best viewed from a distance, from down Lexington Avenue, say, or even from Hollywood: *Ghostbusters, Bonfire of the Vanities,* and the horror flick *Q!* have all featured generous angles of the building. Best is the view you'll get from the observatories at the Empire State Building. The interior, of African marble and chrome steel, is striking, as are the elevators; the mural on the lobby ceiling celebrates transportation and industry.

The Chrysler Building has recently been merged with the former Kent Building on Third Avenue into an entity its developers have dubbed the Chrysler Center. The most notable elements of this new complex are the so-called Chrysler Trylons, 65-foot-tall semireflective blue-glass-and-steel pyramids on 42nd Street to the immediate east of the Chrysler Building. The pyramids represent architect Philip Johnson's witty quote about the older structure's roofline. "It's a monument for 42nd Street," Johnson told the *New York Times,* "to give you the top of the Chrysler Building at street level."

GRAND CENTRAL OYSTER BAR

Tucked in the nether regions of Grand Central Terminal and with the same gorgeous Guastavino-tile ceiling vaults as in the station proper, the Grand Central Oyster Bar and Restaurant (below) is a delightful discovery to the newcomer and an unchangeable Manhattan institution to the regular.

Of the three dining spaces, the open central area is a throwback to the counter joints of old and is perfect for a quick half-dozen Belons—cracked open in front of your eyes—while waiting for a train. The wood-paneled Saloon is more intimate but also has a faintly speakeasy flavor, complete with a secret entry. In contrast, the large Dining Room at the other end of the establishment exudes white-tablecloth formality.

The Oyster Bar takes its name seriously and in a given year dishes up about two million of the bivalves—raw and in celebrated pan roasts and stews. Several dozen seafood offerings appear on the menu. The award-winning wine list, heavy on premier American vintages, usually includes a dozen or more choices by the glass.

Lunchtime, especially at the counters, takes on a velocity well suited to the trains and subways roaring by just yards underneath diners' feet. The more staid Dining Room caters to a power-broker crowd. (Split the difference at the chummy Saloon.) Dinner at the Dining Room is a quieter experience altogether, and a favorite of true seafood gourmands. The service people are known not to suffer fools gladly but coddle regulars like old friends. *Grand Central Terminal, Lower Level; 212-490-6650.*

Just down the block from the Chrysler Building, at 42nd Street and Park Avenue, is one of the architectural, cultural, and transportation anchors of Midtown and of Manhattan itself: **Grand Central Terminal,** constructed between 1903 and 1913. It's a building that manages the unlikely feat of combining Beaux Arts fantasy with pure functionalism—it is, after all, a working train station. More than that, it reminds present-day Manhattan of a more gracious past. Compare it with the "modern" monstrosity of Penn Station, and you'll know why New Yorkers cherish Grand Central.

The station's exterior is studded with sculpture, including one of railroad magnate Commodore Cornelius Vanderbilt, the site's original developer. The massive clock-and-statue grouping on the colonnaded south side, by Jules-Alexis Coutans, is visible all the way down Park Avenue. Grand Central's east side is less embellished by architectural ornament. When the building was erected this side fronted slums, the denizens of which were not thought capable of appreciating beauty.

The interior bears out the promise of Grand Central's marvelous façades. A soaring vault decorated with constellations (painted by Paul Hellau and Charles Basing, complete with over twenty-five hundred trompe l'oeil "stars") watches over the scurryings of a half-million commuters daily. A recent cleaning project by the Metropolitan Transportation Authority, holder of the Grand Central lease, scrubbed away fifty years of soot and grime to reveal a brilliant cerulean "sky."

A stylish boîte for thirsty commuters and nightcrawlers alike is the **Campbell Apartment** (15 Vanderbilt Avenue), a luxurious wood-panel bar that was formerly a businessman's office and apartment right within Grand Central. The bar specializes in vodkatinis (orange vodka, cherry liqueur, and a splash of lime, anyone?).

From the heights to the depths: The station is built over a complex of railway and subway tunnels, and is itself several stories deep. The acoustics along the Guastavino-tile vaults are such that a whisper spoken into one of the corners will magically be heard across the hallway. You'll often see people testing this phenomenon on the lower-level ramp outside the Oyster Bar.

For all the glory of the 75-foot-tall arched windows and the grand staircases, patterned after those at the Paris opera, Grand Central is a building that *works,* and works hard. Subways, commuter trains, and serious Midtown foot traffic converge here, with 32 miles of track in total. Fluid pedestrian movement is maintained by ramps and segregated levels. A marvel of practicality and panache, Grand Central is a railroad terminal against which all others may be measured.

In the late 1960s, it appeared as if Grand Central might go the way of the old Pennsylvania Station, demolished in the name of progress. When the terminal's owners, the Penn Central railroad, wanted to raze it and erect an office tower in its place (in two designs, Marcel Breuer placed a tower over the terminal), Jacqueline Kennedy Onassis and other prominent New Yorkers joined in the battle to preserve it. The legal case went all the way to the Supreme Court, resulting in a six-to-three precedent-setting decision endorsing the concept of landmark preservation.

Directly north of Grand Central is the **MetLife Building** (200 Park Avenue), known to stubborn New Yorkers by its former appellation, the Pan Am Building. Controversial from the first, for usurping the "air rights" of Grand Central, the Pan Am monolith went on to greater notoriety when a helicopter fell off its helipad (since closed) onto unsuspecting pedestrians below.

Like the MetLife Building, the golden-topped **230 Park Avenue** building also stands athwart Park Avenue, but it is much more popular. Designed by the same architects who created Grand Central Terminal, it was built in the late 1920s. In modern times it was absorbed into the hotel and real estate empire of Harry Helmsley and was known during the 1980s and 1990s as the Helmsley Building. The late Helmsley was the husband of Leona, the self-proclaimed "Queen of New York" (others called her the "Queen of Mean"), who was convicted in 1989 for tax evasion and served eighteen months in jail. "Only little people pay taxes," she is said to have proclaimed, before the legal system whittled her down to size.

The United Nations, the Chrysler Building, and Grand Central stand side by side in a neighborhood of superlatives, but if you made us choose the most beautiful structure, it would be the **New York Public Library** (Fifth Avenue and West 42nd Street), designed by the firm of Carrère and Hastings. The site was formerly the Croton Reservoir, an artificial lake with an Egyptian-style parapet 50 feet high and 25 feet thick, around which it was once fashionable to stroll. Improved water delivery systems eventually made the reservoir obsolete, and one of the grandest libraries in the world was built here, financed by the largesse of John Jacob Astor and Samuel J. Tilden, a former New York State governor. The new entity combined the collections of the Astor Library, which at the time was operating out of the Astor Place building that now houses the Public Theater, and the Lenox Library, then located at Fifth Avenue and East 70th Street, in the building that preceded Henry Clay Frick's mansion.

The New York Public Library is a place of quiet repose in the concrete jungle.

As with Grand Central, the architectural style of the library is Beaux Arts, but here the building's utilitarian pursuits don't overwhelm the decorative flourishes quite as much. The library, completed in 1911, is a lyrical white marble temple dedicated to reason, education, and beauty. Outside, two stone lions, named Patience and Fortitude, stand guard.

The ornate façade is set off by two flagpoles, their bases riotously embellished in painted bronze. A pair of fountains, labeled Truth and Beauty ("all ye need to know in life," according to Keats), flanks the grand entrance steps, which are peopled in warm weather by a carnival gallery of lounging, lunch-eating, gawking New Yorkers. Food kiosks supply sandwiches and beverages.

Inside, the gilded opulence of the library's Astor Lobby immediately straightens the spine of everyone who enters. Directly ahead is Gottesman Exhibition Hall—venture in, look up, and admire the superb ceiling. Down the south hall on the first floor is the DeWitt Wallace Periodical Room (eleven thousand periodicals in twenty-two languages from 124 countries), named after the founder of the *Reader's Digest* and graced with great Richard Haas murals celebrating the New York publishing world. A codicil to DeWitt Wallace's will directed that the room be air-conditioned (the only public space in the library that is) in tribute to the long hours he and his wife spent sweating in this room in muggy New York summers, preparing the first issues of what became the world's most popular magazine.

This central research library of the New York Public Library system (eighty-five branches, seven million users annually) does not lend out books; rather, users are permitted to request and peruse them in two grand reading rooms on the third floor. The coffered, 50-foot ceilings of these linked rooms feature superb decorative murals crowded with clouds, flying fish, angels, and satyrs. They are the perfect diversion while you're waiting for your books to arrive from the 92 miles of computerized stacks, with more than three million books tucked out of sight below Bryant Park.

Bryant Park, immediately behind the library to the west, is a great success story of New York renewal. Named for the poet William Cullen Bryant, it was a potter's field (some of the bodies moved from Washington Square wound up here), and then the grounds of the Crystal Palace Exhibition Hall, which burned down in a spectacular conflagration in 1858. Two decades ago, it was a seedy drug bazaar, but in 1989 it was closed and underwent a total makeover. The result is one of the friendliest public spaces in Manhattan, patrolled and kept clean, with lively events

THE NEW CABARET

In the era of nu-metal and progressive house music, something as light and delicately clever as a Cole Porter tune might not be expected to survive. But in a collection of plush boîtes and smoky nightclubs, the joys of Porter and George Gershwin and Kurt Weill—not to mention the newer material of Stephen Sondheim and Julie Gold—are prospering mightily.

This is the celebrated New Cabaret, a self-consciously stylish throwback to Café Society of the 1930s and 1940s. In venues like the history-drenched **Oak Room** (Algonquin Hotel, 59 West 44th Street; 212-840-6800), or the retro-hip **Fez** (Time Cafe, 380 Lafayette Street; 212-533-7000), the pleasure of sipping a dry martini while listening to a sultry singer has been reborn.

New Cabaret runs a gamut of styles. Performers might be straight-ahead elegant, like Julie Wilson. They might play off the conventions, as with the cross-dressing hilarities of Justin Bond, of the popular duo Kiki and Herb. Or they can drag nostalgia kicking and screaming into the age of rock. But the essence of this art is intimacy. This 1939 review in the *New York Times* of the great Greta Keller sounds themes that remain true today: "Ill at ease in the larger sanctums, Miss Keller's peculiar and indefinable quality as a singer needs the intimate surrounding the Algonquin provides. Tales of heartbreak are not easily sung in the great halls, but in a small room Miss Keller can take listeners into her confidence."

Keller's successors take contemporary listeners into their confidence at a number of intimate venues. Bobby Short has become an institution playing piano in his own timeless style at the **Cafe Carlyle,** while across the hall in the smaller **Bemelmans Bar,** things are even more cozy (both bars: Carlyle Hotel, Madison Avenue and East 76th Street; 212-744-1600). The **Chestnut Room** at Tavern on the Green (Central Park West and 67th Street; 212-873-3200) might look like "a hunting lodge decorated by Liberace," as the *New Yorker* has described it, but the live music adds a touch of class.

Something other than nostalgia goes on in these rooms—a devotion to tradition, sure, but also an insistence that the murderous pace and volume of modern life need not have the last word. Instead, like a note hung off the coda of a Cole Porter lyric, New Cabaret can invent the world—or at least an evening—anew.

Other New Cabaret venues to check out include **Cafe Pierre** (2 East 61st Street; 212-940-8185); **Knickerbocker** (33 University Place; 212-228-8490); **Don't Tell Mama** (343 West 46th Street; 212-757-0788); and **Arci's Place** (450 Park Avenue South; 212-532-4370).

Midtown office workers flock to Bryant Park in fine weather.

such as outdoor movies (projected against a giant screen at night) in the summertime. From inside Bryant Park one may meditate on the mysteries of architectural style, since to the south rises the great Gothic pile of the **American Radiator Building** (40 West 40th Street), and to the north, the sleek vertical curve of the **W.R. Grace Building** (1114 Avenue of the Americas).

North of Bryant Park is the "Club Row" of 44th Street: such tony enclaves as the **Yale Club** (50 Vanderbilt Avenue, at East 44th Street), the **Harvard Club** (27 West 44th Street), and the **New York Yacht Club** (37 West 44th Street). Tucked away on the same street is the small gem of the **General Society Library of Mechanics and Tradesmen** (20 West 44th Street), a private book collection open for a nominal fee and one of the great little-known retreats of Midtown.

The **International Center of Photography** (1133 Avenue of the Americas, at 43rd Street), universally known as "ICP," is the most prestigious venue for photography in the city. ICP mounts rotating exhibitions in its cavernous bi-level space. A few blocks north, on 47th Street between Fifth Avenue and the Avenue of the Americas (Sixth Avenue), is the **Diamond District** of mostly wholesale and some retail establishments operated by a hermetic group of dealers, many of them Orthodox Jews. The organizational structure here is tantamount to a medieval guild.

Equally concentrated is what could be labeled the **musical instrument district,** to the west of the Diamond District on 48th Street between the Avenue of the Americas and Seventh Avenue—a mecca for those in search of a perfect Stratocaster, drum kit, or licorice stick. After the MTV studios in Times Square, it's the best place in the city for rock-star gazing.

■ ROCKEFELLER CENTER *map pages 164–165, E-3*

Covering a 22-acre parcel of very expensive real estate is **Rockefeller Center,** which includes much of the land between 47th Street, Fifth Avenue, 52nd Street, and the Avenue of the Americas. Probably the grandest Oedipal monument Manhattan has to offer, it was conceived and built by John D. Rockefeller Jr., who constantly labored in the shadow of his father, the Standard Oil tycoon. Rockefeller Center was going to be Junior's self-validation, the project that would prove his worth.

It almost ended in a disaster. In 1928, Junior paid $3.3 million for a twenty-four-year lease on a parcel of Midtown that in the 19th century was the site of the Elgin Botanic Gardens, and later passed into the hands of Columbia University. Junior planned a development that would be anchored by the Metropolitan Opera, which was casting about for a new home.

Then the Great Depression hit. The front page of the *New York Times* on October 29, 1929, said it all in two headlines: "Stock Prices Slump $14,000,000,000," and a smaller one below, "Architects Picked to Plan Rockefeller Center." John D. Jr.'s timing could not have been worse. The Met bowed out, and the Rockefellers were left holding the bag—and a very expensive bag at that. Only John D.'s doggedness, the immense wealth of the Rockefeller family, and the sheer momentum of the building project saved Rockefeller Center from bankruptcy. It didn't turn a profit until well after World War II.

Nobody can deny the scale of the plan. There were fourteen original buildings, including such New York landmarks as **Radio City Music Hall** (Avenue of the Americas and West 50th Street) and the **G.E. Building** (30 Rockefeller Plaza), formerly the RCA Building. Another five office towers were added along the Avenue of the Americas in a second round of construction beginning in 1957, with Marilyn Monroe throwing the switch to dynamite the hole for the **Time-Life Building** (1271 Avenue of the Americas), whose modern (for its day) lobby merits a peek.

Rockefeller Center is a thriving city within a city, with fifteen million or so square feet of rentable space, about four hundred elevators, and nearly one hundred thousand locks to keep it all safe and secure. Some elements of the original design are ingenious, such as the rooftop lawns, the underground truck delivery bays, and the vast subterranean promenade connecting the buildings, lined with shops and restaurants.

Clever also is the long, sloping design of the **Channel Gardens,** between the **British Empire Building** (620 Fifth Avenue, at West 50th Street) and **La Maison Française** (610 Fifth Avenue, at West 49th Street)—the "Channel" between the British and the French—which employs gravity to draw passersby on Fifth Avenue into the center. The lures here include the famous Christmas tree and skating rink in winter, the annual flower show in spring, and open-air dining in warm weather.

That sunken skating rink is a quintessential Manhattan scene, especially when the huge Rockefeller Center tree is erected over it during the holidays. There always seem to be more than a few smooth professionals among the wobbly-ankled amateurs, and their circuit of the small rink, breath pluming in the cold air, can be mesmerizing. Onlookers line the promenade above, sometimes several deep during the crowded shopping days around Christmas.

The National Broadcasting Company became one of the first tenants of Rockefeller Center, back when radio was king. Entrances to the **NBC Studios** are midblock on the West 49th Street side of the G.E. Building. You can buy tickets to studio tours at the frenetic **NBC Experience** store, also in the GE Building. Across the street is NBC's "window on the world"—huge picture windows fronting on the set of *The Today Show.* Electronic kiosks solicit "people in the street" interviews and passersby can ogle the newscasters inside.

Be sure to note the Jose Maria Sert murals (*American Progress* on the west wall, and *Time* on the ceiling) in the G.E. Building lobby. Sert had the unenviable job of replacing Diego Rivera's controversial 1933 mural, which was originally commissioned for the space. Rivera, a Communist and iconoclast, began an epic panorama featuring a heroic proletariat triumphing over the very kind of capitalists that built Rockefeller Center. Nelson Rockefeller pulled the plug when the Mexican muralist included a glowing portrait of Lenin. To Rockefeller's credit, he tried to move the mural to the Museum of Modern Art, but that proved physically impossible and,

"The view of Rockefeller Center from Fifth Avenue is the most beautiful I have ever seen ever seen ever seen." —Gertrude Stein

The sloping design of the Channel Gardens directs all eyes to the middle of Rockefeller Center.

in any case, Rivera was adamant that the artwork should be shown in the space for which it was created or not at all.

All things considered, Rockefeller Center is a little too cold, a little too clean, to invite an enthusiastic embrace. Appreciation, yes, admiration, maybe—but there are limits to the emotions it sparks in the hearts of New Yorkers. Maybe that's because Rockefeller Center has never strayed far from its corporate genesis; it is, after all, a collection of office buildings, no matter how much art or how many amenities it scatters around for the masses.

The best way to investigate the nooks and crannies of Rockefeller Center is with a self-guided tour. You can pick up maps in the lobby of the G.E. Building.

■ HEART OF MIDTOWN

Also built on a grand scale is Rockefeller Center's neighbor across Fifth Avenue, **St. Patrick's Cathedral** (Fifth Avenue and East 50th Street). Begun in 1858 and opened in 1879 (its spires were added in 1888), St. Patrick's is the spiritual center of New York's vast Catholic population. The interior is even more impressive than the Gothic Revival exterior, especially the Lady Chapel, behind the altar. James Renwick, the primary architect, also designed the Smithsonian Institution in Washington, D.C., and the Episcopal Grace Church near Astor Place.

In the lower level of the nearby Olympic Tower is the well-heeled **Onassis Cultural Center** (645 Fifth Avenue), a museum-quality exhibition space that presents fabulous shows of Greek and Byzantine art.

On Madison Avenue, directly across from St. Patrick's rectory, are the wonderful **Villard Houses** (451 and 455 Madison Avenue). Now partly incorporated into the New York Palace Hotel, these are the surviving pair of five 19th-century brownstones built to resemble an Italian Renaissance palazzo. At number 455 is the legendary Le Cirque restaurant, which moved here in 1997 under the name **Le Cirque 2000.** Inside the north wing is the **Urban Center** (457 Madison Avenue), a research and preservation group that mounts exhibits and has an excellent bookstore specializing in architecture and urban design.

A wonderful place to catch up on all those segments of *The Honeymooners* you missed—as well as other television shows and news reports and radio programs—is the **Museum of Television and Radio.** This marvelously modern shrine to television (and, to a lesser degree, radio) hosts lectures and exhibits, but its great appeal is derived from the screening facilities. *25 West 52nd Street; 212-621-6800.*

After a session chuckling at Lucy or witnessing Walter Cronkite get misty-eyed reporting John F. Kennedy's assassination, you can revive your spirits next door at the famed **"21" Club** (21 West 52nd Street). A speakeasy during Prohibition, these days it's a power brokers' hangout par excellence.

As long as you accept "modern" as applying to a defined period—say, the 1870s to 1950s—the **Museum of Modern Art** (212-708-9400), whose 11 West 53rd Street facility closed in 2002 for a three-year reconstruction and expansion project, is the standard against which all other collections must be measured. MoMA, as it is known in shorthand, was founded in 1929 (by John D. Rockefeller Jr.'s wife, Abby Aldrich Rockefeller, among others). It was the first of its kind, since contemporary art at the time was consigned exclusively to private galleries.

MoMA is justly celebrated for its collection of Impressionist, Cubist, and Modern masters, with van Gogh particularly well represented and some epochal works of Picasso among the holdings. As much as the painting collection shines, though, MoMA's primary contribution to the art world is in enlarging its scope, canonizing works from the disparate fields of design, photography, film, and architecture.

Easter Day Parade revelers take a breather in front of St. Patrick's Cathedral.

MoMA long seemed willing to rest on its considerable laurels, leaving the thrashing and brawlings of the contemporary art scene to other museums. When the expansion is complete, MoMA might be a shade less stodgy, if only because of its merger with the hipper P.S. 1 Contemporary Art Center in Queens. Until MoMA's West 53rd Street digs reopen, the museum has moved its operations—and many of its famous artworks—to the spiffily redesigned former Swingline stapler factory in Queens, rechristened as MoMA QNS (for directions to the facility and other information, see page 289).

Across from MoMA is the **American Craft Museum,** which exhibits ceramics, work in metal and wood, and other media ghettoized under the rubric of "crafts," as opposed to "art." The craft museum announced plans in 2002 to spend $30 million to restore 2 Columbus Circle (see page 250) and move there by mid-decade. *40 West 53rd Street; 212-956-3535.*

The **American Folk Art Museum,** relocated from its uptown home in Lincoln Square, opened to much fanfare in late 2001. The permanent collection here includes a broomstick whirligig, a hand-sewn 1800 glazed-wool quilt, and a black-bellied plover decoy. With its striking contemporary design and whimsical art and artifacts, the museum instantly became a must-stop visit among Midtown art attractions. If you need a breather, you can stop in the downstairs café and contemplate this facility's wealth of scrimshaw and needlepoint samplers. *45 West 53rd Street, near Avenue of the Americas; 212-265-1040.*

Along Fifth and Park Avenues near MoMA are some of Midtown's most notable skyscrapers, and many have additional treasures hidden inside them. Architect Mies van der Rohe's **Seagram Building** (375 Park Avenue) is home to power-dining central—the **Four Seasons** restaurant, designed by Philip Johnson. The nearby **Lever House** (390 Park Avenue), designed by Gordon Bunshaft, and the Seagram are considered the apogee of the International style of "glass box" architecture.

John Burgee teamed with Johnson on the **"Lipstick Building"** (885 Third Avenue), an odd, oval edifice that was once voted the most unpopular skyscraper in Manhattan. Nearby, dwarfed by its towering neighbors, is a two-story holdout from the 19th-century, the small, distinctive saloon **P. J. Clarke's** (915 Third Avenue), which underwent major restoration in 2002. Universally known as P. J.'s, the bar was a key stop in Ray Milland's degenerate pub crawl in the 1945 Billy Wilder film *The Lost Weekend.*

(following pages) Architectural milestones: Seagram Building, Citicorp Center, Lipstick Building, and Lever House.

A distinctive roofline is that of the **Citicorp Center** (153 East 53rd Street), designed by Hugh Stubbins and Associates. Its beveled roof was originally meant to be a solar collector, but the real innovation here is the airy, open base of the building, where a church and shopping bazaar are located. Also famous for its profile is Johnson and Burgee's **Sony Building** (550 Madison Avenue), with its "Chippendale" top. In the spacious ground-floor **Sony Plaza** (entrances off 55th and 56th Streets) is the elevator to the **Sony Wonder Technology Lab,** an engaging interactive electronic exhibit.

On the Fifth Avenue side of the Sony Building block is that great temple of high-end consumerism, **Trump Tower** (725 Fifth Avenue). "The Donald," as the developer Donald Trump is known to gossip columnists and one of his ex-wives, made this glitzy tower of shops, boutiques, and condos his headquarters. For an easy antidote to the glut of modernism, gaze over to the ornate **Crown Building** (730 Fifth Avenue), brilliantly lit at night. On the twelfth floor was the original home of the Museum of Modern Art.

The equestrian statue of General William Tecumseh Sherman in **Grand Army Plaza** (Fifth Avenue and Central Park South) often invokes gasps of astonishment, but the gaudy gold-leafing is part of Augustus Saint-Gaudens's original design. *Pomona,* the mythological lady in the middle of **Pulitzer Fountain,** is only a bit more sedate. The model for the sculpture was the legendary Suzi, a mainstay of the New York Art Students League and here immortalized in bronze.

Grand Army Plaza, known to New Yorkers simply as the Plaza, the name of the hotel that fronts it, is one of the few European-style plazas in the city. It is also one of the few remaining places in the city to get, courtesy of the carriage horses that wait for passengers here, an ammonia-scented whiff of what all New York used to smell like. Watch out—some of these beasts are surly, and will bite. Instead, herd the kids across the street to the world's most famous stuffed animal and gewgaw emporium, **F.A.O. Schwarz** (767 Fifth Avenue).

Coolness and gentility have held sway at **the Plaza** (Fifth Avenue and Central Park South) for so long that they have survived repeated assault—from Eloise, the eponymous heroine of the children's book, who is depicted pouring water down the mail chutes; from the Beatles, whose stay during their original U.S. tour sparked a near riot; and from Donald Trump, who bought the hotel in 1988 and not only failed to transform it into Atlantic City North, as some doomsayers predicted, but with the help of his then-wife Ivana managed to restore its fading grandeur.

THE PLAZA

Even a place as massive and immovable as Manhattan needs anchors, and the Plaza hotel has anchored the southwest corner of Central Park for almost a century now, since 1907. Above and beyond architect Henry J. Hardenbergh's confectionary design, the Plaza, with its air of cultured elegance and grand history of hosting celebrities and showmen, helps sustain the romance of the whole city.

The Plaza's suites, on the hotel's northeast corner, with views of both Fifth Avenue and Central Park, were celebrated in Neil Simon's *Plaza Suite* and still symbolize having arrived. As befitting a hotel whose permanent residents included Vanderbilts and proto-jetsetters, some suites are absolutely palatial, with high ceilings and bathrooms the size of New York City apartments (the Vanderbilt Suite is pictured below).

Luckily, the casual visitor can enjoy the hotel too. Tea, complete with finger sandwiches, in the lobby's central Palm Court has a proper Old World feel. Great murals by Everett Shinn, a painter of the Ashcan School, grace the Oak Bar. Nurse a

manhattan with the blue light of evening falling outside and you'll instantly find yourself transported back to the pre–World War II era of F. Scott Fitzgerald.

The Plaza has occasionally fallen on hard times, but it has done more than survive and endure. It has prospered. "They've tried very hard to get rid of the Plaza," Bette Davis once said, one grande dame commenting on the vicissitudes of another. "That would be the end of New York." *Fifth Avenue and Central Park South; 212-759-3000.*

Window displays at F.A.O. Schwarz tempt children from far and wide.

Fifty-seventh Street, the main crosstown artery of northern Midtown, is known internationally for its art galleries. This is also the street of **Carnegie Hall** (156 West 57th Street). The hall has a rather perfunctory Renaissance Revival exterior, but it's been a venue for superb music ever since it was built in 1891, with Tchaikovsky conducting the debut concert.

Carnegie was always known as a classical hall, with Gustav Mahler, Arturo Toscanini, and Leonard Bernstein all conducting here. The New York Philharmonic was also in residence until it moved to Lincoln Center in the early 1960s—part of the reason Carnegie fell on hard times during this period. The classical "barrier" was broken by the "Father of the Blues," W. C. Handy, in 1928, and Benny Goodman a decade later. Carnegie Hall hosts a wide variety of acts but remains a prime classical venue, especially for visiting orchestras.

Incredibly, the hall never managed to turn a profit. In the early 1960s, it was slated for the wrecking ball, but a group of artists, violinist Isaac Stern chief among them, stepped in to save it. A renovation in the late 1980s cleared away some of the hall's shabbiness, but, say some, damaged its fabled "warm" acoustics—a problem remedied in 1995 when a concrete subfloor beneath the stage was ripped out. To the left of the main entrance, on the second floor, is a small museum that usually has an interesting music-related display.

The Russian Tea Room, the Russian-theme restaurant a few doors east of Carnegie Hall and long a haunt of entertainment celebs, closed its doors in 2002 after a glitzy makeover failed to generate sufficient business. Regulars are hoping someone will revive the restaurant, but in the meantime the blinis and caviar still flow forth at nearby **Petrossian** (Alwyn Court, 182 West 58th Street), a glam excursion best experienced on an expense account.

Also east of Carnegie Hall, two piano stores sit a block apart: **Chickering Hall** (29 West 57th Street) and **Steinway Hall** (109 West 57th Street). From the former, Alexander Graham Bell made the first long-distance telephone call; the latter is still a great place to hear a recital on a freshly minted concert grand.

A block north of Carnegie Hall is the confectionary façade of the **Alwyn Court Apartments** (58th Street and Seventh Avenue), every facet encrusted with terra-cotta ornamentation in the style known as François I. The salamander above the corner entryway (and elsewhere on the façade) is a heraldic reference to the French king. In the building's courtyard is a mural by Richard Haas, who did some of the decorative work in the New York Public Library.

Near the Alwyn is the **Ed Sullivan Theater** (1697 Broadway), whose star tenant, David Letterman, has turned the immediate neighborhood into a sort of talk-show theme park, with visits to area stores and staged events—from dogwalking contests to daredevil dives—that periodically close down West 53rd Street. Competition for tickets to *The Late Show with David Letterman* is fierce, and each day the chosen few assemble under the Sullivan's grand marquee to wait for showtime.

The area immediately to the north of Times Square is Hotel Land, but there are a few sites of casual interest, such as the **Hearst Building** (959 Eighth Avenue). The oddly truncated feel to this elaborately ornamented six-story building can be explained by the fact that it was meant to be the base for a skyscraper, whose builders halted construction when the stock market crashed in 1929. The Hearst Corporation plans to add a crystalline tower designed by the British architect Norman Foster.

Another product of the Depression, this one gloriously realized, is the Thomas Hart Benton mural, *America Today,* inside the north lobby hallway of the **Equitable Center** (787 Seventh Avenue). Moved from the New School for Social Research, where it was installed in 1930, this epic painting perfectly embodies the political and artistic flavor of the Depression years. Compared to it, Roy Lichtenstein's giant *Mural with Blue Brushstroke,* also in the Equitable lobby, is mere decoration.

FOUR SEASONS HOTEL

When the Four Seasons Hotel opened in 1993, it ushered luxury accommodations into the 21st century—a few years ahead of time. The hotel, designed by I.M. Pei, became an instant Manhattan landmark, a soaring presence on East 57th Street.

The stepped exterior with faint echoes of Art Deco is sheathed in the dun-colored Magny limestone that Pei used in his noted pyramidal design at the Louvre in Paris. The hotel continues its dramatic statement inside, with the three-story Grand Foyer, surrounded by terraced restaurants and lounges. The restaurant and bar space in particular, with 16-foot round windows looking out on 58th Street, has been so fervently embraced by New Yorkers and visitors that it is sometimes a battle to get to the rail. The Fifty Seven Fifty Seven Bar, has become Manhattan's martini central.

The experience of lodging at the Four Seasons matches its impressive physical reality. Feather-down pillows, tubs that fill in sixty seconds, and always, always, those views! New York's tallest hotel gives a sense of living in an aerie, with the great Chippendale top of the Sony Building seemingly within reach and the green swath of Central Park visible from half the rooms. The service is thoughtful, prompt, and warm enough to balance out the environment's glossy chill. High-tech touches such as CD players, data ports, and VCRs in every room extend the theme of opulence updated and tailored to modern tastes. *57 East 57th Street, at Madison Avenue; 212-758-5700.*

■ TIMES SQUARE AREA *map pages 164–165, D-4*

The most startling transformation in Manhattan over the last decade has been **Times Square**'s changeover from the gritty to the glitzy, from a neighborhood that was downright dangerous after dark to a clean, safe "urban theme park" on an epic scale. The metamorphosis was so sudden it must have seemed like a thunderclap to the area's street hustler population, the drug dealers and prostitutes who were the symbols of Times Square's decline. A new symbol has taken their place, and it wears mouse ears. Disney's renovation of the New Amsterdam Theater and the opening of the company's store next door on West 42nd Street are largely credited with kicking off the Times Square turnaround.

Many Manhattanites grouse that the new Times Square is too sanitized, that the redevelopment has eliminated the area's rough-edged vivacity. The hordes of new visitors—millions of people come to the Crossroads of the World each year, and the Saturday-night pedestrian traffic at 46th Street and Broadway was recently measured at five thousand people per hour—have simply trampled over the concerns of the naysayers in their eagerness to get to the new attractions of this gussied-up version of Times Square. In fact, approximately eighty percent of all visitors to New York drop by Times Square.

Here is all the commercial dazzle of Manhattan distilled into a bow-tie-shape six-block "advertising park," as one of Times Square's developers labeled it. Everything in the area must be biggest, grandest, best: The biggest music store in the world (the Virgin Megastore); the biggest outdoor LED display; the country's largest theater district; the nation's largest television screen.

What's really biggest and best about Times Square, though, is its brilliant electronic plumage. Huge advertising displays, called supersigns in the slang of the billboard trade, tower over the sidewalks, blasting the brain into consumerist submission, turning night into day. A single supersign—there are more than fifty in the Square—might have as many as thirty-three thousand bulbs, and rent for more than $1 million per year. The pulsing electronic tempo of the area is set by the fabled "Zipper" on 1 Times Square that flashes a continuous—and at times vertiginous—stream of news bulletins to the gape-jawed person-in-the-street. There is always something new in the works—consider Motorola's plan to install gigantic "talking" wireless phones on the face of Broadway's Condé Nast building.

(following pages) The frenzied pace of foot and car traffic in Times Square makes it possible to feel that one is at the center of everything.

Forty-second Street and Broadway is the place where the ball drops every New Year's Eve, the corner where it's said if you wait there for the space of a half-hour, someone you know will eventually pass by. Standing at 1 Times Square and gazing northward at night is one of the great sights that Manhattan has to offer, a glorious blaze of exuberant, incandescent vulgarity, a glitter gulch to rival Las Vegas's. If you could get sunburnt from electronic displays, there would be a lot of red faces around Times Square.

The quarter where Broadway slashes across West 42nd Street and Seventh Avenue was originally a dusty district called the Long Acre (after a London neighborhood), with a concentration of carriage houses and riding stables. This evolved into Longacre Square, changed to its present name in 1904, when the *New York Times* occupied its former headquarters at 1 Times Square. As 1904 gave way to 1905, the paper threw a fireworks celebration welcoming itself to the area, and the tradition of New Year's revelry in Times Square has continued ever since. A globe of one sort or another has been lowered since the dawn of 1907.

Times Square is first and foremost "the Great White Way," a theater district. Since the late 19th century, Manhattan has been the country's premier showcase for drama, comedy, musicals—and, yes, even Shakespearean tragedy. The theater district in Manhattan has been a movable feast—over the years, it has migrated, always in a northerly direction, from lower Broadway and the Bowery to 23rd Street and finally to Times Square. "Broadway" as a theater district was born in 1895, when Oscar Hammerstein I (the grandfather of the famed lyricist) opened the Olympia on Longacre Square. Hammerstein intentionally oversold opening night, so that impatient ticketholders would cause a mini-riot and guarantee him free publicity. They obliged, but he overextended himself and lost the theater a few years later. In 1900, he built the Republic Theater, now the New Victory Theater but a few incarnations before that Minsky's burlesque house, whose star performers included the stripper Gypsy Rose Lee.

In the 1930s and 1940s, so-called "legitimate" theater suffered the indignity of being pushed off Broadway itself by big movie palaces. It was relegated to the side streets of Times Square. There it remains today, forty theaters strong, twenty-two of them landmarked originals. The theater in general is supposed to be chronically wounded in a way that justifies its nickname "the fabulous invalid," but lately it has been showing surprising signs of life. Led by such stunners as *The Lion King* and *The Producers*, Broadway has recently had some of its best years ever. It might not be as vibrant as it was in the glory days of the Bowery, when people killed over casting, or even during the Golden Age of the 1920s, when Eugene O'Neill was reinventing American drama and paving the way for Tennessee Williams, Arthur Miller, Edward Albee, and others. But today's imported musicals, limited-run celebrity showcases, and the occasional serious drama are pleasing more people than ever before.

The phrase "Broadway theater" refers not to geography but to a specific level of theatrical contract: union labor, guild-sanctioned agreements, and—to attract the audience to pay for all this—major talent. As noted, Broadway theater rarely happens on Broadway itself. It is usually in Times Square, but might stray as far as Lincoln Center. Off-Broadway, on the other hand, refers to smaller productions, performed at venues scattered all over town (the theaters must, however, be of at least 100-seat capacity)—though there are more than two dozen such theaters in the Times Square area. Off-Off-Broadway, so-called "Little Theater," is often experimental or exploratory in nature, and performed in anything from theaters to abandoned movie houses to storefronts to art galleries.

The Astor Theatre advertises The Great Ziegfeld *during Broadway's heyday in the 1920s. (Library of Congress)*

One way to cut your entertainment expenses and get a dose of Manhattan street life at the same time is to stand in line at the TKTS booth in **Father Duffy Square** (West 47th Street between Broadway and Seventh Avenue). Duffy Square was named after a notable World War I figure ("The Fighting Priest"), and contains statues of Duffy and the great Broadway producer George M. Cohan. Both statues are somewhat obscured by TKTS (pronounced "tickets"). The booth sells half-price tickets to selected shows on a first-come, first-served basis on the day of the performance, beginning at 10 A.M. for matinees and 3 P.M. for evening performances. Check to see what shows will be available, then take your place in line.

Spend an hour in the TKTS line on a pleasant afternoon and a phantasmagoria of Manhattan street life will pass in parade. Sometimes it's better theater than what you'll see onstage. While you're on line at TKTS, you can look up at the façade of the old **I. Miller Building,** on the northeast corner of 46th Street and Seventh Avenue, to see some of the grande dames of Broadway: statues of stage actress Ethel Barrymore, musical star Marilyn Miller, movie icon Mary Pickford (she got her start on the New York stage), and opera singer Rosa Ponselle are there. I. Miller was a world-famous shoe store, where the stars shopped for footwear.

Across from Duffy Square is the **Times Square Visitors Center** (1560 Broadway, at West 46th Street), a great resource in the Embassy Theater, a small screening room built in 1925 for upscale patrons. The theater has been fully restored to its Louis XVI opulence, and offers such services as ATMs, Broadway ticket sales, sightseeing tours, free Internet access, and rest rooms.

Times Square has become so jammed with visitors that police set up sawhorses on the streets to direct pedestrian traffic. Live appearances by stars only increase the congestion—and the excitement. A recent stroll through the area found actor Russell Crowe attracting a large clot of passersby to the **MTV Studios** (Broadway and West 45th Street), while the rock band No Doubt held forth across Times Square at the **Virgin Megastore** (Seventh Avenue at West 45th Street). Traffic control is often needed inside the gigantic **Toys "R" Us** (Seventh Avenue and West 44th Street) store when the line of kiddies waiting to ride the four-story Ferris wheel gets too long.

The restoration work on Broadway theaters is perhaps the most cheering aspect of the neighborhood's general refurbishment. Disney's groundbreaking facelift of the gorgeous **New Amsterdam** (214 West 42nd Street) led the pack. When

Aglow and on the go in Times Square.

Mickey stepped in, the old home theater of Florenz Ziegfeld and his Follies was in sad disrepair, its roof open to the elements, mushrooms growing among the empty seats. Across 42nd Street is the city's oldest Broadway theater, the **New Victory** (209 West 42nd Street), devoted to children's theater. Next door, the Apollo and Lyric Theaters have been combined into the lavish 1,850-seat **Ford Center for the Performing Arts** (213 West 42nd Street).

Farther down "the Deuce," as the stretch of West 42nd Street between Seventh and Eighth Avenues used to be known, massive new developments offer a battery of attractions, including forty-one movie screens. **Madame Tussaud's Wax Museum** (234 West 42nd Street) has been installed in a sprawling commercial extravaganza on the south side of the street (the old Empire Theater was lifted up and moved a half block west to make room), and on the north side the **E-Walk** (West 42nd Street and Eighth Avenue) complex contains stores, arcades, and restaurants. The capstone to the whole redevelopment effort is the swooping forty-five-story **Westin New York** (255 West 42nd Street) hotel, designed by Arquitectonica with two immense prisms separated by a curved beam of light.

Eighth Avenue north and south of 42nd Street has seen a changing of the guard, as the number of sex emporiums diminishes. But in some cases the sex biz is evolving with the neighborhood. Show World, a longtime New York supermarket of sex, collaborated with the Off-Off-Broadway impresario Aaron Beall on **Nada Show World** (675 Eighth Avenue), which presents adventurous theater and performance pieces on stages once trod by strippers.

Unmissable at Eighth Avenue and West 42nd Street is the **Port Authority Bus Terminal,** a large-scale commuter terminal. Though it's been spruced up, it remains a bit of an eyesore. More pleasing is the **McGraw-Hill Building** (330 West 42nd Street), designed by Raymond Hood, who led the team that created Rockefeller Center. One of Manhattan's architectural gems, the 1931 structure straddles two genres. It's not quite Art Deco, but not quite full-blown modern, either.

■ CLINTON *map pages 164–165, B-3/4*

West of the Port Authority, stretching north to West 59th Street, is the area that used to boast the flavorful moniker of **Hell's Kitchen.** Hell's Kitchen is an old formulation, known in London in the 17th century, but there are some reports that there was a restaurant in the neighborhood, run by a couple named Heil, called Heil's Kitchen—thus the deliberately mispronounced appellation.

Since the 1970s, landlords and most residents have opted for the blander name of Clinton, after a park located on West End Avenue between 52nd and 54th Streets. The park, in turn, was named after Mayor DeWitt Clinton, nephew of Governor George Clinton. A patrician of one of New York's most prominent families, DeWitt Clinton checked the early rise of the Tammany political machine, serving as state legislator and U.S. senator, as well as mayor.

Long a district of freightyards, docks, and light industry, Hell's Kitchen had a reputation in the 19th century as one of the slum-pits of the city. This is the neighborhood of *West Side Story,* and gang activity has often been associated with this turf, during the 20th century in the form of the contract killers named the Westies. The docks remain, and some still play host to transatlantic liners and cruise ships at the **NYC Passenger Ship Terminal** (Piers 88 and 89, at West 49th Street).

Berthed at the western end of 46th Street is the USS *Intrepid,* a decommissioned U.S. Navy aircraft carrier turned into the ***Intrepid* Sea-Air-Space Museum.** The 900-foot World War II veteran flattop is joined by the *Growler,* a nuclear submarine, and the destroyer the *Edson,* all open to the public. On board the *Intrepid* are more than forty aircraft, including a Stealth bomber, as well as space capsules, rockets, and missiles. Also on display are an Iraqi tank captured in the Gulf War and a Russian guided-missile corvette. The unheralded added attractions are the great views of the harbor from the *Intrepid*'s football-field-size deck. *Pier 86; 212-245-2533.*

San Juan Hill, centered around Ninth Avenue and West 57th Street, was an African-American neighborhood in the early 20th century. It was supposedly named for a black regiment in the Spanish-American War, but was also the site of vicious street battles, as marauders from the Irish neighborhoods to the south came north to fight. Thelonious Monk, one of New York's musical heroes, lived in San Juan Hill, and there is now a street, Thelonious Sphere Monk Circle, named after him. Today, Clinton plays host to a couple of entertainment-related landmarks: the **Film Center Building** (630 Ninth Avenue), with a great Art Deco lobby; and the **Actors Studio** (432 West 44th Street), thespian training grounds for stars like Marlon Brando, Dustin Hoffman, and Al Pacino. Of late, the neighborhood has been injected with a new vitality, and boasts an international array of restaurants as well as trendy bars.

CENTRAL PARK

Central Park is the weary city-dweller's salvation. A combination escape hatch and exercise yard, the park is an urbanized Eden that offers everyone a bite of the apple. Two then-obscure geniuses, Frederick Law Olmsted and Calvert Vaux, raised American landscape architecture to an art in the process of fashioning this most cherished of resources. Imagine how impossibly clogged Manhattan would be without it.

Only with great struggle did Central Park come into existence. Beginning in the 1840s, the poet and newspaper editor William Cullen Bryant campaigned hard for the creation of a great park in what was then the hinterlands, beyond the northern edge of the city. He was joined by Washington Irving and other notables, and popular support rallied behind the idea to the degree that both mayoral candidates in the 1850 elections felt obliged to come out in favor of the proposal.

Most of the present 843-acre site was acquired by the city in 1855 for the then-astronomical sum of $5 million. The next step was to perform a topographical survey, hardly an enviable job, given the presence within the park's boundaries of a good population of squatters, who made their living in such esoteric 19th-century pursuits as the boiling of bones. They recognized surveyor Egbert L. Viele as a harbinger of eviction, and gave him the bum's rush the first time he ventured into what was mostly a no-man's-land.

All of the future Central Park was not a wilderness, however. In the late 1990s, a previously suppressed portion of the park's history was revealed. Seneca Village, which stretched from 81st to 89th Streets on the park's west side, was a community mainly of African-Americans, who had been living in the area since the 1820s. Some were, as a plaque in the area now describes them, members of the African Methodist Episcopal Zion Church, the "largest and wealthiest church of coloured people in this city, perhaps in this country." By the time the park surveyor arrived, many Irish and German immigrant families were among the sixteen hundred or so people who lived or worked in Seneca Village, which like other private property within the park tract was appropriated in "eminent domain" proceedings. Landowners were compensated, but everyone was forced to disperse.

The towers of the Beresford apartment building loom over Central Park.

Olmsted, a journalist backed by Bryant and Irving, assumed the somewhat existential position of superintendent for a park that did not yet exist. Vaux (whose name rhymes with "box"), an English-born architect, convinced his friend Olmsted that together they should enter the design competition for the park. Olmsted was busy during the day supervising the clearing of the ground, so the two had many of their conferences at night as they trod the territory by moonlight. The duo's entry, which they dubbed the Greensward Plan, won the $2,000 first prize. With a few notable departures and augmentations, it has been the blueprint of Central Park ever since.

Development moved at a snail's pace until the Panic of 1857, which put such a great number of people out of work that the city's moneyed classes believed they had only two choices: establish a public-works program or face an insurrection. So the monumental task of making the Greensward Plan a reality began in earnest: five million cubic yards of dirt were moved—some of it dislodged by the ten tons of gunpowder exploded—and more than four million trees, plants, and shrubs were planted. Outcroppings of the famous Manhattan schist were dug up and left artfully exposed. Olmsted faced constant sniping on his bureaucratic flank: he and Vaux submitted their resignations several times during the course of the project.

When the job was completed, in 1873, the result was a masterful combination of shaped nature and exuberant wildness. Olmsted's announced goal was to create a place where city dwellers could go to forget all about the city, and to that end he planted the edges and ridges of the site with trees. Over the years, the city grew taller than those screens. Buildings now loom over the park like a far-off barricade.

Modifications of the Greensward Plan have detracted from its original purity of purpose. The automobile has made the most difference, of course, and the rise of team sports has transformed what Olmsted meant as meditative wolds into amateur playing fields. Furthermore, Olmsted detested as "sepulchral" all monuments and statues—suggesting they be best left to cemeteries—but more than a hundred can be found within the park. He viewed all buildings within the park as "deductions" from valuable open space, objecting even to the imposition of the Metropolitan Museum of Art, which to date has eaten up 14 acres of parkland.

Robert Moses, who served as parks commissioner under Mayor Fiorello La Guardia, left his inimitable stamp on Central Park, systematically squaring off the intentionally rough edges of Olmsted and Vaux's plan. One measure Moses took in the mid-1930s, though, was long overdue: elimination of a flock of mutant sheep that roamed a meadow in the park's southern quadrant. Genetically degraded by inbreeding, the animals, which formerly presented a picturesque tableau, by this time resembled something out of a carnival freak show.

In the 1970s, budget difficulties in New York City contributed to the park's neglect. The decline was halted by the efforts of the Central Park Conservancy, a private organization formed in 1980 that raises more than eighty-five percent of the park's operating budget. Particularly welcome was the attention paid to the space north of the Reservoir, originally designated as the "wild" sector in the Greensward Plan. The Conservancy and the Parks Department trimmed the shabby trails and overgrown brush into usable, but still relatively untamed, parkland. Also refurbished were many of the playgrounds. (Olmsted and Vaux never designated any parts of the park as playgrounds per se, but over the years nearly two dozen of them have sprung up.)

More than twenty million people use Central Park each year; on an average spring weekend day, 250,000 children and adults flood into these precincts from all over Manhattan, New York, and the world. The park's reputation for danger is a remnant of bleaker days. Between dawn and dusk it's actually one of the safest places in the city. An awareness of one's surroundings and common sense should suffice to protect the wary.

■ From Central Park South to Bethesda Terrace *map page 210*

The most popular entry point to Central Park is through the Scholar's Gate at West 59th Street and Fifth Avenue, behind the equestrian statue of General William Tecumseh Sherman. (All twenty-two pedestrian entries to the park are occupationally named, e.g., Mariner's Gate, Hunter's Gate, Miner's Gate.) Veering left, or west, at Scholar's Gate you will come up against the preserved enclave of **the Pond** and **Hallett Nature Sanctuary.** It is a paradox that one of the wildest nooks of the park, a small sanctuary alive with birds, abuts one of Manhattan's busiest corners, Grand Army Plaza. *East Side at Central Park South.*

If you walk north from the plaza along East Drive, you'll reach the zoo. Should you get lost and request the location of the **Central Park Wildlife Center,** the facility's official name, you'll draw a blank stare from most New Yorkers. Ask for the "Central Park Zoo," though, and you'll be directed northward, to about 63rd Street. The Central Park Zoo is itself perfectly proportioned for youngsters to enjoy, and just north of it is the lavish **Tisch Children's Zoo,** with fancy simulated trees in its Enchanted Forest. The large central sea lion pool (feeding time, usually at 11:30 A.M., 2 P.M., and

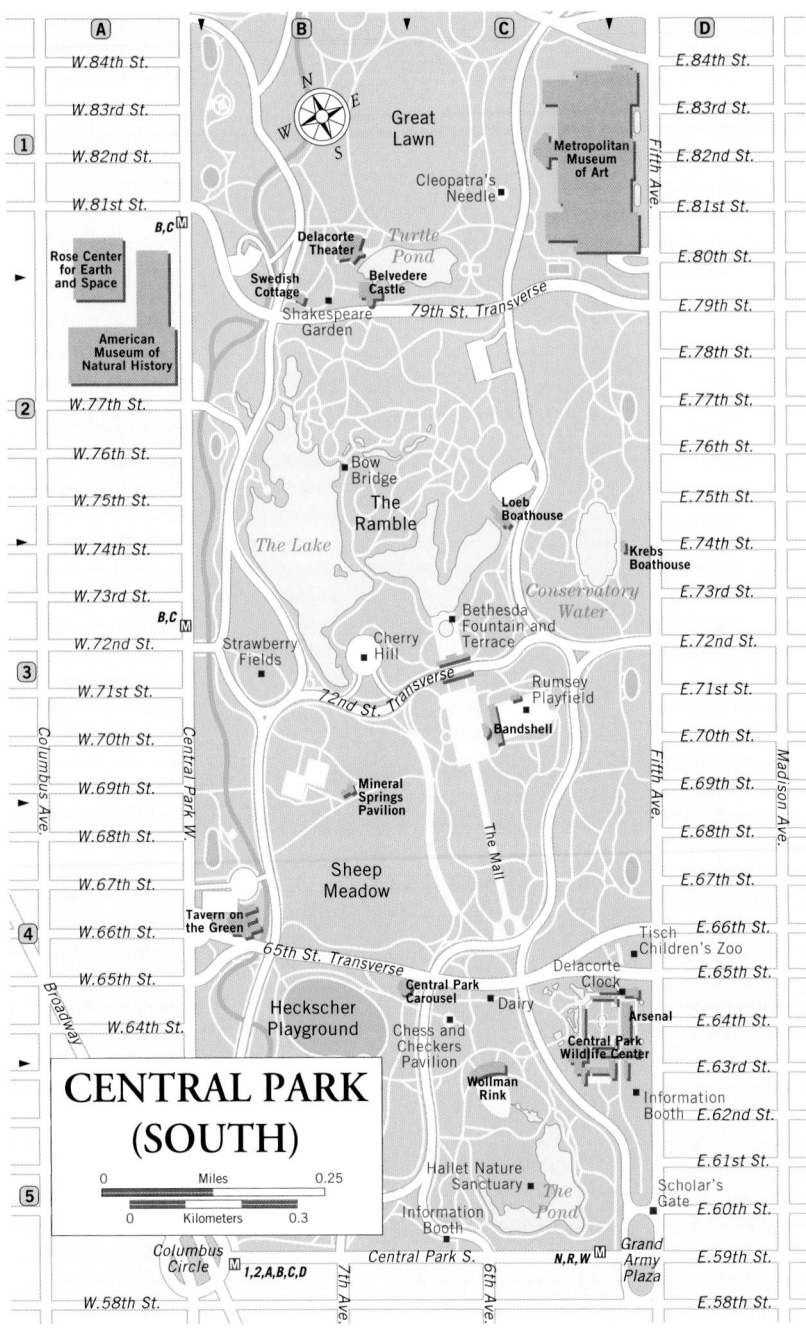

CENTRAL PARK (SOUTH)

4 P.M., is thrilling to watch) is surrounded by three fan-shape environments: the tropics, the temperate zone, and the polar ice cap. This last environment, with a trio of polar bears and a flock of penguins, is a captivating spectacle. *East Side between 63rd and 66th Streets.*

To the east of the zoo, fronting Fifth Avenue, is **the Arsenal,** the only building in the park that predates its founding. Erected between 1847 and 1853, it serves as the headquarters of the Parks and Recreation Department. On the third floor is Olmsted and Vaux's original rendering of the Greensward Plan. *East Side at 64th Street.*

Don't leave the area without waiting for the half-hour and the activation of the **Delacorte Clock,** atop a gate between the children's and main zoos. The clock—decorated with a fanciful bronze mechanical menagerie, including a dancing bear, a kangaroo, and a rhino, all tootling on musical instruments—was presented to the city by the philanthropist George T. Delacorte. *East Side at 65th Street.*

Delacorte also contributed funds for the establishment of a free theater in the park, and he figures in one of the more bitterly ironic episodes in Central Park lore: at 10 A.M. one winter morning in 1985, the ninety-two-year-old Delacorte and his wife were mugged in a pedestrian tunnel near the clock. The incident reportedly did nothing to dim Delacorte's enthusiasm for the park or his daily walks in it, which he continued until his death six years later.

West of the zoo is **the Dairy,** whose staff in the 19th century served glasses of fresh milk as treats for city children (the cows were kept right here). That building now houses the park information center, but today's Dairy retains a kid-friendly slant, offering a few games inside. You can also get free playing pieces for the nearby **Chess and Checkers Pavilion,** a gazebo-like affair with game tables indoors and out. *Mid-park at 65th Street.*

Taking up the pasture where the cows from the Dairy used to graze is **Wollman Rink,** its reconstruction completed with much fanfare (as something like a cross between a public service and a publicity stunt) by developer Donald Trump when the city proved unable to finish the job. *East Side between 62nd and 63rd Streets.*

Past Playmates Arch turns the great **Central Park Carousel,** which previously twirled in Coney Island. The Carousel, created in 1908 by the Stein and Goldstein company of Brooklyn, has fifty eight hand-carved horses. The 1870 original (the current one is the fourth here) was powered by real horses trudging in a circle in a basement pit. *Mid-park at 64th Street.*

(following pages) The competition can be fierce—or not—on Central Park baseball fields.

Southwest of the carousel is **Umpire Rock,** so called because it overlooks the baseball diamonds. The ball fields were not in the original Olmsted-Vaux design, but are nevertheless ragingly popular with players in cut-throat publishing, advertising, media, and theater softball leagues. By the rock, **Heckscher Playground,** a great children's area, allows youngsters to scamper over a 400-million-year-old outcropping of Manhattan schist. *Seventh Avenue and Central Park South.*

North of this is the **Sheep Meadow,** where the ghosts of cacogenic sheep have long since vanished, leaving an open lawn (no dogs, bicycles, or noise from stereos allowed) for picnics, sunbathing, or just lounging. **Tavern on the Green,** originally the Sheepfold, represented another trespass against the original plan when it was erected by Boss Tweed in 1870, but the giddily overdone space has long been one of Manhattan's special-occasion dining palaces. *West Side between 66th and 69th Streets.*

Better suited to the spirit of the park is **Strawberry Fields,** a few blocks north of Tavern on the Green. Honoring John Lennon, who was killed by a crazed fan a

Mall in Central Park *(1913), by Gifford Beal, depicts earlier, genteel times. (National Academy of Design)*

Fancy footwork in Central Park.

block west outside his residence at the Dakota, this beautifully landscaped spot is sponsored by his widow, Yoko Ono, with botanical contributions from nearly every country in the world. A large mosaic set into the sidewalk reads "Imagine," from one of the musician's lyrics. During certain momentous occasions, such as the anniversary of Lennon's death or the passing of celebrities such as Diana, Princess of Wales, or Lennon's Beatles bandmate George Harrison, Strawberry Fields becomes a magnet for people wishing to express grief or solidarity. *West Side between 71st and 74th Streets.*

On the east side of the Sheep Meadow is the **roller-skating concourse,** a riot of skill and exhibitionism that convenes every warm-weather weekend, and on some weekdays as well. To the east of this is a more sedate promenade, one Olmsted and Vaux included in their original plan: **the Mall,** popular when it opened as a place for *tout* Manhattan to see and be seen. The Mall was skewed northwest to provide a prospect of Belvedere Castle, to the north, past the Romantic opulence of Bethesda Terrace. *Mid-park between 66th and 72nd Streets.*

Together, the Mall, Terrace, and Castle are the most formal elements in the Greensward Plan. **Bethesda Terrace** is a natural point to view the rowboats on the Lake and the graceful arc of Vaux's Bow Bridge. The terrace's fountain, the center-

MOVIE STAR

Central Park has been a movie star for more than a century. Thomas Edison and other early filmmakers used the park as a backdrop in the 1890s, and film's first great director, D.W. Griffith, featured Mary Pickford in a short subject set in Central Park in 1909, well before she became American movies' first big star. Even Westerns—of a sort—have been shot here: In *Branding Broadway* (1918), the silent film star William S. Hart makes quick business of a crook, chasing him on horseback through the park, where he ropes and hogties him. The park has represented everything from bucolic perfection, as in Woody Allen's *Everyone Says I Love You* (1996), to apocalyptic hellhole, as in John Carpenter's *Escape from New York* (1981).

Nearly two hundred feature films have been shot in Central Park, not to mention thousands of documentaries, television shows, concerts, and student works. Before the 1960s, the park was often re-created on Hollywood soundstages or on location in southern California, but these days directors tend to prefer the real article. On a fine-weather day, it's not unusual to come across someone filming, with or without a permit. Below are a few additional films with memorable moments set in Central Park:

Angels in America (2003)	*Hair* (1979)
An Affair to Remember (1957)	*I'm Not Rappaport* (1996)
Barefoot in the Park (1967)	*Marathon Man* (1976)
The Best of Everything (1959)	*On the Town* (1949)
Breakfast at Tiffany's (1961)	*The Out-of-Towners* (1970)
Crimes and Misdemeanors (1989)	*Six Degrees of Separation* (1993)
Death Wish (1974)	*Tootsie* (1983)
The Fisher King (1991)	*The Way We Were* (1973)
Ghostbusters (1984)	*When Harry Met Sally* (1989)

piece of a large promenade, was built in 1873 to commemorate those who died at sea during the Civil War. Emma Stebbins, a noted sculptor of her day and the sister of city parks commissioner Henry Stebbins, created the statue that tops the fountain, *The Angel of the Waters.* The statue rates a key mention in *Angels in America,* Tony Kushner's epic drama. *Mid-park at 72nd Street.*

East of Bethesda Terrace is **Rumsey Playfield,** where New York's most fabulous music festival, **Central Park Summerstage,** takes place on summer weekends.

Lights, camera, action: preparing to shoot a scene of Angels in America.

Summerstage features every kind of popular music you can imagine—and some you probably can't—from the world over. And it's free! The music builds to an especially furious crescendo when the players are trying to ward off an afternoon thunderstorm. *Mid-park at 71st Street.*

■ FROM THE LAKE TO THE RESERVOIR *map pages 210 and 218*

The Lake was designed to appear larger than it is by winding around north from Bethesda Terrace. Exploring the Lake's 22 acres by renting a rowboat at **Loeb Boathouse** is one of the most romantic things to do in Manhattan. *Mid-park between 71st and 78th Streets.*

The **Conservatory Water** is a Central Park landmark most New Yorkers know by a less formal name, the Model Boat Pond. Here, serious craftsmen convene every weekend at the Kerbs Memorial Model Boathouse and float their tiny ships. Near this shallow oval of water are two popular children's statues: ***Alice in Wonderland,*** to the north, and ***Hans Christian Andersen,*** to the west. In recent years, the ornithologically curious have gathered near the boat pond to watch a pair of red-tailed hawks raise their young. Their nest has a fashionable address—it's perched on a ledge of a Fifth Avenue apartment building. *East Side between 72nd and 75th Streets.*

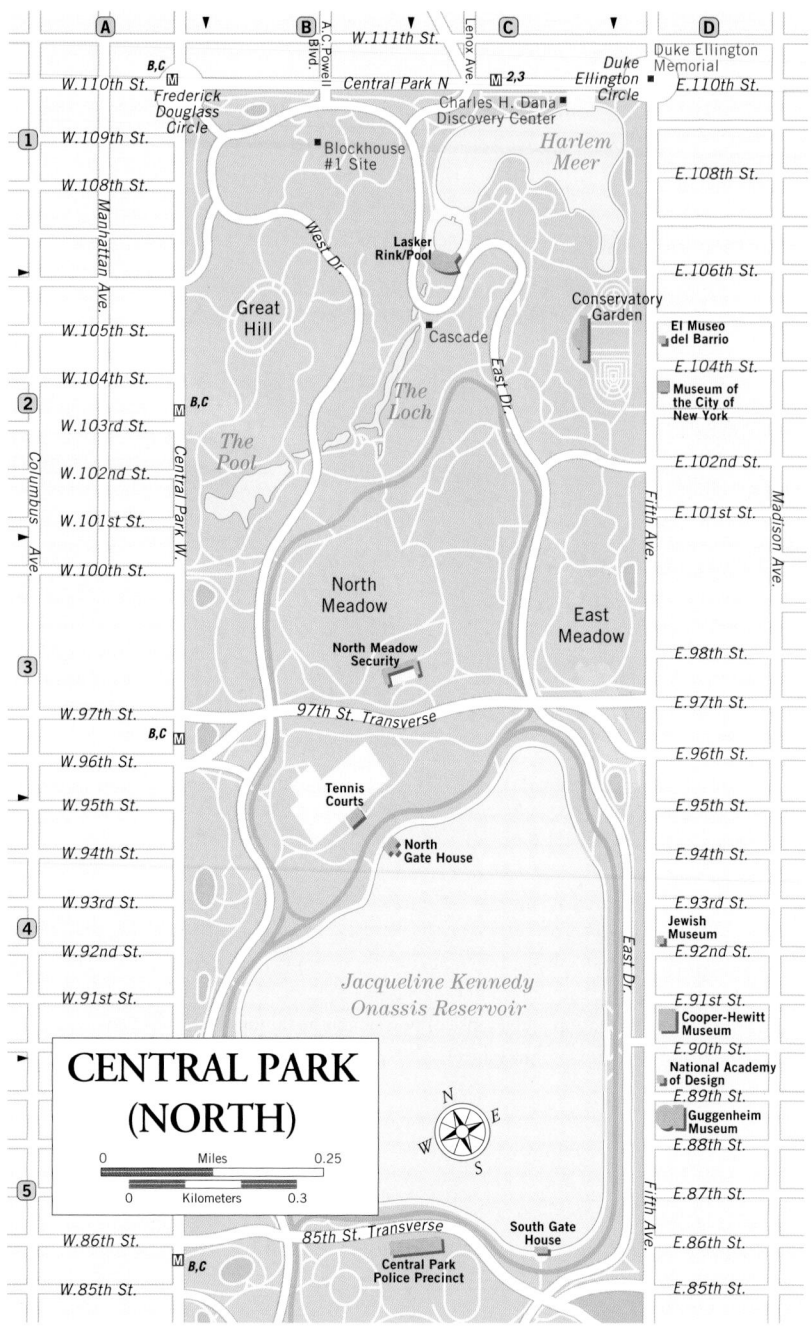

CENTRAL PARK (NORTH)

Miles 0 — 0.25

Kilometers 0 — 0.3

On the north side of the Lake is **the Ramble,** a deliberately less landscaped hill of twisted paths and thickets that comprises a well-known birding mecca, especially for the March 10 "return" of certain birds that show up in the same spots each year. *Mid-park between 73rd and 79th Streets.*

North of the Ramble, across the 79th Street Transverse (all Central Park transverses—there are four—are named for their East Side terminuses; the 79th Street Transverse exits the park at West 81st Street) is **Belvedere Castle,** the headquarters of the Urban Park Rangers Meteorological Station and Learning Center. Head up the castle's narrow spiral staircase for some fine park views, especially to the north. Vaux designed the castle on a small scale to trick perspective, so that it appears farther off than it really is. At the castle, you can borrow guidebooks and binoculars to track migrating raptors in the Ramble. *Mid-park at 79th Street.*

Belvedere Castle is a great stage set for nearby **Delacorte Theater,** another gift to the city from George T. Delacorte and the venue for the free Shakespeare festival put on by the Public Theater each summer. The popular shows usually feature a "name" star or two. *Mid-park at 80th Street.*

ALONE IN CENTRAL PARK

In Central Park the snow had not yet melted on his favorite hill. This hill was in the center of the park, after he had left the circle of the reservoir, where he always found, outside the high wall of crossed wire, ladies, white, in fur coats, walking their great dogs, or old, white gentlemen with canes. At a point that he knew by instinct and by the shape of the buildings surrounding the park, he struck out on a steep path overgrown with trees, and climbed a short distance until he reached the clearing that led to the hill. Before him, then, the slope stretched upward, and above it the brilliant sky, and beyond it, cloudy, and far away, he saw the skyline of New York....[T]here arose in him an exultation and a sense of power, and he ran up the hill like an engine, or a madman, willing to throw himself headlong into the city that glowed before him....

And still, on the summit of that hill he paused. He remembered the people he had seen in that city, whose eyes held no love for him....Then he remembered his father and his mother, and all the arms stretched out to hold him back, to save him from this city where, they said, his soul would find perdition.

—James Baldwin, *Go Tell It on the Mountain,* 1952

West of the castle is the **Swedish Cottage,** where charming old-fashioned marionette shows are put on. The nearby **Shakespeare Garden,** sprouting flowers, plants, and herbs mentioned by the Bard, is one of the park's most contemplative spots. *West Side between 79th and 80th Streets.*

The **Great Lawn,** due north of Belvedere Castle, was once a reservoir; when it was drained in the early 1930s, thousands of homeless drifted into the muddy expanse and set up a Hooverville, one of the Depression-era shantytowns named in mocking tribute to President Herbert Hoover. Now a collection of playing fields in summer, it is the site of free opera and New York Philharmonic concerts. *Mid-park between 79th and 86th Streets.*

North of the Great Lawn is the **Jacqueline Kennedy Onassis Reservoir.** The reservoir's perimeter is Manhattan's most heavily used jogging track, over the years the haunt of Madonna, John F. Kennedy Jr., Dustin Hoffman (at least in the movie *Marathon Man*), and other stars. Directly north of the 97th Street Transverse is the North Meadow Recreation Center, which offers classes in bouldering. *Mid-park between 85th and 96th Streets.*

The Great Lawn in Central Park hosts performances by the Metropolitan Opera and the New York Philharmonic. It's also a great place for a game of Frisbee.

■ THE UPPER PARK *map page 218*

Olmsted and Vaux intended the northern section of the park to be wilder than the rest of it. Unfortunately, this and the poverty of nearby neighborhoods have contributed to neglect that only in recent years has been remedied.

One exception has always been the **Conservatory Garden** on the East Side, entered through Vanderbilt Gate at East 105th Street and Fifth Avenue. Robert Moses added this small paradise after a glass-roof conservatory building was torn down. The resulting formal gardens, with their fountains and pergola, reflect the taste of their progenitor in their elegance and beauty. Spring is a spectacular time to visit the Conservatory Garden, when twenty thousand tulips, along with other bulbs, are in bloom. And for a short window of time, usually in late April, blizzards of white petals fly in the crabapple allées. But special floral displays happen through most of the year, from hellebores in February to Korean chrysanthemums in late October. *East Side between 104th and 106th Streets.*

The park's northern end has always held some of its most romantic topography, with the outcroppings of Manhattan schist accentuating and forming the backdrop

Birds from far-flung regions of the world have been spotted in Central Park, especially in spring.

BIRD-WATCHING

Central Park's prime bird-watching season is springtime, when species from as far north as the Arctic Circle may be seen passing through, and species from other points nest here, including cardinals, downy woodpeckers, eastern kingbirds, gray catbirds, and mallard ducks. The park's four best birding areas include the promontory of the Pond near the southeast entrance, the Reservoir, the Loch, and the wild-and-woodsy Ramble on the north shore of the Lake. Park rangers conduct bird walks year-round.

In February, look for fish crows and iridescent common grackles; in March, American robins and American woodcocks; in April, ruby-crowned kinglets, blue-gray gnatcatchers, yellow-rumped warblers, brown creepers, black-and-white warblers, and hermit thrushes; and in May, orioles, scarlet tanagers, rose-breasted grosbeaks, indigo buntings, and brightly colored warblers. The fall migration is less concentrated and less colorful because the birds aren't in their mating plumage.

Other good birding spots in Manhattan are Riverside Park and the Heather Garden in Fort Tryon Park. To find out what's been seen where, call the Rare Bird Alert (212-979-3070).

for landscaped effects. The **Harlem Meer** (*meer* is Dutch for "small sea") curls northward from the Conservatory Garden, its western shore flanked by steep, rocky bluffs that saw action during the Revolutionary War. Fortifications from the War of 1812 remain to this day. The Meer is stocked with fish, and fishing has become a popular pastime with neighborhood kids. Fishing poles are available for loan in the **Charles H. Dana Discovery Center,** on the northern shore of the Harlem Meer. The center's ecology exhibits attract students, birders, and other naturalists. *East Side between 106th and 110th Streets.*

Just outside the park, at its northeastern corner, is the 25-foot-tall **Duke Ellington Memorial,** which pays tribute to the great composer and musician Edward Kennedy "Duke" Ellington. In Robert Graham's monumental sculpture, three 10-foot columns, each topped with female figures representing the muses, support a platform on which Duke Ellington stands next to a grand piano. *East Side, Duke Ellington Circle, Fifth Avenue and 110th Street.*

Casting a line into Harlem Meer.

Lasker Rink and Pool serves double duty as a skating rink (if Wollman Rink is too crowded, head up here) in winter and a swimming pool in summer. *Mid-park between 106th and 108th Streets.*

Paths south of Lasker Rink and Pool wind west to **the Loch,** fed by water from the 4-foot pipe that also feeds **the Pool.** At certain times of the year, when the colors are just right and the willow branches droop languidly over the water, the Pool looks like something right out of a Maxfield Parrish painting. If you walk between Lasker and the Pool, you'll partake in a little of what Olmsted and Vaux worked so hard to develop in the entire park: a mixture of the wild and the refined, with the traffic routed so as not to encroach too severely on the parkgoing experience. *West Side between 100th and 103rd Streets.*

The pastoral atmosphere continues on the **Great Hill,** one of the park's highest points and a mecca for picnickers. **Great Jazz on the Great Hill** is a popular summer event that attracts players like Wynton Marsalis. *West Side between 103rd and 107th Streets.*

CHILDREN IN MANHATTAN

One of the truly great things about being brought up in New York City is that it allows you to go through life with an open mind. —Jimmy Breslin

Children love New York City. They tune in to its frantic pace, its energy, its unpredictability. Central Park is a natural for kids, but the whole city's a playground.

Small children can ricochet from a horse-drawn carriage ride in Central Park (from Central Park South, about $40 per twenty minutes, plus tip) to the dinosaur exhibits in the **American Museum of Natural History** (see page 259) to **Serendipity 3** (225 East 60th Street; 212-838-3531) for an ice-cream sundae.

Teenagers can take in one of Midtown's theme restaurants—among them the **Hard Rock Cafe** (221 West 57th Street; 212-489-6565), the **Harley-Davidson Cafe** (1370 Avenue of the Americas; 212-245-6000), the "haunted" **Jekyll & Hyde Club** (1409 Avenue of the Americas; 212-541-9505), and sci-fi **Mars 2112** (1633 Broadway; 212-582-2112)—and bounce over to **Sony Wonder Technology Lab** (see next page) for a quick mixing session in the recording studio, and then prove they are never too old for **F.A.O. Schwarz** (767 Fifth Avenue).

The New York of the new millennium is a more family-oriented place than the "Fun City" businessman's playground of decades past. Nowhere is the change more apparent than in **Times Square,** that neon amusement park the whole family can enjoy. From the giant Ferris wheel inside **Toys "R" Us** to the raucous displays outside the **MTV studios** to the flashing lights and bustling masses, Times Square ceaselessly stimulates.

A day spent touring the **Statue of Liberty** and **Ellis Island** is still one of the best hands-on history lessons any American city can offer, and the experience can be sugar-coated for restless youngsters by packing along a picnic lunch and scheduling plenty of outside run-around time. The view from the observation deck of the **Empire State Building** provides a young mind with a perspective on just how wide and teeming the world really is.

A visit to New York puts some steam in the step of even the most jaded adolescent. Walking a single block in **Midtown** or the **Village,** or visiting **Chinatown** or **125th Street,** can be a real eye-opener. What New York offers children above all is a vision of life as crowded with experience, rich with people, and energized by human industry.

Special Places for Children

Bronx Zoo. The largest metropolitan zoo in the nation and a pioneer in creating natural habitats for animals. *2300 Southern Boulevard, Bronx; 718-367-1010.*

Central Park Wildlife Center. Fun and manageable. (See page 209.)

Children's Museum of Manhattan. Kids get a taste of the arts here, with many spoonfuls of sugar. *212 West 83rd Street, Upper West Side; 212-721-1234.*

Intrepid **Sea-Air-Space Museum.** Military hardware, up close. (See page 205.)

New York Aquarium. Nose-up-against-the-glass thrills with dolphins, sharks, and more than three hundred other marine species. *West Eighth Street, Coney Island; 718-265-3474.*

New York Hall of Science. A great New York City diorama, plus hands-on science exhibits in a parklike setting. *Flushing Meadows, Queens; 718-699-0005.*

Rose Center for Earth and Space. A showpiece of galactic splendor to wow the astronomically inclined. (See page 260.)

Sony Wonder Technology Lab. All the bells and whistles of the technology era, with only a slight host-company emphasis. *550 Madison Avenue, at East 56th Street, Midtown; 212-833-8100.*

The polar bear habitat at the Central Park Wildlife Center.

UPPER EAST SIDE

For a certain species of class-conscious New Yorkers, there is simply no other place to live. The West Side is too parvenu, too bourgeois; the Village has all those neo-bohemian flavorings that make it unseemly; everywhere else is out of the question.

Which leaves only the elite Upper East Side. Since early in the 20th century it has been *the* place for Manhattanites who feel themselves defined by their addresses. According to recent statistics, the blocks between East 59th and East 110th Streets, from Fifth Avenue to the East River, have the highest per-capita income of any urban quarter in the nation. Not surprisingly, the area is thick with fine restaurants, boasts a world-class shopping strip on Madison Avenue, and attracts other businesses whose purpose is to serve the rich.

The residential palaces of families like the Astors, the Whitneys, and the Vanderbilts once graced this neighborhood, and some of the structures that remain have been transformed into museums containing great treasures. **Museum Mile** (much of which was known as Millionaires' Row a century ago) runs along Fifth Avenue roughly from East 70th Street to East 104th Street.

A traditional bifurcation of the district is now fading: the Upper East Side (north of 86th Street or so) and the plain old East Side have become more or less interchangeable, the distinction vital only to an earlier generation of Manhattanites. These days, Upper East Side generally refers to any address due east of Central Park.

Here are a few salient dates in the neighborhood's development as Manhattan's Gold Coast:

1896 Caroline Webster Schermerhorn Astor moves to her mansion at Fifth Avenue and East 65th Street; after her comes the deluge of society, making upper Fifth Avenue the fashionable address it remains today.

1901 Steel magnate Andrew Carnegie occupies his mansion at Fifth Avenue and East 91st Street, further extending the boundaries of the acceptable. The neighborhood becomes known as Carnegie Hill.

1907 The New York Central Railroad electrifies the trains that plow down Park Avenue toward Grand Central Station, with a railroad tunnel subsequently built beneath the street.

Andrew Carnegie's mansion is one of many Upper East Side residences that have been converted into museums. (Cooper-Hewitt National Design Museum)

The railroad tracks were along a sooty, unsightly boundary that separated the wealthy (west from Park Avenue to Fifth Avenue) from the poor (east to Yorkville and the East River). When the tracks were buried, Park Avenue was transformed into one of the city's most prestigious residential addresses. The riff-raff were subsequently chased out of Yorkville by high rents, and the Upper East Side became solidly middle and upper class.

■ FIFTH AVENUE AND EAST OF EDEN

The old world of privilege and exclusivity survives on the Upper East Side; this is Clubland, though not in the sense that Elvis Costello sings about. The **Metropolitan Club** (1 East 60th Street), the **Harmonie Club** (4 East 60th Street), the **Knickerbocker Club** (2 East 62nd Street), the **Lotos Club** (5 East 66th Street), the **Union Club** (101 East 69th Street), the **Colony Club** (564 Park Avenue), and the **Cosmopolitan Club** (122 East 66th Street)—these last two primarily for women—are membership-only havens, most inside fine old mansions. The irony about these clubs, with their air of inaccessibility, is that many were formed by people who were kept out of other clubs: J. P. Morgan, for example, founded the Metropolitan Club when the Union Club stiffed him.

A stroll up Fifth Avenue is instructive, just to see how the upper crust lived—and to some extent still lives today. This neighborhood contains much originally residential architecture, with many of the old mansions since converted into consulates, offices, schools, and clubs. At 810 Fifth Avenue was the penthouse-cum-aerie of Nelson Rockefeller, the longtime governor of New York and heir to one of the largest fortunes assembled by one family. As governor, Rockefeller once wanted to clear an entire West Side block for a plaza. Aides were mystified by his insistence on the plan (eventually thwarted), but they should have stood in Rocky's apartment: with the block across the park leveled, he would have had a clear view of the Chagall murals he had donated to the Metropolitan Opera at Lincoln Center.

A couple of blocks north of Rocky's roost is **Temple Emanu-El** (1 East 65th Street), the city's most esteemed Jewish congregation. The temple is on the site of the Caroline Astor mansion that prompted the stampede of society folk to the Upper East Side. Also on the street is the **China Institute Gallery** (125 East 65th Street), a great repository of Chinese art guarded by a pair of fierce-looking stone lions (and well worth a stop if you are interested in the subject).

Those afflicted with altitude sickness over this stretch of Fifth Avenue would do well to head further east, to the area around **Bloomingdale's** (Lexington Avenue and East 59th Street) department store and the **Roosevelt Island Tram** (Second Avenue and East 60th Street). For all its upward mobility, the area is referred to as East of Eden.

One indication of the relatively rootless nature of the population is the strip of singles bars along First and Second Avenues near the Queensboro Bridge. They cater to the upwardly mobile and unattached who, seeking the prestige and relative cleanliness and safety of the East Side, flooded into the area during the 1970s and 1980s.

The middle-class flavor of Queens wafting across the **Queensboro Bridge** (Second Avenue and East 59th Street) may clear your head, and may even leave you feelin' groovy, à la Simon and Garfunkel's "59th Street Bridge Song." While you're flashing back to the title credits of the television show *Taxi* (the cab crosses the bridge), you can admire the 1909 cantilevered span itself. Notice the bizarre finials. Under the bridge's Manhattan terminus is the spectacular space known as **Bridgemarket** (First Avenue and East 59th Street), with high-end shops and a restaurant called Guastavino's, after Rafael Guastavino, the Catalan architect whose namesake tiles contribute to the grandeur of Bridgemarket's soaring vaults. Bridgemarket was a farmers market from the 1910s to the 1930s, after which it became a Department of Transportation facility.

North of the bridge, filling the space between York Avenue and FDR Drive, is **Hospital Row,** a concentration of research and health-care facilities. The **Sloan-Kettering Cancer Center** (1275 York Avenue) has a worldwide reputation; it was here that the late Shah of Iran came for treatment, setting the stage for the Iranian hostage crisis.

Rockefeller University (York Avenue and East 66th Street) was originally endowed by John D. Rockefeller Sr. as the Institute for Medical Research. It was put on a graduate-university footing by his grandson, David, and today ranks as one of the most prestigious medical research facilities in the nation. The grounds, which it shares with the **Cornell Medical Center,** are capacious, but the splendid gardens open to the public only on special occasions. This area was once part of Jones Wood, a huge park that extended from the East River to Third Avenue in the mid-1800s and was proposed as an alternative to Central Park.

What is now the **Asia Society and Museum** was a pet project of John D. Rockefeller III, or JDR III, as he liked to be called. (The five sons of John D.

GUASTAVINO TILES

Guastavino is not a name that rings a bell for the majority of Manhattan visitors, but to the cognoscenti it sounds a theme basic to the New York experience: an immigrant innovator, who through sheer brilliance and determination transforms the whole city.

When architect and engineer Rafael Guastavino arrived in America in 1881, he brought with him an age-old secret from his native Catalonia: a mortar-and-tile vaulting system with Spanish and Middle Eastern origins, which he had applied with great success in Barcelona.

In the 1880s Guastavino first tried out what would become his patented style of ceramic coursing on a synagogue and several residential projects on the Upper West Side, some of which survive to this day. Laminating layers of rectangular, interlocking terra cotta tile in Portland cement, Guastavino created vaults, domes, and arches that were strong, fireproof, and only inches thin.

Guastavino gave wings to the ambitious architects of Manhattan's golden age, among them Richard Morris Hunt and Cass Gilbert and the designers at McKim, Mead & White. His firm, the Guastavino Fireproof Construction Company, became builder of choice for major projects such as Grant's Tomb, the Great Hall at Ellis Island, Grand Central Terminal (including the Oyster Bar, pictured below), Carnegie Hall, the Federal Reserve Bank, the ceilings of the Columbia University chapel, and our personal favorite, the Elephant House at the Bronx Zoo.

Guastavino and his namesake son contributed to more than four hundred projects in New York, more than in any other city. The recently restored vaults beneath the Queensboro bridge, formerly a farmers market and today the Bridgemarket restaurant and shopping mecca, are an excellent example of the work of a genius who left an indelible mark on Manhattan.

Rockefeller Jr. supposedly once had a conversation whereby they divided the world: Nelson "got" South America, David got Africa, Laurance got Europe, and JDR III got Asia. Winthrop, the black sheep, was given the army as his purlieu.) By all accounts, JDR III had a true sympathy for the refined aestheticism of Japan and other Eastern cultures, and it resulted in a lifelong fascination with Asian art. Visitors reap the rewards here, with galleries, films, lectures, theater events, and a bookstore and gift shop on the premises. A major renova-

Members of the Seventh Regiment. The gentleman seated on the left is Charles W. Clinton, the designer of the Armory.

tion to the museum completed in 2001 has made the exhibition spaces more user-friendly than they were. *725 Park Avenue, at East 70th Street; 212-288-6400.*

The **Seventh Regiment Armory** (East 67th Street and Park Avenue) embraces disparate elements of the Upper East Side mystique within an imposing red-brick fortress. The site of the tony Winter Antiques Show, with an interior that contains detailing by Louis Comfort Tiffany, the Armory remains an active National Guard training site. Troops used the facility extensively after the World Trade Center attack. Nearby, in Central Park, is the **Seventh Regiment memorial** (Fifth Avenue and East 67th Street).

Which Upper East Side block best represents the neighborhood's residential architecture is debatable. The stretch of **East 67th Street off Fifth Avenue** gets votes for its many Renaissance Revival limestone façades. And **East 70th Street between Park and Lexington Avenues** has adherents, for its wonderful diversity of architectural styles: English Gothic, Italianate palazzo, neo-Georgian, Modern, and French provincial, as well as assorted others, all within one block!

The Upper East Side is known for being staid, but life-of-the-party types—in real life and fiction—have hung their hats here. **Andy Warhol's residence** for the last years of his life was a townhouse at 57 East 66th Street. The townhouse at 171 East 71st Street is instantly recognizable as **Holly Golightly's digs** in the movie version of Truman Capote's novel *Breakfast at Tiffany's*.

■ MUSEUM MILE

So many *objets,* so little time. Museum Mile—roughly from the Frick Collection at East 70th Street to El Museo del Barrio at East 104th Street—is actually somewhat longer than a mile, more like two. The concentration of world-class art museums along this stretch can turn Fifth Avenue into something of a cultural marathon. The best advice is not to attempt too much. Check the schedules before you go, not only for special exhibits, but also for hours. Some museums are closed for as many as three days a week. Stop and smell the flowers at Central Park's exquisite Conservatory Garden. Take your time. Don't overload. Wear comfortable shoes.

■ FRICK COLLECTION *map page 228, A-5*

Can a bad man make a good art museum? The answer is yes in the case of Henry Clay Frick and the **Frick Collection.** Frick was one of the most obdurate of the late-19th-century capitalists. As Andrew Carnegie's hatchet man at U.S. Steel, he exploited workers mercilessly, spied on his employees in search of signs of unionism, broke strikes with smug relish, and survived numerous assassination attempts. So you may want to pause at the portal to the Frick Collection, housed in the industrialist's Fifth Avenue mansion, and meditate on his indifference to misery. Then put it out of your mind and enjoy one of the most perfect art experiences Manhattan has to offer.

The Frick Collection is a private home's private gallery raised to sublime heights by the magic of money and good taste. Sit yourself down, says the Frick, make yourself at home, bowl a few frames. It's true: in the basement is Henry Frick's private bowling alley, a manual one, no doubt meant to be operated by a nonunion pin-boy. (This is all off-limits to the public, of course, but just knowing it's there adds to the wonder of the place.) The Frick's spectacular building, designed by the architectural firm of Carrère and Hastings, which was also responsible for the New

(following pages) The Fragonard Room. (© The Frick Collection)

York Public Library, includes a skylit courtyard that has to rank among the city's most perfect spots for romance. One of the best ways to appreciate the atmosphere is with a soundtrack, via the occasional Sunday afternoon chamber orchestra concerts. Lean back, close your eyes, inhale the gardenias.

The collection centers on Old Masters from the 14th to 19th century, with special attention paid to the Italian Renaissance. Jean-Honore Fragonard's *The Progress of Love* has a whole room to itself. The gleaming, confectionary glaze of the French court shines from every panel of the series, which was commissioned by Madame du Barry, mistress of France's King Louis XV. Rembrandt's exquisite *The Polish Rider* is here too, along with masterworks from Van Dyck, Holbein, Titian, El Greco, Fra Filippo Lippi, Turner, Corot, Gainsborough, and Vermeer. What's most impressive about the Frick is not who is represented but the works Frick selected: many of the paintings here are pivotal examples of their creators' artistry. *1 East 70th Street, at Fifth Avenue; 212-288-0700.*

The Frick's Garden Court. (© The Frick Collection)

■ Whitney Museum of American Art *map page 228, A-4*

The beetling, forbidding façade of the **Whitney Museum of American Art** belies the egalitarian ideals of its designer, the Bauhaus master Marcel Breuer, and suggests a futuristic castle—complete with moat—rather than a warm and inviting space for viewing art. Started by Gertrude Vanderbilt Whitney, a sculptor and renowned art collector, the museum owns and exhibits modern American sculpture, painting, and photography, as well as film, video, and new media works.

The Whitney strives to be brash and iconoclastic, fresh and irreverent. In its struggle to remain current, the Whitney sometimes strays into the peculiar, but the spectacle of a major arts institution embarrassing itself is not entirely unappealing; at its best the museum manages to stir the froth of modern American art into something resembling life. The Whitney Biennial, mounted in the spring of even-numbered years, is intended by the museum to be a plenary look at what's happening on the art scene at that particular time. Taking potshots at the Biennial lineup is a major cottage industry among art critics, but the show consistently commands attention. *945 Madison Avenue, at East 75th Street; 212-570-3676.*

■ Metropolitan Museum of Art *map page 228, A-3*

The dilemma here is a glorious one: too much choice. With more than three million objects in the **Metropolitan Museum of Art,** how can one avoid being buried under the avalanche of culture?

Give yourself time, try to go when you won't be battling crowds—nonsummer weekday mornings are a good bet—and allow yourself the luxury of chance meetings with an Etruscan sculpture, a Flemish masterwork, a delicate Chinese vase. Serendipity is an essential part of the Met experience, and to let yourself wander through these halls is one of life's great pleasures.

Begin with the Met's setting: a healthy tract of precious Central Park land. Frederick Law Olmsted regretted giving the park over to the Metropolitan's use, but despite the institution's explosive growth, this has been a happy marriage of art and open space.

Several of New York's architectural all-stars have contributed to the museum's design over the years, with Calvert Vaux's original 1880 building having long since been engulfed by subsequent additions. Richard Morris Hunt, who designed the base of the Statue of Liberty, and his son, also named Richard,

(following pages) The Temple of Dendur. (Metropolitan Museum of Art)

created the grand stairway and main Fifth Avenue section; the architects at McKim, Mead & White, responsible for several nearby mansions (as was the elder Hunt), designed the side wings. The building is most impressive when entered by the front steps (you can sometimes enter more quickly through an entrance at 81st Street). Above the entrance are great stone blocks, originally meant to be statues, left uncarved due to the vagaries of time and economics.

As you enter the museum's Great Hall through the main entrance, you can get a sense of the type of benefactors the Met has—just to keep this superb room in fresh flowers requires a huge endowment. And the list of art givers is a veritable roll call of heavyweights: Rockefeller, Morgan, Mellon, and, more recently, Walter Annenberg, the *TV Guide* and *Racing Form* mogul. "Strength goes to strength," explained Annenberg when asked why he donated his vast collection of Impressionist paintings and other priceless art to the Met.

Lately, with gifts like Annenberg's and that of *Reader's Digest* cofounder Lila Acheson Wallace, the Met has been increasing its 20th-century holdings. It already has the world's greatest collection of medieval antiquities, a gift of financier J. P. Morgan. Also impressive is the Egyptian collection, crowned by the Temple of Dendur, built by the Roman emperor Augustus in 15 B.C. The sandstone building, which would have been submerged by water held back by the Aswan Dam, was given to the United States by the Egyptian government in the 1960s. Kevin Roche John Dinkeloo & Associates, the architectural firm that has designed the museum's additions and remodelings during the past five decades, created the massive wing that houses the temple.

For many people, the first thing to do at the Met is to head straight up the main stairway and enter the European painting galleries. The Dutch masters are well represented here, with Vermeer, Hals, and Rembrandt leading the way. In gallery after gallery, the Met's collection unfolds like a rose: English painting by Gainsborough and Sir Thomas Lawrence, Italian Renaissance masterworks by Raphael and Botticelli, priceless Spanish canvases by El Greco and Velázquez. But you're not done yet, for the petals part to reveal an astounding array of Impressionist paintings by Manet, Monet, Cézanne, Degas, Renoir, and Gauguin.

Strength goes to strength. That's the whole story of the Met collection. Just when you think you've plumbed its depths, you round a corner and another priceless treasure greets you. The 19th-century American paintings on exhibit give a precise measure of the glories and limits of the nation's art during that period. The medieval collection, built upon Morgan's original gift, is so extensive that portions can be housed both here and uptown at the Cloisters with no discernible diminishment to either display.

The museum's Asian art is arranged around a re-creation of a Chinese scholar's courtyard. The Chinese and Japanese holdings are particularly strong, and there are noteworthy pieces from India, Tibet, Nepal, and other lands.

The Michael C. Rockefeller Wing (named for Nelson Rockefeller's son, who disappeared on an art-gathering trip to New Guinea in 1961, and who was, some say, eaten by either sharks or cannibals) contains a wealth of art from traditional cultures, displayed in coolly correct surroundings.

The Met collection sprawls, and there are those who complain that it is not organized in a totally logical manner. Because of the bequest that spawned the Lehman Pavilion, for example, there are European paintings here that might better be displayed with other Continental works. But one could also conclude that logical organization is impossible with such a large collection.

The Met is so huge that it has forgotten corners—like the pistol range in the basement, usually off-limits to the public. The period rooms in the American wing, perhaps not crowd favorites, can nonetheless transport a visitor as surely as any time machine. The sculpture court, full of Rodin bronzes, is a gentle place to linger.

The best thing about the Met is that it allows you to develop your own tastes, no matter how idiosyncratic. At the top of the main stairway to the left is a vitrine of Chinese porcelain. Many people pass by it on their way to the Impressionist wing or the current special exhibition. But we've formed an attachment to this glass case of small, perfect pottery, to the degree that no visit to the Met is complete without it. One expert called it "a sorbet for the eyes, something to clean the palate between courses." Another description is closer to how these vases hit us: "This is the kind of sculpture they have in heaven." The Met is filled with such transcendent objects.

The Met is open on Friday and Saturday evenings. A string quartet plays on the balcony, and potential lovers eye each other. Another special occasion is the weekend brunch in the members dining room, normally closed to the public. The museum's restaurant, arranged around a sunken fountain, is at times hectic, but is a good place to recharge one's batteries. In summer, be sure to visit the rooftop garden. In addition to a major sculptural exhibit, you can take in views of Central Park. *Fifth Avenue and East 82nd Street; 212-535-7710.*

■ GUGGENHEIM MUSEUM *map page 228, A-2*

Officially called the **Solomon R. Guggenheim Museum,** this modern-art mecca is as famous for its building as for its collection. Frank Lloyd Wright, who professed to hate cities, got a chance to alter the look of one with his monumental swirl of alabaster concrete. It bulges atop its one-story plinth like a beehive on a gravestone. The Guggenheim represents something of a road not taken for Wright, who perhaps could have rivaled Le Corbusier in forging the modern cityscape.

Inside, the main gallery follows Wright's ramplike spiral around the outside of the five-floor atrium. Solomon Guggenheim was one of the most voracious collectors of the 1920s and 1930s, and the permanent exhibit is full of masterpieces by Chagall, Léger, and Kandinsky. For a long time, space considerations kept many of the Guggenheim's treasures locked away (Wright being a better conceptual architect than a practical one), but an addition completed in the 1990s doubled the available gallery space, allowing more works to be shown. Look for the early Picassos in particular. *1071 Fifth Avenue, at East 89th Street; 212-423-3500.*

(opposite) In summer, the Met uses its roof garden for changing installations, such as this one from "Oldenburg and Van Bruggen on the Roof." (Metropolitan Museum of Art) (above) The Guggenheim's curving exterior. (Solomon R. Guggenheim Foundation)

■ **CARNEGIE HILL MUSEUMS** *map page 228, A-1/3*

The rise of land from East 86th to East 96th Street between Fifth and Lexington Avenues was named Carnegie Hill after Andrew Carnegie's residence. Participants in the New York City Marathon have another name for Carnegie Hill. Because it is near the end of the route, and they arrive exhausted, the runners call this gentle rise "the Wall."

Carnegie's mansion is now the **Cooper-Hewitt National Design Museum,** a branch of the Smithsonian Institution devoted to historical and contemporary design. On display might be avant-garde glass, contemporary furniture, ancient textiles, architectural drawings, and decorative metalwork. The curators do a splendid job of making the design arts accessible to the layperson. In fine weather you can sit in the large garden, which overlooks Fifth Avenue. *2 East 91st Street, at Fifth Avenue; 212-860-6868.*

The stunning **Neue Galerie,** a boutique museum specializing in early modernist German and Austrian fine and decorative arts, opened to great and deserved fanfare in 2001. As with the Frick, the mansion the Neue Galerie occupies was designed by the firm of Carrère and Hastings, and a visit here provides a glimpse of the opulence with which rich New Yorkers surrounded themselves. The Café Sabarsky, a replica of a Viennese café circa 1900, has become a popular destination in its own right. *1048 Fifth Avenue, at East 86th Street; 212-628-6200.*

Furniture, textiles, architectural drawings, and even fanciful china are typically on display at the Cooper-Hewitt. (Cooper-Hewitt National Design Museum)

Samuel F. B. Morse might seem an odd person to have founded the **National Academy of Design,** but the inventor of the telegraph was also a painter, and in 1825 he realized his life's dream to build a school for artists, run by the artists themselves. (The original building was at East 23rd Street and Park Avenue and survives in another incarnation as the façade of Our Lady of Lourdes Church in Hamilton Heights.) The academy presents exhibitions and supports a School of Fine Arts, around the corner on 89th Street. *1083 Fifth Avenue, at East 89th Street; 212-369-4880.*

The **Jewish Museum,** inside a lyrically designed mansion that imitates French Gothic châteaus of the Loire Valley, mounts interesting historical and contemporary exhibits related to the Jewish diaspora. The museum's permanent exhibition, *Culture and Continuity: The Jewish Journey,* surveys the Jewish experience from ancient times to the present. The Cafe Weissman is one of the best museum restaurants in town. *1109 Fifth Avenue, at East 92nd Street; 212-423-3200.*

The **Museum of the City of New York** provides a charming tour of the past, as shown through etchings, paintings, and other artworks and artifacts. The charred remnant of Adrian Block's *Tyger,* the first ship to circumnavigate Manhattan, is on display here, brought from where it was discovered during the excavations for the World Trade Center. John D. Rockefeller Sr.'s bedchamber is available for inspection; it and the dressing room he and his wife shared were removed from his townhouse at 4 West 55th Street and meticulously reconstructed here. Another show-stopper is the *Broadway! The History of American Theater* exhibit. *1220 Fifth Avenue, at East 103rd Street; 212-534-1672.*

Marking the upper reach of Museum Mile is **El Museo del Barrio,** well situated at the portal to Spanish (East) Harlem. The museum exhibits the works of Puerto Rican and other Hispanic artists and displays cultural and historical artifacts from New York's huge and varied Latino population. *1230 Fifth Avenue, at East 104th Street; 212-831-7272.*

The massive red-brick castle on Madison Avenue at East 94th Street is actually a trick of architecture. What you see here is, indeed, the old **Squadron A Armory,** but it's only the shell of the turreted, crenellated, machicolated fortress. On the eastern side, a more modern building takes over: Intermediate School 29, also known as Hunter High School. Nearby is another massive architectural fantasy, the **Synod of Russian Orthodox Bishops** (1180 Park Avenue), originally a private residence, incredibly enough.

Bedroom suite of John D. Rockefeller Sr. (Museum of the City of New York)

One of the wellsprings of the neighborhood—culturally, socially, and physically—is the **92nd Street Y** (1395 Lexington Avenue). As famous for its lectures and classical concerts as it is for its aerobics and gyms, this Y is a branch of the Young Men's and Women's Hebrew Association. A short distance away is the **Islamic Culture Center** (201 East 96th Street, at Third Avenue), designed by Skidmore, Owings & Merrill (the minaret is by Swank, Hayden, Cornell) and completed in 1991. The building's erection addressed the somewhat embarrassing lack of a world-class Islamic house of worship in Manhattan. The building is situated on the site so that it faces Mecca.

■ **YORKVILLE** *map page 228, B-2/3*

Yorkville, stretching north from Midtown along York Avenue, was originally a 19th-century German-American community, discrete from the rest of New York and centered at East 86th Street and Third Avenue. In those days York Avenue was called Avenue A—its present-day name derives not from the city's moniker but from World War I hero Alvin C. York. Why did a German neighborhood rename its main drag after a man known for having wiped out thirty-five German machine-gun nests in one day? To defuse anti-German feelings, perhaps?

There are but faint reminders of Yorkville's immigrant past today, but check out **Schaller & Weber** (1654 Second Avenue), an amazing sausage cornucopia that typifies the neighborhood's previous Germanic flavor. Also recalling a bygone era are the charming Queen Anne–style row houses in a cul-de-sac off East 86th Street near East End Avenue known as **Henderson Place.**

Across East End Avenue from Henderson Place is **Carl Schurz Park,** a riverfront esplanade named for a German immigrant who was a prominent newspaper editor in the 19th century. Note the sheet-metal cutouts that line the southern part of the esplanade between 81st and 84th Streets—officially called **Jack Finley Walk,** after yet another newspaper editor, this one from the *New York Times.* The best thing about the park is the view of Hell Gate, the roiling part of the East River where Long Island Sound and the Harlem River meet in a riot of crosscurrents. Across the river is the Roosevelt Island Lighthouse; to the north are Randalls and Wards Islands and the Triborough Bridge.

The northern boundary of Carl Schurz Park abuts the grounds of **Gracie Mansion,** the official residence of New York's mayor since the days of Fiorello La Guardia. (The current mayor, Michael Bloomberg, who lives on East 79th Street, only uses Gracie Mansion for formal government occasions.) The homey, rather homely farmhouse contains elements of the original, an out-of-the-way summer cottage built in 1799 by Archibald Gracie, a Scottish émigré who had made his fortune in shipping. Expanded and refurbished—with the help of the Gracie Mansion Conservancy, which runs a delightful tour of the place—the residence remains unprepossessing, a house rather than a mansion. Yet the sight of a woodframe house with its new yard, so rare in Manhattan, is altogether enchanting. *East 88th Street and East End Avenue.*

The distinctive parabolic roofline of **Asphalt Green,** a former asphalt plant recycled into a deluxe public gymnasium and community center, is visible from nearby FDR Drive. The huge natatorium next door has given the neighborhood's Olympic hopefuls a place to work out. *655 East 90th Street.*

If you happen to pass the unassuming tenement house at 179 East 93rd Street, you might want to bow your head—or, more appropriately, raise it and emit a horse-laugh—in acknowledgment of the **boyhood home of the Marx Brothers,** Chico, Harpo, Groucho, and Zeppo, who grew up here. The quartet made their splash on Times Square vaudeville stages before conquering Hollywood.

UPPER WEST SIDE

For a long time the Upper West Side was the Upper East Side's poor relation, later to develop and lacking the elite cachet of the neighborhood across the park. Today it presents itself as a less stuffy alternative to the Upper East Side, a family haven filled with cultural opportunities and egalitarian pleasures.

The district that would come to be known as the Upper West Side began its urban life as part of the Thousand-Acre Tract, granted to rich landowners by the first English governor of New York. An old Indian trail bisected the area, and several hamlets and villages grew up along it, among them Bloomingdale, an Anglicization of the Dutch town of Bloemendael. Through the 18th and much of the 19th century, the area was sleepy, peaceful, inhabited by poor farmers, and overrun by goats.

The coming of mass transit—the Ninth Avenue Elevated in 1879 and the IRT subway in 1904—precipitated a mad rush of development. An indication of how much of an outpost the area remained is the Dakota apartment building, completed in 1881 and so called because it was "far enough from the center of town to be in Dakota." Broadway was still Bloomingdale Road then (and afterward, briefly, "the Boulevard"), before it was widened and linked to the downtown thoroughfare.

Development continued in fits and starts throughout the early 20th century. The lag behind the Upper East Side might have actually benefited the neighborhood, because by the time it was built up the city's urban lifestyle had undergone a key shift. Before the mid-19th century it was not considered proper for more than one family to share a roof—that was for the lower classes, who lived in the tenements. But relentless population pressure forced a change and gave birth to the apartment building. To entice the burgeoning middle class into apartment buildings, developers provided exceptional luxuries, such as marble lobbies, richly ornamented exteriors, and modern amenities.

Thus the Upper West Side was built up not by millionaire mansions, as were Fifth Avenue and Carnegie Hill, but by classic apartment houses. The Dakota, the Ansonia, the Belnord, the Kenilworth, the Apthorp—along Central Park West and Broadway these magnificent structures survive, testimony to a new order of urban existence.

The area west of Broadway, however, was left to degenerate into a slum. To create Lincoln Center, one of the largest and most high-handed urban renewal projects of 20th-century Manhattan, the city cleared a vast swath of those slums, dropping an enormous cultural complex down in their place. John D. Rockefeller III followed in his father's Rockefeller Center footsteps here, with master builder Robert Moses as his éminence grise. The Upper West Side, long a neighborhood of artists, became a neighborhood of the performing arts as well.

The Upper West Side is bounded by 59th Street to the south and 110th Street (Cathedral Parkway) to the north, braced by Central Park on the east and Riverside Park along the Hudson. Some even include Morningside Heights and Columbia University—up to around West 120th Street. As with the Upper East Side, previous generations of New Yorkers made more of a distinction between the southern and northern parts of the district, calling the portion from 59th Street up to around 86th Street or so the West Side and reserving the term Upper West Side for the parts to the north. But these days the area above 59th Street west of Central Park generally goes by the name Upper West Side.

■ COLUMBUS CIRCLE *map page 251, D-5*

Casting a shadow over the southwest corner of Central Park is the **Trump International Hotel and Tower,** formerly the Paramount Communications Building and, before that, Gulf & Western Plaza. Developer Donald Trump, with help from

The Dakota apartment building rises on the West Side overlooking skaters in Central Park, ca. 1890. (New-York Historical Society)

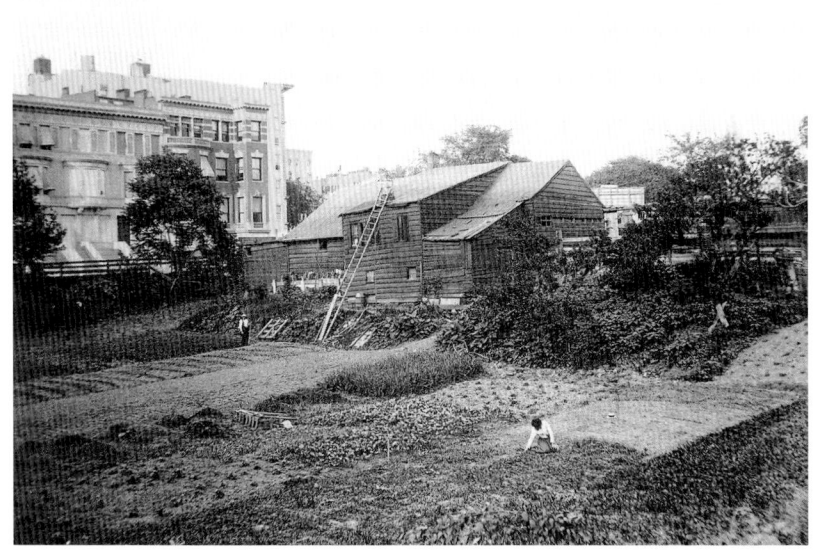

West End Avenue at 89th Street, 1902. (New-York Historical Society)

architect Philip Johnson, renovated what was the shoddiest skyscraper in town (pieces used to fall off into the street below). Now it's Trump glitzy, with a huge gilt globe that has been known to blind cab drivers when it catches the morning sun.

On street level, **Columbus Circle** represents the intersection of Broadway, West 59th Street, Eighth Avenue, Central Park West, and Central Park South. To get across it is a major test of one's urban survival skills. The rotary used to be called Grand Circle, but in its center is the reason for the renaming: the monument to Christopher Columbus. A majestic obelisk visible all the way down Eighth Avenue, the 80-foot-tall, 700-ton statue-topped monument was erected in 1892 with donations from New York's Italian-American community, to commemorate the 400th anniversary of the explorer's voyage to North America.

The distinctive building on the circle's south side, **2 Columbus Circle,** was completed in the mid-1960s and had a brief life as the home of the Gallery of Modern Art—the A&P grocery heir Huntington Hartford's iconoclastic answer to what he perceived as MoMA orthodoxy. Edward Durrell Stone, a contributing architect on MoMA's 1939 building as well as the General Motors Building,

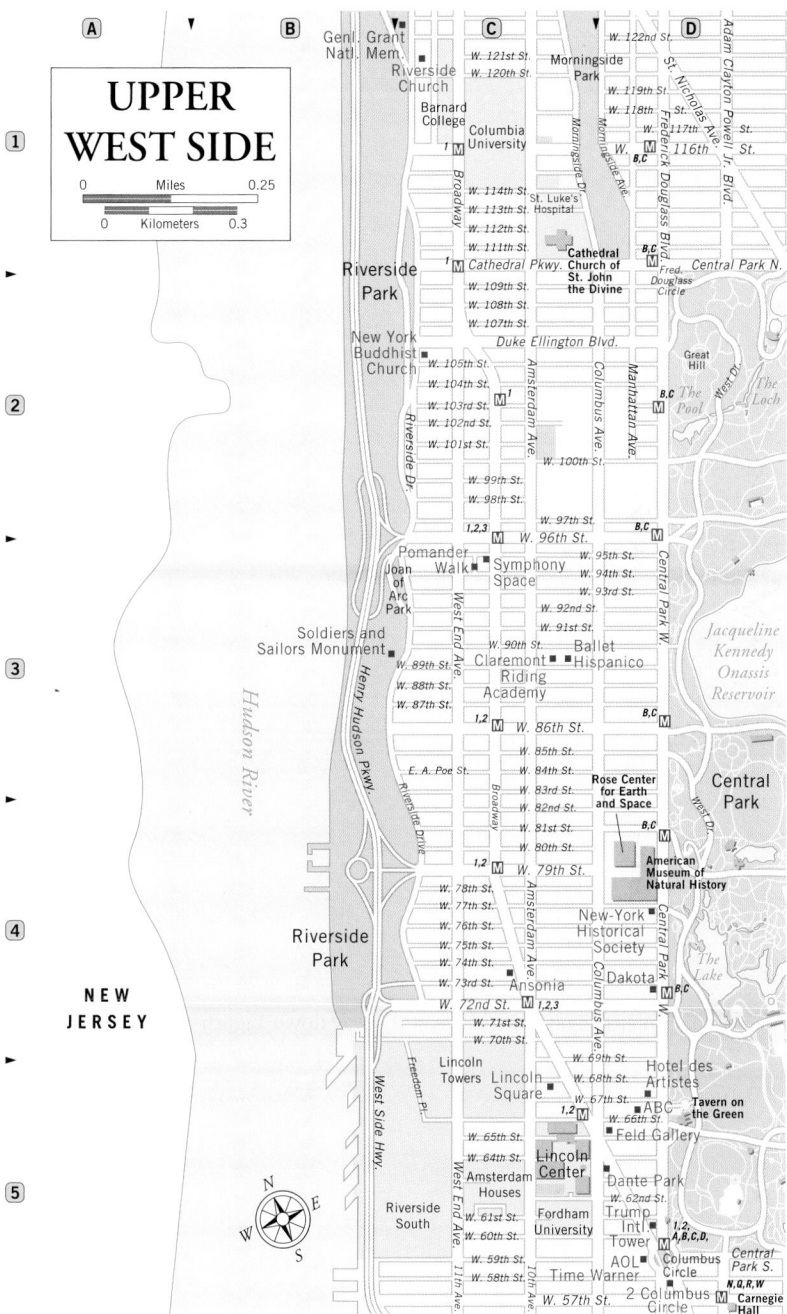

created the quirky, vaguely Moorish structure, which is slated to become the new home of the American Craft Museum. On the circle's west side, the New York Coliseum exhibition space, which nobody but Robert Moses loved, fell, unlamented, to the wrecker's ball. In its place soars the new AOL Time Warner headquarters building.

■ LINCOLN CENTER *map page 251, 5-C*

Just up Broadway from Columbus Circle is the cultural enclave of **Lincoln Center,** created in 1957 when a board member of the Metropolitan Opera suggested to John D. Rockefeller III that interesting shifts were afoot in Manhattan's cultural and real estate worlds. The New York Philharmonic was getting the boot from Carnegie Hall, and the Metropolitan Opera was looking to move from its longtime home on West 39th Street. Meanwhile, master builder Robert Moses was razing an expanse of tenements on the West Side that might provide the perfect site for both cultural institutions. JDR III donated almost $45 million of Rockefeller family money ($10 million of it his own) and, with Robert Moses acting as midwife, ushered Lincoln Center

The Metropolitan Opera occupies center stage in Lincoln Center.

through the birthing process. The project grew until it included not only the Philharmonic and the Met but a grab bag of cultural institutions, including the Juilliard School of Music, the New York City Opera, the New York City Ballet, and the Film Society of Lincoln Center.

Moses's slum-clearance project created great controversy. When eighteen square blocks were razed, more than eight hundred businesses were displaced and seven thousand families lost their homes. The eerie sense of a neighborhood sucked dry of life is captured in the film version of *West Side Story* (1961), which was shot on the deserted streets before Moses brought in the bulldozers. Whatever its origins, the development of Lincoln Center altered the entire social equation of Manhattan and provided a transforming boost to the Upper West Side.

It's there, it's used, but is it loved? The angular, travertine chilliness of Lincoln Center's buildings—some of them built in a style so austere it is called Brutalist — has always tempered the feelings New Yorkers hold for their cultural Acropolis. The complex of theaters, auditoriums, libraries, and cultural facilities represents convenience above all—one-stop shopping for the arts.

Lincoln Center's most prestigious tenant is the **Metropolitan Opera,** which moved into its impressive quarters in 1966. The Met (it shares the appellation with the art museum across town, so context determines which one you are talking about) has prospered in Lincoln Center and ranks among the world's leading opera companies.

The Met faces Columbus Avenue, presenting its ten-story fenestrated façade to the plaza, fountain, and passersby. In the morning, the windows are shaded to protect the priceless artworks within: huge, vibrant murals by Marc Chagall that at night transform the building into an oasis of color. Inside, all is elegance and high culture, the royal red carpet set off by starburst chandeliers. The four-tier theater is plush but not elaborately ornamented—an opera house brought successfully into the modern era. When the chandeliers ascend to the ceiling like angels at the start of each performance, clearing the sight lines and at the same time dimming the interior, it is difficult not to feel a corresponding rise in expectation. With its enormous stage and even bigger budget, the Met mounts productions that tend to be grand and diva-studded.

Performing cater-corner at the **New York State Theater** is the New York City Ballet. Under the leadership of George Balanchine, NYCB became internationally known for the precision and depth of its corps de ballet. Also performing at the State Theater is the New York City Opera, which performs standard works from the operatic repertoire in addition to small-scale (at least by comparison with the Met)

Baroque operas and lesser-known works by 20th century composers. In early May, after the opera season has ended, the American Ballet Theatre takes the stage until June. Known for its star dancers and renditions of story ballets, ABT spends much of the year touring with a wide-ranging repertoire.

Avery Fisher Hall, opposite the New York State Theater, is the home of the New York Philharmonic as well as such crowd pleasers as the Mostly Mozart Festival. **Alice Tully Hall** is an intimate hall for recitals and chamber music. For a long time it was also the home of the Film Society of Lincoln Center, but that is now headquartered at the **Walter Reade Theater,** part of the Lincoln Center North development. Some screenings of the society's popular New York Film Festival, an early fall event, take place at Tully, though.

Also part of the Lincoln Center complex are the **Juilliard School** and the **New York Public Library Performing Arts** branch. Two theaters, the **Vivian Beaumont,** a 1,050-seat Broadway venue, and the 299-seat **Mitzi E. Newhouse,** are nestled behind a reflecting pool that features a Henry Moore sculpture. *Contact,* which won the 2000 Tony Award for best musical, had its world premiere at the Beaumont. The Newhouse is the Beaumont's somewhat more adventuresome sidekick, mounting such productions as *Waiting for Godot* played as it was written—as comedy—with Robin Williams and Steve Martin, as well as producing revivals such as Eugene O'Neill's *Ah, Wilderness!* and sending plays such as Wendy Wasserstein's *The Sisters Rosensweig* to Broadway.

Lincoln Square, the intersection of Broadway and Columbus Avenue, from which Lincoln Center takes its name, has been the focus of some intense high-rise development. The homey **Eva and Morris Feld Gallery** (2 Lincoln Square, at West 66th Street; 212-595-5933), formerly the main facility of the American Folk Art Museum, which moved to Midtown in 2001, offers a welcome counterpoint to the hustle-bustle of the urban square outside. The gallery's window panes and interior design represent a modern take on the Shaker quilting tradition. The exhibits inside focus on actual quilts and other folk art.

Across the avenues from Lincoln Center, past the sculpture of Dante holding his *Commedia* in **Dante Park** (West 63rd Street and Broadway), is the block that was slated for Nelson Rockefeller's Lincoln Plaza project, the abandoned plan that would have cleared the space to improve Rocky's view from across Central Park. The **Westside YMCA** (5 West 63rd Street) was the block's only tenant to refuse to budge, and thus scuttled the whole deal. Contributing a pop-culture veneer to the neighborhood are the ABC and WABC headquarters, at 30 West 67th Street and 56 West 66th Street.

More stately, and right down the street from ABC, is the **Hotel des Artistes** (1 West 67th Street), proof that the area's artistic bent predates Lincoln Center. Completed in 1918 with double-height ceilings to accommodate painters' studios, and not a hotel at all but an apartment building, it has played host to such celebrity tenants as Norman Rockwell, Noel Coward, and Isadora Duncan. One resident, the pin-up illustrator Howard Chandler Christy, painted the extravagant murals in the building's famed restaurant, **Café des Artistes.** The whole block was called Studio Row, for the half-dozen buildings that were designed as artists' studios.

Nothing on the island is quite like **Riverside South,** the monster development Donald Trump is building on the site of the old New York Central Railroad freight yards, which stretch from 59th Street all the way to 72nd Street along the Hudson River and are the last major vacant land parcel in Manhattan below Harlem. In the mid-1980s, Trump announced that he would erect something he called Television City, a sprawling communications, commercial, and residential complex that would include the world's tallest building. Community and financial pressure have since tempered the developer's grandiose vision, but Riverside South still entails constructing a 57-acre mini-city.

■ CENTRAL PARK WEST *map page 251, D-2/5*

At West 72nd Street and Central Park West is the famous **Dakota** (1 West 72nd Street). The apartment house's notoriety stems not only from having been the centerpiece of films like *Rosemary's Baby* and *House of Strangers,* as well as the cult novel *Time After Time,* but also because in 1980 John Lennon was shot to death in the 72nd Street driveway. Other residents over the years have included Judy Garland, Boris Karloff, Leonard Bernstein, and Lauren Bacall.

The Dakota was built by the Singer Sewing Machine heir Edward S. Clark, who had the sense of humor to turn a barb about the place's far-flung location into its actual name. The building, designed by Henry J. Hardenbergh—who also whipped up the equally ornate Plaza hotel—has marvelous architectural details, some with a Wild West theme (in jocular reference to its name) and others baroquely neoclassical, like the Zeus sculptures on the balustrade.

A walk along this section of Central Park West (or CPW, as it's known in Manhattan shorthand) north from the Dakota yields glimpses of some classic apartment buildings, all built in the early years of the 20th century, including the **Langham** (135 CPW) and the **Kenilworth** (151 CPW).

CAFÉ DES ARTISTES

Recipe for a prized Manhattan moment: stroll away an afternoon in Central Park, taking in the antic machinations of the Delacorte Clock, watching the rollerbladers near the bandshell, catching the view from Belvedere Castle, and wandering the Ramble. When late afternoon rolls around, work your way over to the West Side and Café des Artistes.

A restaurant full of cozy alcoves, with the tiny Parlor drink-and-coffee bar across the lobby, Café des Artistes has a long and interesting history—not least as the home restaurant of its building, Hotel des Artistes, built in the mid-1910s. Long before Lincoln Center turned the neighborhood into art central, the block of West 67th Street between Central Park West and Columbus Avenue was known as Studio Row for its preponderance of artist studios. Hotel des Artistes—not a hotel at all, but a residential apartment building complete with a swimming pool, a squash court, and a private ballroom—hosted many artists, including the top illustrator and portraitist of his day, Howard Chandler Christy.

Beginning in the early 1930s, Christy created the murals that grace the Café today, cheerfully naughty nudes with names like "The Parrot Girl," "The Swing Girl," and "The Fountain of Youth." In eras past, the regulars included author Fannie Hurst, artist Marcel Duchamp, and dancer Isadora Duncan. Nowadays you might encounter Paul Newman or news anchor Peter Jennings (ABC has television studios across the street).

The Café's menu was formerly modeled on the style of the English bistro called the Ordinary and has never been the strongest draw of the place. Come instead for coffee, drinks, or dessert, for the surroundings, and for the indubitable air of joie de vivre that permeates the place. *1 West 67th Street, at Central Park West; 212-877-3500.*

(above) Decorous dining at Café des Artistes. (opposite) Detail from Howard Chandler Christy's mural The Parrot Girl. *(Café des Artistes)*

Most impressive for its bulk, but also for the trend it set on Central Park West for twin-towered silhouettes, is the **San Remo** (145–146 CPW). Once in the news because its co-op board turned down an application from Madonna (fearing she would attract too many screaming fans), the San Remo has been the East Coast home to Hollywood celebs like Steve Martin and Dustin Hoffman; Bruce Willis and Demi Moore lived here before their divorce.

Farther north at 170 CPW is the **New-York Historical Society,** a superb archive of documents relating to the history of the city and state of "New-York," as the name used to be written. The treasures here include original watercolors by the naturalist John James Audubon.

■ AMERICAN MUSEUM OF NATURAL HISTORY *map page 251, D-4*

Across West 77th Street from the historical society is the sprawling **American Museum of Natural History,** a hulking Barosaurus of a place that ate four square blocks. The repository of an astounding thirty-five million objects of potential interest to the anthropologist, archaeologist, naturalist, or anyone curious about the world, this museum needs even more space. Many of the exhibits have been updated in recent years, but certain sections of the museum retain an anachronistic, daffy charm, especially the rooms with exquisitely painted dioramas behind animals stuffed six or more decades ago. And though gallery after gallery here seems devoted to dead things, many others sparkle with liveliness—if not *life.*

In the Hall of Minerals, priceless gems (including the glowing Star of India sapphire) and glittering geodes fill the glass cases. We like the West 77th Street entrance, not only because that whole side of the museum is a red-brick Romanesque delight, but because lines there are usually shorter. The main entrance on Central Park West is watched over by an equestrian statue of Teddy Roosevelt, whose father was among those who founded the museum in 1869. Check out the other statues on the pediment, ranked above the entrance like sentries.

A group of three dinosaur skeletons in the main entrance hall welcomes visitors and immediately demonstrates the staggering size of these beasts. A *tableau vivant* features a gape-jawed Tyrannosaurus rex about to devour a baby Barosaurus, and a mother Barosaurus rearing up on her hind legs to defend her offspring. Little matter that some paleontologists debate whether the huge, hulking Barosaurus could, in fact, rear up at all—the arrangement is a spectacular opening to the treasures of the museum.

Rosemary's Baby, *among other films, was shot at the famous Dakota.*

To see the dioramas, such as the African mammals room, head straight past the Barosaurus from the main entrance. The real dinosaur stomping ground is on the fourth floor—not the musty-but-beloved exhibits of yesteryear but a remounted and redesigned scientific extravaganza, funded in part by Steven Spielberg's donated profits from the film *Jurassic Park*. The Hall of Mammals has been redone in a glitzy, high-tech marriage of the ancient past and the future present. The revamping also included clearing of windows in the galleries, providing more natural light (and lovely views of Central Park) to wanderers here. One great attraction of this museum, as with the Met, is exploring its out-of-the-way spaces. Strolling through the Hall of Biodiversity on a gloomy winter day, one feels transported, not necessarily to a Central African rain forest or other ecosytem, but to some twilight zone out of time—or at least out of Manhattan. In the tropical climes of the Butterfly Conservatory, free lepidoptoras alight on shrubbery, flowers—and you.

The latest jewel in the museum's crown is the **Rose Center for Earth and Space,** which includes the Hall of Planet Earth and the reconceived Hayden Planetarium. The projector used for the space shows here is encaged in a huge orb with a glass-skinned outer shell. Supergalaxies in the dome above zoom by at trillions of times the speed of light. There's also a walkway called Scales of the Universe, which displays the relative sizes of stars, planets, and atoms. *CPW and West 79th Street; 212-313-7278.*

■ NORTH ON BROADWAY   *map page 251, C-3/4*

Broadway has its share of classic constructions from the golden age of the apartment building, none of them finer than the **Ansonia** (2109 Broadway), which rises like an astonishing vision, its history every bit as outrageous as its Beaux Arts ornamentation. Its developer, William Earle Dodge Stokes, heir to a mining fortune, was an iron-willed eccentric who kept a whole menagerie on the Ansonia's roof: five hundred chickens—he sold eggs for half-price to his tenants—a tame bear, and a flock of hybrid geese that used to fly over and terrorize Central Park, biting passersby. Seals cavorted in a pool in the lobby. Eventually the health department forced him to give up his animals.

Stokes demanded that the Ansonia be not only fire-resistant but fireproof. His precautions were so thorough that for years fire insurance wasn't required. The building's 3-foot-thick walls, part of the fireproofing scheme, made the rooms virtually

The Rose Center lends the Upper West Side an otherworldly glow at night.
(© American Museum of Natural History)

(opposite) A Beaux Arts masterpiece, the Ansonia has a history as rich as its densely ornamented exterior. (above) Interior view of the apartment building.

impervious to sound, a feature that attracted a musical clientele. Arturo Toscanini, Igor Stravinsky, and Lily Pons stayed here. Impresarios Florenz Ziegfeld and Sol Hurok were also longtime tenants. (By one account, when Hurok was evicted in the late 1920s because of financial setbacks, he lived for a spell in Central Park.)

In the 1960s, the basement swimming pool, the wonder of Manhattan when the Ansonia opened, was turned into a gay bathhouse, the Continental Baths. Bette Midler got her start here, performing cabaret (Barry Manilow accompanied her on piano) for the betoweled patrons. In the 1970s, after the baths closed, came Plato's Retreat, a heterosexual swingers' club. The Ansonia starred in the movies *Three Days of the Condor, Single White Female,* and *The Paper.*

Broadway north of the Ansonia, like the parallel stretch of Columbus Avenue one block over, is redolent with Upper West Side flavor and includes many shops that are neighborhood favorites. **Fairway** (2127 Broadway) is worth a step inside just to see how crazy and exhilarating the simple act of produce shopping can get in Manhattan. Aficionados of **H&H Bagels** (2239 Broadway) swear by the product—the shop sends orders by FedEx all over the world. **Zabar's** (2245 Broadway) is an internationally

Zabar's purportedly sells a thousand pounds of smoked salmon each week.

known emporium for cookware (second floor) and, more to the point, smoked fish and other comestibles (ground floor). Zabar's—pronounced "ZAY-bars"—reportedly sells a thousand pounds of smoked salmon a week.

■ LOWER RIVERSIDE PARK *map page 251, B-3/4*

Riverside Park, which undulates along the Hudson on the western flank of the West Side, runs all the way from 72nd to 159th Street, more than 4 miles. Designed by Calvert Vaux and Frederick Law Olmsted, this park has wide promenades punctuated by monuments and memorials, including a statue of Eleanor Roosevelt (Riverside Drive and West 72nd Street), one of the few statues in the city to honor a 20th-century woman.

The **Soldiers and Sailors Monument** (Riverside Drive and West 89th Street), with its huge Corinthian columns, massive dome, and stern eagles, has an empty niche once filled by a life-size bronze sculpture of George Washington, since removed to the safety of City Hall. South of the monument, at West 83rd Street, is **"Mount Tom,"** named by Edgar Allan Poe after his landlord's son, and a place where the author of "The Raven" used to go to contemplate the Hudson.

Something of a historical throwback is the **Claremont Riding Academy and Stables** (175 West 89th Street), a place to get horses for the bridle paths of Central Park. Also near the park, at West 94th Street and Broadway, is one of those charming hideaway mews that are sprinkled all over Manhattan. This one, **Pomander Walk,** is modeled after a stage set of the popular play of the same name, which opened on Broadway in 1911.

Symphony Space was the brainchild of Oscar-winning director Allen Miller and radio personality Isaiah Sheffer, who took a run-down movie theater and transformed it into a landmark concert and lecture hall that fostered a cultural revival in the neighborhood. In 2002, Symphony Space expanded into the long-closed (and much-beloved) Thalia art-house cinema, now called the Leonard Nimoy Thalia after the actor who plays *Star Trek*'s pointy-eared Vulcan—he provided the bulk of the funds to revamp the space. The combined complex, now officially named Peter Norton Symphony Space, for another major benefactor, is famous for hosting daylong classical concerts (usually concentrating on a single composer), an annual dramatic reading of James Joyce's *Ulysses,* and short-story fests. *2537 Broadway, at West 95th Street; 212-864-1414.*

In general, the Upper West Side north of West 86th Street is more ethnically diverse and less homogenized than the sections to the south. The neighborhood still struggles to balance the social needs of its citizenry with the quality-of-life issues that make some of the blocks here resemble open-air mental clinics. But there are some startling finds here, such as the huge statue of Buddha, said to be the largest in Manhattan, that greets passersby at the **New York Buddhist Church** (Riverside Drive and West 106th Street).

The housing projects of Manhattan Valley, as the area around 100th Street and CPW is known, symbolize an old-style government approach to the area's social diversity. Somewhat more human-scale is the huge government project designated the West Side Urban Renewal Area: it resulted in the renovation of side-street brownstones, landmark status for Claremont Stables, and a new home for **Ballet Hispanico,** in two renovated carriage houses at 167 West 89th Street.

HARLEM AND
UPPER MANHATTAN

Whole blocks, whole neighborhoods of Harlem rank among the most beautiful in Manhattan and would grace any district of the city. But these areas go unnoticed because of Harlem's reputation as a crime-ridden ghetto. Despite dangers real or imagined, there is a burning curiosity about Harlem on the part of tourists and residents alike, a sense of longing on the part of those looking across the fence of race and suspicion. If this largely untapped desire to know more were fulfilled, Harlem would become even more popular as a tourist destination than it already is.

More than a third of the length, if not the area, of Manhattan lies to the north of Cathedral Parkway, or 110th Street. Here topography has defeated the best efforts to subdue it, and the island retains many of the dips and hills that were leveled out during the development of its lower two-thirds. The far upper reaches finally vanquish the grid plan altogether, with the streets surrendering to the contours of the land.

Dutch settlers claimed Harlem Valley in 1636 as a tobacco plantation on the site of an abandoned Indian village. Peter Stuyvesant, the governor general of the colony, stepped in when area farmers lobbied to name the place after their own home towns in Holland. None of them came from the Dutch city of Haarlem, though, so

Some of the rooftops of Harlem show the neighborhood's early Dutch influence.

Stuyvesant named the area Nieuw Haarlem to avoid a squabble. In the 1840s, after rail service connected it to downtown, **Harlem** became New York's first suburban community. Rich downtowners fled the heat of the city to access the river-cooled breezes on the ridges of the heights along the Hudson. These would soon be known as **Morningside, Hamilton, and Washington Heights,** each a distinctive neighborhood with superb views.

The IRT subway extension in 1904 prompted another wave of speculation, but this time the developers overbuilt. As their new apartment houses stood empty, their only option was to rent to Manhattan's burgeoning African-American population, which they did, at three times the normal rate: the black capital of America was born out of rent-gouging landlords' cold hearts. A suitable enough genesis, some say, given that real estate manipulations have plagued the area ever since.

The period immediately preceding and following World War I was the heyday of Harlem, but though its reputation for partying was unsurpassed, the neighborhood, as Alain Locke wrote in 1925, signified something far deeper for African Americans:

> If we were to offer a symbol of what Harlem has come to mean in
> the short span of twenty years it would be another statue of liberty
> on the landward side of New York. It stands for a folk-movement
> which in human significance can be compared only with the pushing
> back of the western frontier in the first half of the last century, or the
> waves of immigration which have swept in from overseas in the last
> half…. Each group has come with its own separate motives and for
> its own special ends, but their greatest experience has been the find-
> ing of one another.

The migration continued after World War II, with a tremendous influx of southern rural blacks. What people of African descent found during both eras were economic apartheid and a Jim Crowism venomous enough for the newcomers to label their new home "Up South"—same bigotry, different latitude. Despite adversity, Harlem prospered as a center of black life, eventually consuming precincts to the east, Italian Harlem and Spanish Harlem.

A lot has been made of "Harlem light," a quality of airiness and openness unmatched anywhere else on Manhattan. This has much to do with the wide boulevards and the relative lack of high-rise buildings, but the exposed topography contributes as well.

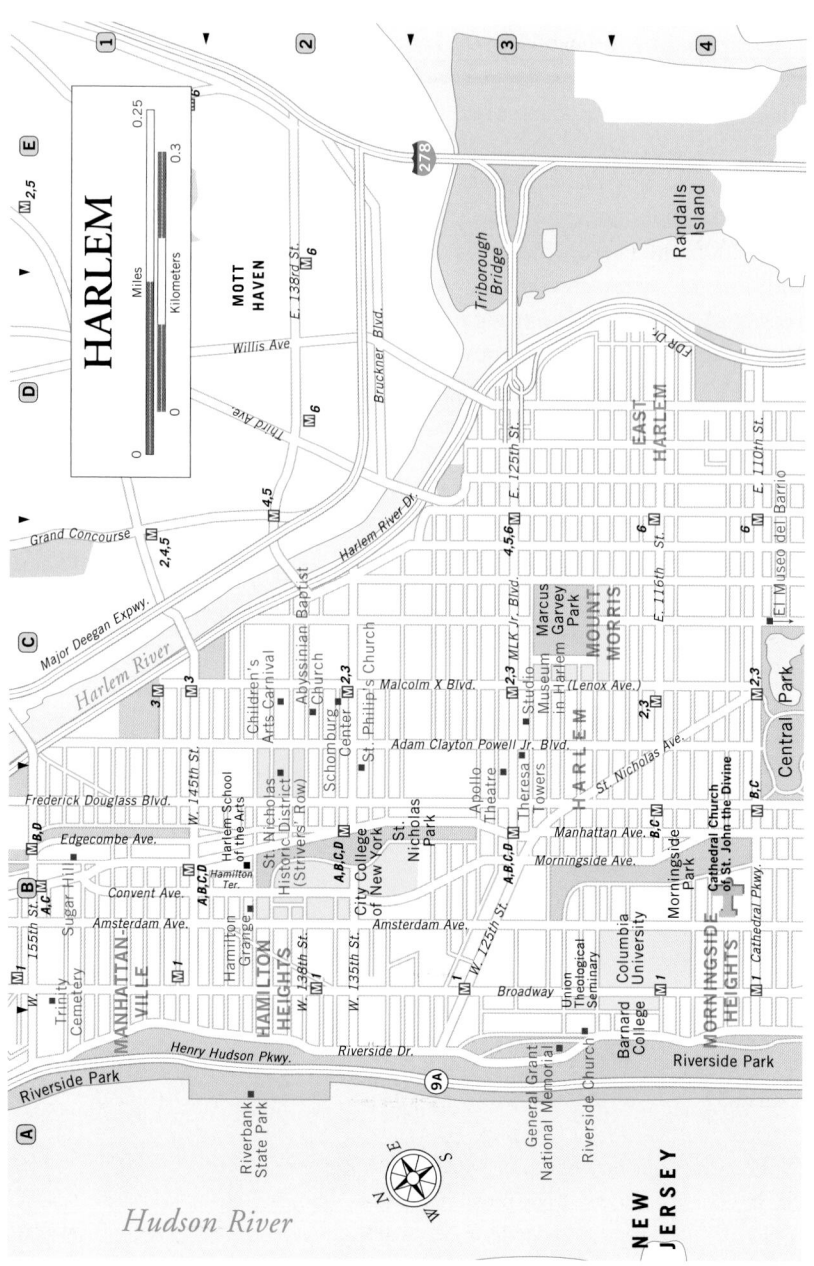

Today, the area is roughly divided between East and West Harlem by the commuter rail tracks of Park Avenue, with 125th Street (Martin Luther King Jr. Boulevard) running the width of the island as a main economic thoroughfare. East Harlem is a little more Hispanic, its black districts a little more poverty-stricken than those in West Harlem, which has more middle-class neighborhoods and a greater preponderance of historical sites.

As is happening elsewhere in New York, a battle continues over Harlem's future, with groups in favor of more landmarking and low-rise zoning facing off against real estate interests. The opening of Bill Clinton's post-presidential offices at 55 West 125th Street, coming on the heels of new malls and shops on 125th, signaled to many longtime residents that another speculative boom was about to begin.

On the district's western edge, rising above the Hudson River, are **Morningside Heights,** the home of Columbia University, and **Hamilton Heights,** the home of City College of New York. Together, Morningside and Hamilton Heights constitute Harlem Heights; farther north the same ridgeline is called **Washington Heights.** At Manhattan's northern tip is Inwood, more topographically varied than the rest of the island. With rude outcroppings of **Inwood** marble and Fordham gneiss, this neighborhood is probably the only place in Manhattan where one can experience the land the way the Algonquins saw it.

■ MORNINGSIDE HEIGHTS *map page 268, B-4*

Constructed in fits and starts since 1892 and still unfinished, the **Cathedral Church of St. John the Divine** rides the crest of Morningside Heights like a celestial spaceship. This Episcopalian edifice bills itself as the largest cathedral in the world—it's smaller than St. Peter's Basilica in Rome, but that is technically not a cathedral. Work on the structure halted during the Depression and World War II but has lately recommenced in earnest. A master English stonemason, Simon Verity, trained a corps of neighborhood youths in the fine art of gargoyle production from 1978 to 1994. The gargoyles are crafted following a French Gothic master design modified from the original by Ralph Adams Cram in 1911. Cram, the cathedral's architect, proved true to his name, cramming an enormous amount of ornamentation onto the building.

The fact that their house of worship is a work in progress has not halted the St. John's congregation from pursuing a vigorous course of social and ecumenical activism. This includes a wide menu of events, concerts, theater, and lectures.

During the annual Blessing of the Animals, neighborhood residents turn out with their pets in tow. Classical and jazz concerts within the soaring space of the cathedral's interior are also widely popular. *Amsterdam Avenue and West 112th Street; 212-316-7540.*

If the cathedral is the gateway to Morningside Heights, **Columbia University,** which lends an Ivy League cachet to the more fundamental education that comes with living in Manhattan, is the neighborhood's principal tenant. The main campus officially stretches between West 114th and West 120th Streets and Amsterdam Avenue and Broadway, but as the neighborhood's largest landlord, Columbia's influence extends well beyond the campus borders.

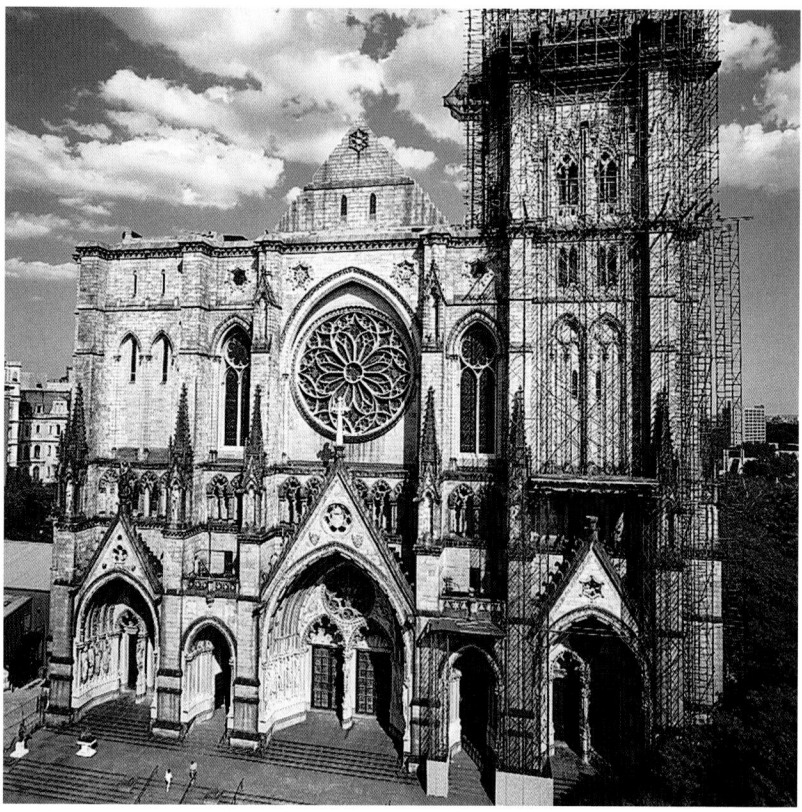

St. John the Divine cathedral has been under construction since 1892.

The central conduit of the campus is **College Walk,** a pedestrian extension of West 116th Street. Low Memorial Library, now the main administration building, lies across a stately plaza from Butler Library. The plaza sits atop underground steam and electrical tunnels that honeycomb the campus. These came of use to students protesting the war in Vietnam. When they took over the campus in 1968, the protesters circumvented police barricades by using the tunnels to get from building to building.

Cross to the west side of Broadway to enter the **Barnard College** campus; the main gate is at West 117th Street. Barnard, one of several schools that make up Columbia University, is one of the few remaining women-only undergraduate schools in the nation.

The northwest corner of Barnard abuts two magnificent specimens of religious architecture, both of them Gothic adaptations. The interior courtyard at the **Union Theological Seminary** (Broadway and West 120th Street) seems miles removed from the city outside. John D. Rockefeller Jr. funded the **Riverside Church** (490 Riverside Drive, at West 120th Street), whose carillon bell tower has an observation deck (closed for renovations until at least 2004) with excellent views of Manhattan, the Palisades in New Jersey, the Hudson River, and the George Washington Bridge. The carillon includes a 20-ton bell, the world's largest carillon bell.

The subject of the famous trivia question—Who is buried in Grant's Tomb?— lies in repose in Riverside Park, near the church. The colossal **General Grant National Memorial,** once one of New York's most popular attractions but now well out of the top ten, contains the matching black tombs of Ulysses S. Grant and his wife, Julia Dent Grant—hence the trick to the quiz. The benches of the plaza outside the mausoleum were covered with mosaics by local youngsters. *Riverside Drive and West 122nd Street.*

■ MANHATTANVILLE AND WEST HARLEM

map page 268, B/C-3

Through a gap in Morningside Heights ran an old road that led to the docks for the New Jersey ferry, and along this road a village called Manhattanville grew up. The gap represents a geologic fault line—not, thankfully, an active one. Today, that road has become the western dogleg of Martin Luther King Jr. Boulevard. Manhattanville has survived as a neighborhood but not as an identity separate from Harlem itself.

The time to visit **125th Street** is on a weekend day, when the street takes on the flavor of a bazaar. Apart from the name, the present-day incarnation of the **Cotton Club** (666 West 125th Street; 212-663-7980) has not much in common with the classic Jazz Age nightclub on Lenox Avenue, aka Malcolm X Boulevard. Events at the club include a gospel-music brunch. **Theresa Towers** (2090 Adam Clayton Powell Jr. Boulevard), now an office building, has a storied past. As the Hotel Theresa, it was where Fidel Castro stayed during his tempestuous visit to the United Nations in 1960, in a snub to the "capitalist" hotels of Midtown. It is slated to reopen again as a hotel.

THE HARLEM DANCER

Applauding youths laughed with young prostitutes
And watched her perfect, half-clothed body sway;
Her voice was like the sound of blended flutes
Blown by black players upon a picnic day.
She sang and danced on gracefully and calm,
The light gauze hanging loose about her form;
To me she seemed a proudly-swaying palm
Grown lovelier for passing through a storm.
Upon her swarthy neck black shiny curls
Luxuriant fell; and tossing coins in praise,
The wine-flushed, bold-eyed boys, and even the girls,
Devoured her shape with eager, passionate gaze;
But looking at her falsely-smiling face,
I knew her self was not in that strange place.

—Claude McKay, 1922

The **Apollo Theatre** (253 West 125th Street; 212-531-5300) still hosts a raucous amateur night every Wednesday and remains a cultural landmark. When Elvis Presley first came to New York, the Apollo was the one place he wanted to see; likewise with the Beatles. It opened in 1914 as a whites-only house, showcasing performers like Bessie Smith, Duke Ellington, and Louis Armstrong. New owners took over in 1934, allowed blacks to patronize the club, and it took off like a rocket. Great talents have performed at the Apollo over the years, including Billie Holiday, James Brown, Diana Ross, Michael Jackson, and George Clinton.

Like most of New York, the Apollo hit hard times in the 1970s, closing briefly before being saved by Harlem mover and shaker Percy Sutton. The reign of Sutton ended in controversy in the 1990s, and a consortium that includes AOL Time

Students hang out across from Columbia University's Butler Library.

Warner now operates the greatly refurbished venue. The theater changed its policy in 2002 and booked a three-day-a-week show, *Harlem Song,* a Broadway-style musical about Harlem during the 20th century. The show's backers had high hopes the musical would settle in for a multiyear run, but whether it succeeds or fails the theater looks well-positioned for the new millennium.

Despite the renovations, some age-old talismans remain. Backstage is the preserved trunk of the famous "tree of hope," touched for luck by performers in the 1920s (when it stood in front of another club) and now used for the same purpose by the Apollo's rap, comedy, soul, and other acts. Most likely in need of a good-luck charm are the brave souls who venture out on amateur night: audience derision can be scathing.

Harlem has other performance venues as well. The **Lenox Lounge** (288 Malcolm X Boulevard; 212-427-0253) is an atmospheric jazz club (Billie Holiday played the Zebra Room here), as is mellow **St. Nick's Pub** (773 St. Nicholas Avenue; 212-283-9728). The **Sugar Shack** (2611 Frederick Douglass Boulevard; 212-491-4422) serves up local poetry and music. **Minton's Playhouse** (210 West

Young Harlemite strikes an enigmatic pose.

Harlem Street, 8th Avenue and West 140th Street *(1938), by Berenice Abbott.*
(Museum of the City of New York)

118th Street), where modern jazz was invented at late-night jam sessions in the 1940s, still sports its original neon signs. Plans are afoot to reopen the club. A nearby cultural mecca is the **Studio Museum in Harlem** (144 West 125th Street; 212-864-4500), a prestigious showcase for African and African-American art. The **Schomburg Center for Research in Black Culture** (103 West 135th Street; 212-491-2200), a branch of the New York Public Library, houses the research collection of Arthur A. Schomburg, who had the foresight and tenacity to collect documents pertaining to African-American history when it was being largely ignored by white academia. This is where Alex Haley researched much of his book *Roots*. Schomburg's original collection of ten thousand books, manuscripts, and artifacts has grown to more than five million items, including runaway-slave notices, the first black newspaper *(Freedom's Journal),* the manuscript of Richard Wright's *Native Son,* and many of Duke Ellington's original scores. The exhibitions here are top-notch.

Around the corner, at **187 West 135th Street,** is where author James Weldon Johnson lived when he wrote "Lift Up Every Voice and Sing," now known as the black national anthem. Adam Clayton Powell Jr. Boulevard, originally Seventh Avenue and renamed for the crusading mid-20th-century U.S. congressman, embraces a historic stretch of former speakeasies and nightclubs that was known as "Harlem's Beale Street" or "Jungle Alley" during the height of the Jazz Age.

THE NEGRO DIGS UP HIS PAST

In the first paragraph of this essay in the Survey Graphic, March 1925, *collector Arthur A. Schomburg stresses the importance of history for African Americans:*

The American Negro must remake his past in order to make his future. Though it is orthodox to think of America as the one country where it is unnecessary to have a past, what is a luxury for the nation as a whole becomes a prime social necessity for the Negro. For him, a group tradition must supply compensation for persecution, and pride of race the antidote for prejudice. History must restore what slavery took away, for it is the social damage of slavery that the present generations must repair and offset. So among the rising democratic millions we find the Negro thinking more collectively, more retrospectively than the rest, and apt out of the very pressure of the present to become the most enthusiastic antiquarian of them all.

Strivers' Row townhouses.

Nearby, at Adam Clayton Powell Jr. Boulevard, is **St. Philip's Church,** one of the reasons Harlem is what it is today. St. Philip's was formerly located in the Tenderloin, on the site of what was to become Penn Station. In the early 1900s, the congregation was bought out for the construction of the station, and it moved up here and purchased a large stretch of 135th Street. The housing that church members built formed the core of the neighborhood out of which arose the famed Harlem Renaissance of the 1920s. *204 West 134th Street.*

A few streets north and encompassing two blocks, the **St. Nicholas Historic District** is better known to nonresidents by the patronizing nickname of **Strivers' Row.** The townhouses were designed by three different architects; Stanford White, of McKim, Mead & White, designed much of the north side of West 139th Street. Note the sign on Gate No. 6 on West 138th Street: "Walk your horses." These blocks have something most of the rest of Manhattan lacks, something taken for granted in many urban areas: alleys, which allow deliveries and garbage disposal through back doors, thereby decreasing traffic jams and litter. The St. Nicholas Historic District has been enthusiastically adopted by urban professionals, from surgeons to rap stars. The townhouse-lined streets are among the prettiest and most serene on the island. *West 138th and 139th Streets between Adam Clayton Powell Jr. and Frederick Douglass Boulevards.*

East of the St. Nicholas district is the **Abyssinian Baptist Church,** long a religious and political locus of Harlem life and the pulpit of such high-profile pastors as Adam Clayton Powell Jr., his father before him, and the present-day activist Calvin Butts. The baptismal font here features a Coptic Cross brought from Ethiopia by Emperor Haile Selassie. The Abyssinian choir is justly famous for its stupendous renderings of gospel hymns. *132 West 138th Street.*

Growing out of a church into a blockbuster cultural and educational force, the **Harlem School of the Arts** occupies old St. James Presbyterian Church but has sprawled to encompass much of the block. The school's Suzuki classes are famed for teaching youngsters the violin and other classical instruments. *645 St. Nicholas Avenue.*

■ **HAMILTON HEIGHTS** *map page 268, B-1/2*

Dominating the ridgeline of Hamilton Heights is **City College of New York,** part of the City University of New York. The Gothic eruptions of college buildings like Shepard Hall are visible from all over Harlem Valley. The darker stones are Manhattan schist, excavated during the building of the IRT subway line; the lighter limestone was quarried by the inmates of Sing-Sing penitentiary.

Hamilton Grange, Alexander Hamilton's country home, is crammed onto the grounds of St. Luke's Episcopal Church. The church fathers bought the house, originally 100 yards to the north, and moved it here for use as a rectory, lopping off the porches and reorienting it, front to back, in the process. The Grange was Hamilton's home during the last years of his life, before his fatal duel with Aaron Burr. There is a proposal afoot to move the place to St. Nicholas Park; as it is now, under the custodial care of the National Park Service, the house is much diminished inside and out. *287 Convent Avenue.*

Convent Avenue is also known for its terrific concentration of row houses, whose style and coloration vary subtly. The residential architecture on the blocks of Convent between West 140th and West 144th Streets is among the finest in Manhattan. At nearby Hamilton Terrace is the **Children's Arts Carnival** (62 Hamilton Terrace), where many Harlem youths get their first exposure to arts and crafts. Vertner W. Tandy, New York State's first registered African-American architect and a resident of Strivers' Row, designed the modernist **Ivey Delph Apartments** (19 Hamilton Terrace).

Sugar Hill, on the Hamilton Heights ridgeline north of West 145th Street, was the most prestigious address in the Harlem of the 1920s. Cab Calloway, Duke Ellington, Thurgood Marshall, W.E.B. Dubois, and Langston Hughes all lived here. Sugar Hill overlooked the **Polo Grounds,** on 155th Street along the Harlem River, the home of the New York Giants baseball team before it moved to San Francisco in the late 1950s. A housing project now stands on the site of some of baseball's most dramatic moments, including Bobby Thomson's famed "Shot Heard 'Round the World" homer against the Brooklyn Dodgers.

Along the Hudson River in West Harlem is a most peculiar hybrid public structure: **Riverbank State Park,** which sits atop a sewage treatment plant. Underneath the ballparks, swimming pool, and playgrounds of this concrete platform is the North River Water Pollution Control Plant. The park was intended to appease community activists who had protested siting the waste plant in the neighborhood, but the plant continued to emit foul odors, and the city had to outlay large amounts of money to render the park usable. *Along the Hudson River between West 137th and 145th Streets.*

Many members of the celebrated "400" of 19th-century society, including Astors, Schermerhorns, and Bleeckers, came to rest at **Trinity Cemetery,** on the former farm of naturalist and ornithologist John James Audubon, who is also buried here. Every Christmas season, carolers visit the grave of Clement Clarke Moore, though perhaps the numbers will diminish, given the revelation that he probably wasn't the author of "A Visit from St. Nicholas." *Riverside Drive West between West 153rd and 155th Streets.*

(above) Alexander Hamilton's country home stood in what is now a Harlem neighborhood. (Library of Congress)

North of the graveyard is **Audubon Terrace,** a collection of Beaux Arts buildings housing the American Academy of Arts and Letters and the **Hispanic Society of America,** a free museum and reference library for the study of the arts and cultures of Spain, Portugal, and Latin America. The museum's collection includes paintings by El Greco, Velázquez, and Goya. *West 155th Street and Broadway.*

The genteel Federal-style **Morris-Jumel Mansion** has stunning views and twelve period-decorated rooms you can tour. Built as a summer home for the Roger Morris family, it was taken over by George Washington during his doomed defense of Manhattan in the fall of 1776. The mansion was later owned by Stephen Jumel, a wine merchant, and his celebrated beauty of a wife, Elizabeth Bowen, who allegedly faked a deathbed scene to get him to propose. When

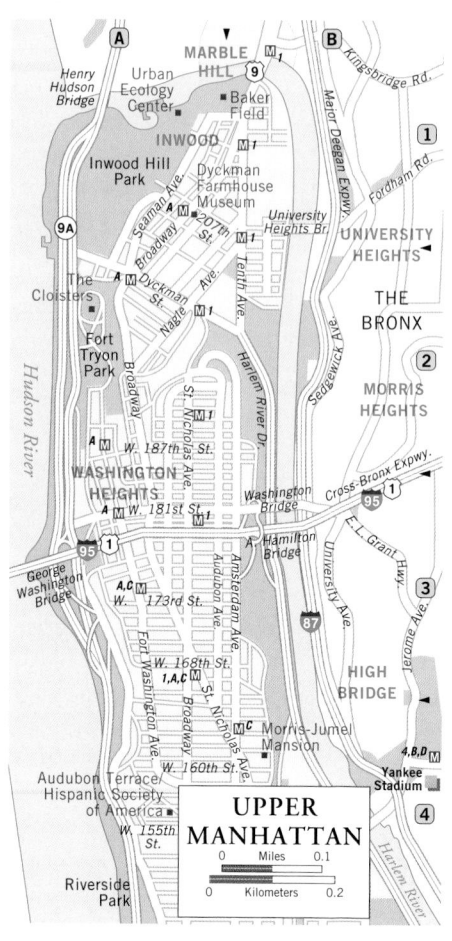

Jumel died, he left Bowen the mansion and a sizable fortune. She went on to marry and then immediately divorce Aaron Burr, her longtime beau. *1785 Jumel Terrace, at West 161st Street and Edgecombe Avenue; 212-923-8008.*

The townhouses, private residences, and row houses surrounding the Morris-Jumel Mansion lend the neighborhood a 19th-century feel. Jumel Terrace, Sylvan Terrace, and West 160th Street are worth a stroll just to soak in the atmosphere of a bygone era. This far north, Manhattan is barely 2,000 yards wide, and from the Morris-Jumel Mansion you can easily sight the **Highbridge Tower,** along the Harlem River at West 174th Street, once part of the city's water supply system.

■ EAST HARLEM *map page 268, C/D-3/4*

El Barrio means "the neighborhood" in Spanish, and East Harlem has had a large Hispanic population since just after World War II, when many Puerto Ricans moved to the city. The new arrivals displaced the residents of Italian Harlem and blended into black Harlem to the north and west.

El Museo del Barrio (1230 Fifth Avenue), the neighborhood's traditional anchor, is a cultural center as much as a museum (see page 245). The district that stretches north from here is a relatively flat area of housing projects, with schemes to exploit the Harlem River waterfront delayed in eternal planning stages. A literal bright spot is the footbridge to Wards Island, at East 103rd Street, which gets periodic coats of Day-Glo paint.

Just south of 125th Street, athwart Fifth Avenue, is **Marcus Garvey Memorial Park.** Marcus Garvey, the black nationalist of the early 20th century who founded a popular "back to Africa" movement, was long associated with Harlem: he had his offices here, and his followers conducted many parades and rallies in the area. Built around **Mount Morris,** which the Dutch called Snake Hill, the park named after

Taino: Ancient Voyagers of the Caribbean, *a permanent exhibition at El Museo del Barrio.*

him anchors a neighborhood of townhouses and churches. On top of Mount Morris is the city's only remaining fire tower, an elegant cast-iron concoction with a spiral staircase and bell, visible from all over the surrounding area.

■ WASHINGTON HEIGHTS AND INWOOD *map page 280, A-1/2*

Glance at a map of Manhattan and you'll see that the city's vaunted street grid system stutters and stops at West 179th Street, north of the approach to the George Washington Bridge. The hills of this part of Manhattan confounded the linear pattern planned for them. Broadway, a rogue thoroughfare in itself, makes a startling turn east. The northern tip of the island, a favorite haunt of the Algonquins, has been given over to wild parkland. It's as though the urban impulse had exhausted itself through too much exertion farther south.

The major boundary line for this neighborhood is the slash of the Cross-Bronx Expressway (here briefly and optimistically called the Trans-Manhattan Expressway), a habitually clotted artery that leads to the **George Washington Bridge.** The soaring suspension bridge architecturally rivals the Brooklyn Bridge as the finest link to Manhattan, and echoes the distant catenaries of the Verrazano-Narrows Bridge to the south. In this neighborhood, though, the bridge stands alone and steals the show, a marvel of engineering and design. Lighting on the interior of the bridge's towers shows off the structure to spectacular effect, and here you will see what is said to be the world's largest free-flying American flag.

When it was completed in 1931, the bridge had one level. The lower level, which New Yorkers snidely dubbed "Martha Washington," was added in 1962. A prime New York experience, but one not for the faint of heart, is to step across the pedestrian walkway, facing into the swirling winds of the harbor. Beneath the bridge, invisible to those who are rushing across it, is the Jeffries Hook Lighthouse, famous from the children's book, *The Little Red Lighthouse and the Great Gray Bridge,* by Hildegarde Hoyt Swift and Lynd Ward.

To the northeast of the bridge is swinging **Washington Heights.** The Dominican Republic has sent a wave of immigrants to New York City in recent years, and many of them have settled here, transforming the neighborhood. St. Nicholas Avenue near the 181st Street subway station throbs with color and life. You'll swear you're in Santo Domingo.

Fort Tryon Park, at West 192nd Street from Broadway to Riverside Drive (the entrance is on Fort Washington Street), graces the ridge of Washington Heights.

The George Washington Bridge crosses the Hudson River in Upper Manhattan.

Here, General Washington made his last stand against the Hessian troops who were dogging his footsteps north as he tried to move his army from New York in the fall of 1776. A Revolutionary War heroine was born during that battle, when Margaret Corbin took over her fallen husband's gun mount and fought for a full day before being wounded.

Fort Tryon Park is a gift to the public from the ubiquitous Mr. Rockefeller (John D. Sr., this time), in exchange for which the city did him a favor: it eliminated traffic thoroughfares through the campus of his Institute for Medical Research (later Rockefeller University). Beautiful flower gardens are what Fort Tryon is known for—that and for being the site of yet another Rockefeller bequest, the Cloisters.

■ THE CLOISTERS *map page 280, A-2*

What a few dollars will buy you: **the Cloisters,** part of the Metropolitan Museum of Art, is an assemblage of elements of medieval church architecture. Purchased by John D. Rockefeller Jr., the component parts were hauled over from France and

---

STRANGE CASE OF MARBLE HILL

When is Manhattan not Manhattan? When it's in the Bronx.

That's the bizarre predicament of Marble Hill, which used to be a proud part of Manhattan Island. In 1895, however, the Army Corps of Engineers rechanneled the meandering Spuyten Duyvil Creek, lopping off Marble Hill from the rest of Manhattan, joining it to the Bronx with landfill from the excavation for Grand Central Terminal. Politically, Marble Hill is still considered part of Manhattan. People living here vote in Manhattan elections and are considered residents of the borough. But geographically, Marble Hill is part of the South Bronx, a neighborhood betrayed by its stream.

Spain and reconstructed on the northern tip of Manhattan. J. P. Morgan's medieval art collection—rare pieces of incalculable value—was donated to the Metropolitan Museum in 1917 and is mostly housed here.

The one-two punch of Rockefeller and Morgan produced a serene refuge unlike any other museum in Manhattan. Even the grounds, meticulously planted with herbs and flowers, impart a sense of order and anachronism. Rockefeller also owned the land across the Hudson from Fort Tryon Park, so there are no messy developments to mar the spectacular river views.

The galleries follow one another in chronological order. The Unicorn Tapestries are brilliantly alive and justly celebrated, but the spectral sepulcher of Ermengol VII is impressive in a darker way. The Treasury has a book of hours that is one of the world's finest illuminated manuscripts. Other oddities in the Treasury—like a single rosary bead upon which the whole scene of the Passion of Christ is carved— demonstrate the strange medieval turn of mind. *West 190th Street and Fort Washington Avenue; 212-923-3700.*

Near the Cloisters is one of the few surviving symbols of Dutch Manhattan: the **Dyckman Farmhouse Museum.** The last 18th-century Dutch farmhouse on the island, it was rebuilt by William Dyckman in 1783 after the British burned the original during the Revolutionary War. A real plus is the interior, filled with Dyckman family furniture and other period pieces. The floor is made of varying widths of chestnut planks. *4881 Broadway, at 204th Street; 212-304-9422.*

The tower of the Cloisters rises above the trees in Fort Tryon Park.

BOROUGHS AND ISLANDS

We've gotten off on the wrong foot right from the start. The folks who live in the Bronx, Queens, Brooklyn, and Staten Island might take umbrage at the term "the boroughs." After all, Manhattan itself is a borough.

In the constantly shifting allegiances of New York City, Manhattan is a source of both resentment and pride to those who live in the "outer boroughs" (again, a Manhattan-centric phrase). They wince at the sneer that they're only "BTs": bridge and tunnel people. But the fact remains that when a Queens resident (or one from the Bronx, Brooklyn, or Staten Island) travels to Manhattan, he or she will often say, "I'm going into the City."

To many visitors, the other boroughs are known primarily by reputation, which is a shame, because each is characterized by such variety that it is difficult for any one rubric to encompass it. The boroughs are simply governmental jurisdictions—each borough is the equivalent of a county or parish. But political boundaries have hardened into stereotypes.

The Bronx, for example, is widely known for the urban wasteland of its southern tier—the rubble-strewn lots of such movies as *Fort Apache, the Bronx*. Yet the borough also has some of the most countrified neighborhoods in the city, suburban oases where raccoons are not unknown. **Queens** is stereotyped as a vast middle-class sprawl, "a little bit of Akron picked up and dumped in the middle of New York City," as Jimmy Breslin once wrote. But it also has ethnically mixed neighborhoods, like Astoria and Flushing.

Brooklyn is perhaps the most famous of the boroughs, or more accurately, the most famous borough from which to come. The "City of Churches" has played mother to a host of errant children, among them Woody Allen, Mel Brooks, Barbra Streisand, Eddie Murphy, Mae West, and Beverly Sills. Finally, **Staten Island** (or Richmond, as it is classically known), is the wallflower of the boroughs—but paradoxically, the first one to talk about leaving home. Home to Mafia dons and New York's largest garbage dump (the now-closed Fresh Kills landfill, the highest promontory on the Atlantic coastline), Staten Island is a region of calm amid the amphetamine hustle of New York City.

The pronounced focus of this book on Manhattan is not meant to indicate any lack of marvelous attractions in her sister boroughs. We'll plead space limitations, and point out that the sites of interest in the outer boroughs are spread out across the city's low-density sprawl. Here's a short inventory of the best of them, listed alphabetically by boroughs.

■ BEST OF THE BOROUGHS

■ THE BRONX

Bronx Zoo. Also known as the International Wildlife Conservation Park, this is one of the best zoos on the East Coast. Along with many in situ animal displays, the zoo has a monorail ride through an "Asian" forest and a great children's petting zoo. *Fordham Road and Bronx River Parkway; 718-367-1010.*

New York Botanical Garden. A lovely haven on the northern edge of the Bronx, the garden has special shows and exhibits throughout the year. *Southern Boulevard and 200th Street; 718-817-8705.*

Bronx Zoo is one of the East Coast's best menageries. (Wildlife Conservation Society)

Summer fun at the Redhook Recreation and Fitness Center in Brooklyn.

■ BROOKLYN

Brooklyn Botanic Garden. Near Prospect Park, the Brooklyn Library, and the Brooklyn Museum of Art, the garden is a walled enclave in the middle of the borough. *1000 Washington Avenue; 718-622-4433.*

Coney Island. Though this landmark has faded, some of the old rides are still here, and there's always the beach. *Take D subway train from Manhattan.*

New York Aquarium. With a population of twenty thousand aquatic creatures, headed up by performing dolphins, seals, and beluga whales, the aquarium isn't just a collection of fish tanks, but a spirited and energetic introduction to the wide world of sea life. *Surf Avenue at West Eighth Street, Coney Island; 718-265-3400.*

Prospect Park. With more than 500 acres, Prospect Park is another masterpiece from Olmsted and Vaux, the team that brought you Central Park. Wilder and more forested than Central Park, this park also has a great children-oriented zoo. *Take the 2 or 3 subway train to Grand Army Plaza.*

Cherry-blossom time. (Brooklyn Botanic Garden)

■ QUEENS

American Museum of the Moving Image. Television, video, and film are all heralded not far from where early movies were made. *36-01 35th Avenue, at 36th Street, Astoria; 718-784-0077.*

Isamu Noguchi Garden Museum. In the famed sculptor's former workshop, exhibits of his graceful, elegant sculpture are displayed in a loft and outdoor garden. The museum reopens in 2003. *32–37 Vernon Boulevard, Long Island City; 718-204-7088.*

MoMA QNS (Museum of Modern Art in Queens). While MoMA's main Manhattan facility undergoes a major reconstruction and expansion that will keep it closed until 2005, the museum is displaying many of MoMA's spectacular artworks in an old Swingline stapler factory, redesigned by architect Michael Maltzan. MoMA QNS also mounts major temporary exhibitions. *45-20 33rd Street, at Queens Boulevard (take the 7 subway train five stops from Grand Central Terminal and follow signs in station); 212-708-9400.*

P.S. 1 Contemporary Art Center. This MoMA affiliate showcases emerging and established talents in a space not far from MoMA QNS. *22–25 Jackson Avenue, at 46th Avenue; 718-784-2084.*

Visitors relax in the P.S. 1 courtyard during a summer event.

Queens Artlink. On Saturdays and Sundays, a shuttle bus loops between Manhattan and the major Queens arts institutions, including the American Museum of the Moving Image, MoMA QNS, the Noguchi Museum, and P.S. 1. *212-708-9750.*

World's Fair site. The ghost of the 1939 World's Fair still haunts this site, with the Unisphere from the 1964 reprise still standing. Check out the Queen's Museum of Art (718-592-2405), with its amazing New York Panorama—a small-scale reproduction of New York City. *Flushing Meadow–Corona Park, entrance at 49th Avenue and 111th Street, Flushing.*

■ STATEN ISLAND

Jacques Marchais Center for Tibetan Art. This gallery-size institution is a pearl hidden in the residential anonymity of Richmond. *338 Lighthouse Avenue; 718-987-3500.*

Richmondtown Restoration. This concentration of restored historical buildings dates from colonial and Revolutionary War times. Some activities—blacksmithing, milling, and carpentry, among them—are re-created by workers in period dress. *441 Clarke Avenue, at Arthur Kill Road; 718-351-1611.*

■ IN NEW JERSEY

Liberty Science Center. Okay, so it's not strictly in a New York borough, but it's just across the river in New Jersey, opposite the Statue of Liberty. This opulent museum, with intriguing exhibits, many of them interactive, is worth the journey, especially for youngsters. *Liberty State Park, 251 Phillip Street, Jersey City; 201-200-1000.*

■ OTHER ISLANDS

Test your knowledge of geography: Which of the five boroughs of New York City is not located on an island? Manhattan we know is, and Staten Island gives itself away. Of the other three, only the Bronx is on the mainland—Queens and Brooklyn represent the western extremity of Long Island.

Manhattan is surrounded by islands large and small. **Ellis and Liberty Islands** are covered in the Lower Manhattan chapter, but the rest are listed here. Some of them figure in area history, and some are just green flecks in the stream that prompt the occasional passerby to wonder, "What's that little island called?"

■ GOVERNORS ISLAND

Long the province of the U.S. Coast Guard, serene Governors Island will undergo major changes in the new millennium. The latest plan (though, as with all proposals in New York City, political maneuvering may kill the deal) is for the island to become a campus of the City University of New York. The island was called Nooten Eylandt (Nut Island) by the Dutch for the trees that grew there, and it was actually where the first colonizers settled—before they moved over to Manhattan. In 1698 it was set aside as a sort of personal bailiwick of New York's governors. Later, it was fortified with Castle Williams during the War of 1812. As with its twin, Castle Clinton in Battery Park, no shots were ever fired from here. The fort, nicknamed "the Cheesebox" and clearly visible from Lower Manhattan, was designed by Benjamin Franklin's nephew, Lieutenant Colonel Jonathan Williams, for whom Williamsburg, Brooklyn, is named.

■ ROOSEVELT ISLAND

It is not recorded what the Algonquins called the pencil of land in the East River, but European settlers named it Blackwell's Island, after a farm family who lived there from 1660 until 1828. Later on, as the city used it as a dumping ground for public works projects, it held a smallpox quarantine station, poorhouses, asylums, hospitals, and jails—thereby earning itself the appellation of Welfare Island.

But that much real estate that close to the East Side was too hard for developers to resist. You can still see the remains of the smallpox hospital at the island's southern tip, Manhattan's only landmarked ruin, and Blackwell's farmhouse has been preserved. The most salient features of Roosevelt Island today, though, are the residential developments erected, beginning in the 1970s, by New York State's Urban Development Corporation.

These came in two successive waves, representing Southtown and Northtown, and are connected by a vehicle-less thoroughfare called—of course—Main Street. In fact, although there is a bridge connecting Roosevelt Island with Queens, cars are relegated to a main garage (called Motorgate) and banned on island streets. Banned also are garbage trucks, due to Roosevelt's ingenious system of zapping its refuse from each apartment house to a central receiving station via pneumatic tubes.

One of the best things about Roosevelt Island is the ride over, via a Swiss-designed aerial tram that departs from East 60th Street and Second Avenue. One of Manhattan's cheapest thrills—it costs the same as a subway trip—the tram has been featured in several films, among them *Spider-Man*. The promenades that encircle the inhabited part of Roosevelt Island provide great views of the Upper East Side. On the northern tip of the island stands a lighthouse that was, legend has it, the work of an inmate of the insane asylum.

■ MILL ROCK

Due east of 96th Street in the East River, Mill Rock is less than an acre even at low tide, and identified on maps as a park. A park for whom, or what, is not explained. Seagulls, perhaps?

■ U THANT ISLAND

Opposite the United Nations in the East River, and originally called Belmont Island, this island was renamed in 1971 upon the retirement of the Secretary General of the United Nations, U Thant, who succeeded Dag Hammarskjold after the latter died in a plane crash. U Thant played a key role in lessening tensions between the United States and the Soviet Union during the Cuban missile crisis in 1962.

■ WARDS AND RANDALLS ISLANDS

These were originally two separate islands, but now they are joined by landfill. Most New Yorkers consider them simply part of the support structure for the Triborough Bridge, which crosses over Randalls. But Downing Stadium, on Randalls, hosts soccer meets and the annual Festival of San Juan, the patron saint of Puerto Rico. On Wards Island are the training center for the city's firefighters, the Manhattan Psychiatric Center, and perhaps the saddest structure in all Manhattan, the Children's Treatment Center for retarded, insane, and emotionally disturbed kids.

PRACTICAL INFORMATION

■ AREA CODES AND TIME ZONE

Manhattan's main area code is 212. The borough's other code is 646. The area codes in the Bronx, Brooklyn, Queens, and Staten Island are 718 and 347, and 917 is a citywide code. New York City is in the Eastern time zone.

■ METRIC CONVERSIONS

1 foot	=	.304 meters (m)
1 mile	=	1.6 kilometers (km)
1 acre	=	.4 hectares (ha)
1 pound	=	.45 kilograms (kg)

■ CLIMATE

Manhattan weather can be a study in extremes, especially during the sopping, muggy heat of August or the cold snaps of February. Yet the city is livable for long stretches of time. Manhattan's prime periods are fall and spring. September brings a palpable excitement over the dawn of a new cultural "season." In May there is the sense of having shucked off winter, and the street scenes become livelier.

■ GETTING THERE

■ BY AIR

Three major airports—John F. Kennedy International (JFK), La Guardia (LGA), and Newark (EWR)—serve New York City. At the Ground Transportation Center booths near the baggage claim areas of the airports' terminals, you can make reservations for buses and shared vans to the city and find out where to catch public transportation. *Call 800-247-7433 for information about ground transportation and the parking lots at all three airports.*

John F. Kennedy International Airport, in southern Queens, handles arrivals from other countries and some domestic flights. **New York Airport Service** (212-875-8200) operates buses from Kennedy to Grand Central Terminal, Pennsylvania Station, and other locations. A free shuttle bus (blue and yellow) to the Howard

| | AVERAGE MAXIMUM | | AVERAGE MINIMUM | |
	Fahrenheit	Centigrade	Fahrenheit	Centigrade
January	39°	4°	26°	-3°
February	40°	5°	27°	-3°
March	48°	8°	34°	1°
April	61°	16°	44°	6°
May	71°	21°	53°	11°
June	81°	27°	63°	17°
July	85°	29°	68°	19°
August	83°	28°	66°	18°
September	77°	25°	60°	16°
October	67°	19°	51°	10°
November	54°	12°	41°	5°
December	41°	5°	30°	-1°

Beach **subway** station stops at all terminals. (Catch the A train, which travels up Manhattan's West Side, stopping at Times Square and several other stations). Allow at least two hours to get to Midtown by subway. A **taxi ride** from Kennedy to Manhattan is a flat-fare $35, plus tolls and tip. **Gray Line Air Shuttle** (212-315-3006 or 800-451-0455) and **SuperShuttle** (212-258-3826) provide shared-van service. *718-244-4444, general information; 718-244-4168, parking.*

La Guardia Airport, in northern Queens, the most intimate airport and the closest in of the three, is near the Triborough Bridge, providing access to all areas of the city. **New York Airport Service** (212-875-8200) operates buses from La Guardia to Grand Central Terminal, Pennsylvania Station, and other locations. Buses connect to the the Main Street/Flushing **subway** station (Take the 7 train to Grand Central, Times Square, and other Midtown stops). A **taxi ride** from La Guardia to Midtown should cost between $25 and $30, including tolls and tip, depending on traffic. **Gray Line Air Shuttle** (212-315-3006 or 800-451-0455) and **SuperShuttle** (212-258-3826) provide shared-van service. *718-533-3400, general information; 718-533-3850, parking; 718-533-3766, ground transportation.*

Newark International Airport, in New Jersey, is an alternative for international and domestic arrivals, though it is farther from Manhattan than either La Guardia or Kennedy. The easiest way to get to Midtown is to catch the **Airtrain,** a direct New Jersey Transit (800-247-7433) connection between the airport and Pennsylvania Station. **Amtrak** (800-872-7245) also operates trains between the airport and Midtown, but tickets for these cost more than ones for the Airtrain. **Olympia Trails** (212-964-6233) runs buses between the airport and Grand Central Terminal, Pennsylvania Station, and other locations. Taxis are usually non-New York City cabs; it is best to establish the price beforehand. A ride to Midtown should cost between $40 and $50, plus tolls and tip. **Gray Line Air Shuttle** (212-315-3006 or 800-451-0455) and **SuperShuttle** (212-258-3826) provide shared-van service. *973-961-6000, general information; 973-961-4751, parking.*

■ By Bus

The **Port Authority Bus Terminal** (Eighth Avenue and West 42nd Street; 212-564-8484) has three dozen bus lines operating out of it. You can make connections at the terminal to many subway lines.

■ By Train

Amtrak (800-872-7245) trains serve Pennsylvania Station (Seventh Avenue and West 33rd Street). Commuter rail lines serve the metropolitan area from Pennsylvania Station and Grand Central Terminal (East 42nd Street and Park Avenue). They include Metro-North (212-532-4900), from Grand Central; and the Long Island Railroad (718-217-5477) and New Jersey Transit (973-762-5100) from Pennsylvania Station.

The trains of **PATH** (Port Authority Trans-Hudson; 800-234-7284), a commuter line, connect New Jersey (Hoboken, Jersey City, and Newark) with Manhattan's West Side (stations along Sixth Avenue at 33rd, 23rd, 14th, Ninth, and Christopher Streets).

■ By Car

Don't bring one. Fleets of taxis wait to take you wherever you want to go; limousines are at your beck and call. Parking in a garage is expensive. Parking on the street is a nightmare. If you must drive, traffic reports are available on WINS (1010 AM). Driving on Manhattan streets is not for the timid.

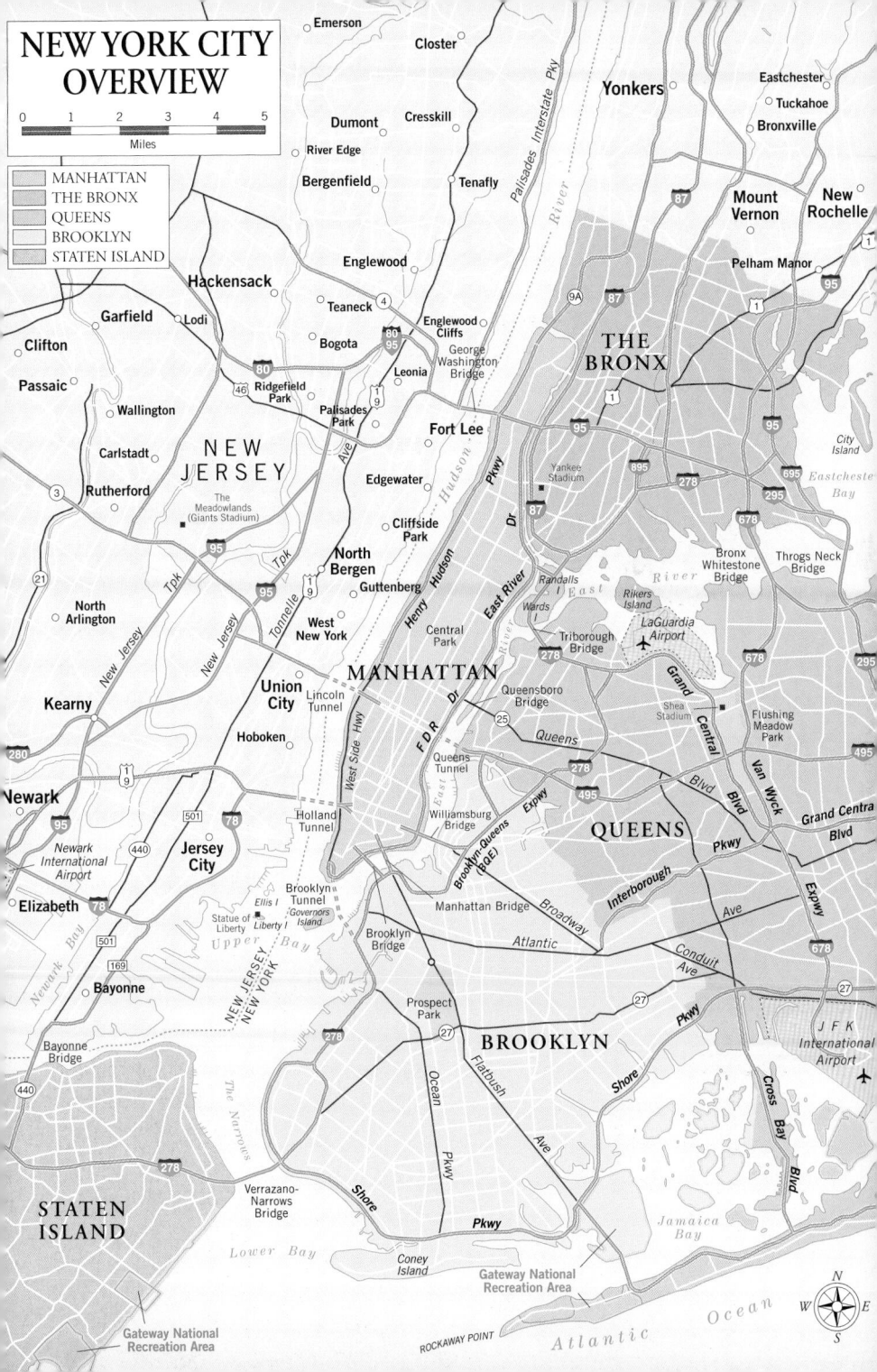

■ Getting Around

■ By Subway

The subway is cheap, reliable, and the most convenient way to traverse the city. Subway trains will get you to most of the major attractions. Though riding the subway is relatively safe, you must take precautions. It's a good idea not to wear flashy jewelry, and late at night you should ride near the middle car, where the conductor sits. MetroCards (good for a ride plus a bus transfer within two hours) and tokens are available at the stations, as are subway maps. A good bargain for visitors is the one-day "Fun Pass" or the one-week MetroCard. You can buy MetroCards in vending machines at most stations and at toll booths and shops. *212-330-1234.*

■ By Taxi

Today's taxi driver is sometimes a newly arrived immigrant, experiencing difficulty with both English and the layout of the city streets. But drivers are just as likely to be consummate professionals who have been driving all their lives. For safety's sake and in case you leave something behind, it's a good idea to note the medallion number of the taxi you are getting into, prominently displayed on the rooftop light. The rooftop light also indicates whether the cab is available (when the middle portion is lit), occupied (the light is off), or off-duty (off-duty light is on). There are some areas of Midtown, such as Grand Central Terminal, where taxis may stop only in specified zones. From 8 P.M. to 6 A.M. there is a 50-cent surcharge. *212-221-8294 (NYC Taxi and Limousine Commission).*

■ By Car/Livery Service

Though not allowed to pick up street hails, livery cab drivers often do. Legally, drivers of yellow cabs may not refuse to take you anywhere within the boroughs or Westchester and Nassau Counties, or to Newark International Airport, but it can be difficult to get a yellow cab to take you to an outlying address. Livery cabs serve many neighborhoods that yellow cabs decline to tread.

■ By Bus

New York City has an extensive bus service, slower than the subway but a great way to view the passing parade of New York life. Tokens, MetroCards, or exact change are required, and paper bills are not accepted. *718-330-1234.*

Riding the new luxury-lighted subway train, 1950. (Library of Congress)

■ ACCOMMODATIONS

There is no feeling in the world like checking into a Manhattan hotel, with evening about to unfold, lights switching on in buildings outside your window, and room service on the way. In recent years, a revolution has occurred in Manhattan hostelries—several revolutions, as a matter of fact. Both the type and location of places to stay in the city have increased. You'll have plenty of choice about where to stay and how you'll be pampered.

The city's classic hotel district is just north of Times Square. If you're planning your first visit to Manhattan around the Broadway theater experience and excursions to Rockefeller Center and the Empire State Building, a Times Square–area lodging could be your best bet.

Some hotels, like the **Algonquin Hotel** (59 West 44th Street, near Fifth Avenue; 212-840-6800), just east of Times Square, have moved beyond the level of mere accommodation to that of myth. No hotel lobby bar in the city is more comfortable for cocktails and chatting than the Algonquin's, with its deep armchairs and the echoes of Dorothy Parker's Round Table laughter.

Hotelier Ian Schrager pioneered the boutique hotel concept with his Philippe Starck–designed **Paramount** (235 West 46th Street, near Broadway; 212-764-5500), following it up with the **Royalton** (44 West 44th Street, at Fifth Avenue; 212-869-4400). The idea was that high design could elevate a small hotel to world-class status—or at least attract beautiful people to its bars and restaurants.

But Manhattan's new hotel landscape means there are offerings in almost every neighborhood, and the traveler need not be limited to Times Square. The **SoHo Grand** (310 West Broadway, at Canal Street; 212-965-3000) led the charge into SoHo, venturing into what was previously a no-rooms-at-the-inn wasteland and becoming instantly hip in the process. The **Mercer Hotel** (147 Mercer Street, at Prince Street; 212-966-6060) is a more recent but equally upscale addition. If shopping and experiencing SoHo or neighboring TriBeCa are your aim—or if business will take you farther downtown, but the business-oriented hotels of Lower Manhattan are not to your liking—then the SoHo Grand or the Mercer would be a good choice.

If your axis will be more uptown, say, along Museum Mile, try the older, more established **Stanhope** (995 Fifth Avenue, at East 81st Street; 212-288-5800). For a slightly hipper ambience, cop a chic suite at the **Mark** (25 East 77th Street, at Madison Avenue; 212-744-4300).

Contrary to popular belief, there are affordable and even what might be termed budget accommodations in Manhattan. The **Carlton Arms** (160 East 25th Street, at Lexington Avenue; 212-679-0680) is known as a poor man's **Chelsea Hotel** (see page 144), if you can imagine that, with many rooms decorated by local artists. You have to share a bathroom at the **Larchmont** (27 West 11th Street, near Fifth Avenue; 212-989-9333), but the hotel is handsomely appointed and centrally located in Greenwich Village. The YMCA is another good option; the two best Y's are the **Vanderbilt YMCA** (224 East 47th Street, near Third Avenue; 212-756-9600) and the **YMCA West Side** (5 West 63rd Street, at Central Park West; 212-875-4100). And the hostel option is alive and well in Manhattan, if a little more expensive than in other parts of the world: try the **Chelsea International Hostel** (251 West 20th Street, near Eighth Avenue; 212-647-0010).

For more lodging suggestions, visit www.fodors.com/nyc. Below are some hotel and motel chains that operate in Manhattan:

■ HOTEL AND MOTEL CHAINS

Best Western. *800-528-1234; www.bestwestern.com*
Days Inn. *800-329-7466; www.daysinn.com*
Doubletree. *800-222-8733; www.doubletree.com*
Four Seasons. *800-332-3443; www.fourseasons.com*
Hilton. *800-445-8667; www.hiltons.com*
Holiday Inn. *800-465-4329; www.6c.com*
Hyatt. *800-233-1234; www.hyatt.com*
Inter-Continental. *800-327-0200; www.interconti.com*
Marriott. *800-228-9290; www.marriott.com*
Radisson. *800-333-3333; www.radisson.com*
Ramada Inn. *800-272-6232; www.ramada.com*
Renaissance. *888-236-2427; www.marriott.com*
Ritz-Carlton. *800-241-3333; www.ritzcarlton.com*
Sheraton. *800-325-3535; www.sheraton.com*
Travelodge. *800-835-2424; www.travelodge.com*
W Hotels. *877-946-8357; www.whotels.com*
Westin Hotels. *800-228-3000; www.westin.com*

■ Dining

New Yorkers just love food, whether standing up, sitting down, eating in, ordering out, or taking out to eat in the park. You can actually find people eating while they walk, which most of the world finds completely disgusting. People think it's because New Yorkers are in a rush—it's not. New Yorkers just don't want to stop. They don't want to stop eating. —Hal Rubenstein, *New York* magazine restaurant critic

Along with talking and making money, consuming food is part of Manhattan's holy trinity. It was always thus: when you hear stories of Diamond Jim Brady devouring twenty-six dozen oysters in one sitting (along with various steaks, chops, and fowls), and that his prowess with a knife and fork somehow translated into renown as a gambler, satyr, and bon vivant, you know the 19th century was not for the gustatorily timid.

Like Diamond Jim shoveling it in, New York is a great consumer not only of food but of cuisines. There is no such thing as "New York food" or a "Manhattan" restaurant in the way a place can be a French restaurant. That's because all food — from French *cordon bleu* to Jamaican jerk chicken—is New York food. New York's trademark eats, the bagel and the knish, are products of an immigrant culture. Some folks insist you cannot get a good version of either west of the Hudson. Even something as foreign to New York as California cuisine has found a home here—and not a few artful practitioners.

Manhattan knows all, embraces all. The "foodies" of the island sniff out new trends and are on them like white on rice. Not for nothing was the *Zagat Guide* born here, a kind of gourmet grapevine in book form, wherein restaurants are voted upon by those who actually patronize them, and the consensus is tabulated as if the process were a political election or a popularity contest.

In a sense, it is. When Chinese food grabbed the attention of food trendies in the 1970s, the Asian community suddenly found that restaurant jobs were plentiful, and there was a resulting infusion of money into the immigrant community. Even the rats in Chinatown got plumper. The stomach, as Bertolt Brecht pointed out, is a political organ.

Mostly, Manhattan avoids the garnish and goes straight for the main course. Street food is a prime anomaly of the island, not found to such a degree elsewhere, not even in the other boroughs. Italian, Chinese, Korean, Thai, Indian, soul,

Japanese, Jewish, Ukrainian, Mexican, Tex-Mex, and even such unlikely but delicious New York–bred amalgams as Cuban-Chinese all crowd the island with heady flavors. The city's French restaurants have long been justly hailed as among the best in the world.

■ Authors' Favorite Restaurants

The following are a few cherished favorites of ours—restaurants with great food, atmosphere, or both. The prices listed below are meant to be a general guide and are for a three-course meal for one, excluding drinks and tip.

$ = under $10   **$$** = $10–$20   **$$$** = $20–$35   **$$$$** = $35–$50   **$$$$$** = over $50

Aquavit. It's hard to decide which is more magnificent at this restaurant—the superbly crafted modern Scandinavian meals or the austerely modernist setting inside Nelson Rockefeller's spacious townhouse. *13 West 54th Street, at Fifth Avenue; 212-307-7311. Scandinavian* **$$$$$**

Le Bernardin. For those who don't believe that food preparation is an art, we recommend a dinner here. It's sure to make a believer out of you. The freshest of seafood dishes are prepared in this kitchen, often in the most imaginative ways. The brilliant desserts are meant to be lingered over. *155 West 51st Street, at Avenue of the Americas, Midtown; 212-489-1515. French/Eclectic* **$$$$$**

Boathouse Café. Location is everything, and you can't beat this restaurant's view of the rowboats on the Lake. *East Park Drive and East 72nd Street, Central Park; 212-517-3623. American* **$$$**

Brasserie. This is one of the city's best bistros, with a stellar interior design by Diller and Scofidio. *100 East 53rd Street, at Park Avenue, Midtown; 212-751-4840. Eclectic* **$$**

Café Con Leche. The oxtail stew is heaven at this upscale version of the Dominican coffee shop. *424 Amsterdam Avenue, at West 81st Street, Upper West Side; 212-595-7000. Caribbean* **$$$**

Café des Artistes. See sidebar on page 256. *Hotel des Artistes, 1 West 67th Street, at Central Park West, Upper West Side; 212-877-3500. Continental.* **$$$$**

Café Un Deux Trois. Crowded and urbane, this classic café serves basic *frites*-style bistro food to pre- and post-theater crowds. *123 West 44th Street, at Avenue of the Americas, Midtown; 212-354-4148. French/Eclectic* **$$**

Carnegie Deli. Is that a Buick or a sandwich? Huge portions of classic fare are served at this survivor of the eternal deli wars. *854 Seventh Avenue, at West 54th Street, Midtown; 212-757-2245. Deli* **$–$$**

Chumley's. You slip into this former speakeasy through the unmarked Bedford Street entrance. Blazing fireplaces, decent pub grub, and sawdust on the floor transport you decades back. On the walls are book jackets by F. Scott Fitzgerald and many other famous authors who wrote or ate here. *86 Bedford Street, near Seventh Avenue, West Village; 212-675-4449. American/Tavern* **$$**

Florent. A lifeline tossed into the black sea of late-night club-crawlers, this bistro remains the hit of the meat market. *69 Gansevoort Street, near Washington Street, West Village; 212-989-5779. French* **$$$**

Four Seasons. The service here is grand yet effortless, and the menu is cool enough to satisfy the many power-broker patrons. The beaded window curtains undulate, the ice rattles in your glass, and waiters lay down delectable seasonal offerings. *99 East 52nd Street, at Park Avenue, Midtown; 212-754-9494. Eclectic* **$$$$$** *(prix fixe* **$$$***)*

Gray's Papaya. Some New Yorkers say the franks here are better than filet mignon. Know what? For the price, they are. Outlets of the chain can be found all over Manhattan. *2090 Broadway, at West 72nd Street, Upper West Side; 212-799-0243. American/Casual* **$**

Grand Central Oyster Bar and Restaurant. See sidebar on page 174. *Grand Central Terminal, Dining Concourse Level, East 42nd Street, Midtown; 212-490-6650. Seafood* **$–$$$$**

Il Vagabondo. It's a little weird having a boccie court in a restaurant, but it is fun. Get a table in the narrow dining room beside the court, and after the regulars leave, toss a few balls yourself. *351 East 62nd Street, at Second Avenue, Upper East Side; 212-832-9221. Italian* **$$**

Luna's. This old standby has great pastas. Be prepared to stand in line. *112 Mulberry Street, Little Italy; 212-226-8657. Italian* **$$**

Odeon. Andy Warhol and friends made this late-night bistro famous back in the 1970s. It still cooks. *145 West Broadway, near Duane Street, TriBeCa; 212-233-0507. French/American* **$$$**

Raoul's. Classy, intimate, and energetic, Raoul's offers straightforward French cuisine. *180 Prince Street, at Sullivan Street, SoHo; 212-966-3518. French* **$$$**

Sucelt. Boxes of sugarcane are stacked up in the corner of this shoebox-size counter spot. You can order one of ten or more different tamales, a hearty soup, or the quivering octopus salad, but leave room for the fruit shake called a *batido*. *200 West 14th Street, at Sixth Avenue, West Village; 212-242-0593. Central American* **$**

Sun Lok Kee. For years it was known only as "the fish place" where Mayor Ed Koch had to be Heimliched out of his pork chow mein. The sign outside is new, but the Cantonese seafood is as magnificent as ever. The mussels in black bean sauce are good, but try the kang poi steak too. *13 Mott Street, near Pell Street, Chinatown; 212-732-7295. Chinese* **$**

Supreme Macaroni Co. This atmospheric hideaway sells groceries up front and serves delicious pasta in a restaurant in back. *511 Ninth Avenue, at West 38th Street, Midtown; 212-502-4842. Italian* **$$**

Sylvia's Restaurant. One bite of the fall-off-the-bone ribs and you'll know why this place is a New York institution. *328 Malcolm X Boulevard (Lenox Avenue), at West 126th Street, Harlem; 212-996-0660. American* **$$$**

"21" Club. In the 1920s, "21" was a swank speakeasy; now it's where Midtown movers and shakers chow down and chew the fat. *21 West 52nd Street, at Fifth Avenue, Midtown; 212-582-7200. American* **$$$$**

Two Boots. The "two boots" are Louisiana and Italy, whose cuisines are blended in dishes like spicy crawfish-topped pizza. Kids are welcome here. *37 Avenue A, at East Third Street, East Village; 212-505-2276. Cajun/Italian* **$**

Union Square Café. See sidebar on page 139. *21 East 16th Street, between Fifth Avenue and Union Square West; 212/243-4020. American* **$**

Veselka. Generations of bohemians have filled up on the hearty food here. *144 Second Avenue, at East Ninth Street, East Village; 212-228-9682. Ukrainian* **$**

■ MUSEUMS

For descriptions of Manhattan's most famous museums—the Frick Collection, Metropolitan Museum of Art, Whitney, Guggenheim, and others—see the index or the "Museum Mile" section in the Upper East Side chapter (see page 233).

American Academy of Arts and Letters. *Audubon Terrace, Broadway and West 155th Street, Upper Manhattan; 212-368-5900.*

American Craft Museum. *40 West 53rd Street, near Fifth Avenue, Midtown; 212-956-3535.*

American Folk Art Museum. *45 West 53rd Street, near Avenue of the Americas, Midtown; 212-265-1040.*

American Museum of the Moving Image. *35th Avenue at 36th Street, Astoria, Queens; 718-784-0077.*

American Museum of Natural History. *Central Park West and West 79th Street, Upper West Side; 212-769-5100.*

American Numismatic Society. *Audubon Terrace, Broadway and West 155th Street, Upper Manhattan; 212-234-3130.*

Asia Society and Museum. *725 Park Avenue, at East 70th Street, Upper East Side; 212-288-6400.*

Brooklyn Museum of Art. *200 Eastern Parkway, Brooklyn; 718-638-5000.*

Children's Museum of Manhattan. *212 West 83rd Street, at Broadway, Upper West Side; 212-721-1223.*

China Institute Gallery. *125 East 65th Street, at Lexington Avenue, Upper East Side; 212-744-8181.*

The Cloisters. *Fort Tryon Park, West 190th Street and Fort Washington Avenue, Upper Manhattan; 212-923-3700.*

Cooper-Hewitt National Design Museum. *2 East 91st Street, at Fifth Avenue, Upper East Side; 212-849-8400.*

Dahesh Museum. *601 Fifth Avenue, at East 48th Street, Midtown; 212-759-0606.*

Dia Center for the Arts. *548 West 22nd Street, Chelsea; 212-989-5566.*

Ellis Island Museum of Immigration. *New York Harbor; 212-363-3200.*

Federal Hall National Memorial. *26 Wall Street, at Nassau Street, Lower Manhattan; 212-825-6888.*

Forbes Magazine Galleries. *62 Fifth Avenue, at West 12th Street, West Village; 212-206-5548.*

Fraunces Tavern Museum. *54 Pearl Street, at Broad Street, Lower Manhattan; 212-425-1778.*

Frick Collection. *1 East 70th Street, at Fifth Avenue, Upper East Side; 212-288-0700.*

Guggenheim (Solomon R. Guggenheim) Museum. *1071 Fifth Avenue, at East 88th Street, Upper East Side; 212-423-3500.*

Hispanic Society of America. *Audubon Terrace, Broadway at West 155th Street, Upper Manhattan; 212-926-2234.*

International Center of Photography. *1133 Avenue of the Americas, at West 43rd Street, Midtown; 212-860-1777.*

***Intrepid* Sea-Air-Space Museum.** *Pier 86, West 46th Street at the Hudson River, Midtown; 212-245-2533.*

Isamu Noguchi Garden Museum. *32-37 Vernon Boulevard, Long Island City, Queens; 718-204-7088. (Reopens at this location in 2003.)*

Jacques Marchais Museum of Tibetan Art. *338 Lighthouse Avenue, Staten Island; 718-987-3500.*

Jewish Museum. *1109 Fifth Avenue, at East 92nd Street, Upper East Side; 212-423-3200.*

Lower East Side Tenement Museum. *97 Orchard Street, at Broome Street, Lower East Side; 212-431-0233.*

Metropolitan Museum of Art. *Fifth Avenue and East 82nd Street, Upper East Side; 212-535-7710.*

MoMA QNS *(Museum of Modern Art).* *45-20 33rd Street, at Queens Boulevard, Queens; 212-708-9400.*

Morgan Library. *29 East 36th Street, at Madison Avenue, Murray Hill; 212-685-0610.*

Mount Vernon Hotel Museum and Garden. *421 East 61st Street, at First Avenue, Upper East Side; 212-838-6878.*

El Museo del Barrio. *1230 Fifth Avenue, at East 104th Street, Upper East Side; 212-831-7272.*

Museum at FIT *(Fashion Institute of Technology). 27 West 27th Street, at Seventh Avenue, Chelsea; 212-217-5970.*

Museum for African Art. *593 Broadway, at Prince Street, SoHo; 212-966-1313.*

Museum of American Financial History. *28 Broadway, south of Morris Street, Lower Manhattan; 212-908-4519.*

Museum of Chinese in the Americas. *70 Mulberry Street, Second Floor, Chinatown; 212-619-4785.*

Museum of the City of New York. *1220 Fifth Avenue, at East 103rd Street, Upper East Side; 212-534-1672.*

Museum of Jewish Heritage. *18 First Place, at Battery Place, Battery Park City; 212-509-6130.*

Museum of Modern Art. *11 West 53rd Street, at Fifth Avenue, Midtown; 212-708-9400. (Closed until 2005; see MoMA QNS, above.)*

Museum of Television and Radio. *25 West 52nd Street, at Fifth Avenue, Midtown; 212-621-6800.*

National Museum of the American Indian. *Alexander Hamilton U.S. Custom House, 1 Bowling Green, at State Street, Lower Manhattan; 212-514-3700.*

National Academy of Design. *1083 Fifth Avenue, at East 89th Street, Upper East Side; 212-369-4880.*

Neue Galerie. *1048 Fifth Avenue, at East 86th Street, Upper East Side; 212-628-6200.*

New Museum of Contemporary Art. *583 Broadway, at Prince Street, SoHo; 212-219-1355.*

New York City Fire Museum. *278 Spring Street, at Varick Street, SoHo; 212-691-1303.*

New York City Police Museum. *100 Old Slip, at Front Street, Lower Manhattan; 212-480-3100.*

New-York Historical Society. *170 Central Park West, at West 77th Street, Upper West Side; 212-873-3400.*

New York Unearthed. *17 State Street, at Pearl Street, Lower Manhattan; 212-748-8628.*

Old Merchant's House Museum. *29 East Fourth Street, at Lafayette Street, East Village; 212-777-1089.*

Onassis Cultural Center. *Olympic Tower, 645 Fifth Avenue, at East 51st Street; 212-486-4448.*

Schomburg Center for Research in Black Culture. *515 Malcolm X Boulevard (Lenox Avenue), at West 135th Street, Harlem; 212-491-2200.*

Skyscraper Museum. *Ritz-Carlton New York, Battery Park, 2 West Street, Lower Manhattan; 212-344-0800.*

Society of Illustrators' Museum of American Illustration. *128 East 63rd Street, at Park Avenue, Upper East Side; 212-838-2560.*

Sony Wonder Technology Lab. *550 Madison Avenue, at East 56th Street, Midtown; 212-833-5414.*

South Street Seaport Museum. *Fulton and South Streets, Lower Manhattan; 212-669-9400.*

Studio Museum in Harlem. *144 West 125th Street, at Malcolm X Boulevard, Harlem; 212-864-4500.*

Theodore Roosevelt Birthplace. *28 East 20th Street, at Park Avenue South, Gramercy Park; 212-260-1616.*

Ukrainian Museum. *203 Second Avenue, at East 12th Street, East Village; 212-228-0110.*

Urban Center Galleries. *457 Madison Avenue, at East 50th Street, Midtown; 212-935-3960.*

Whitney Museum of American Art. *945 Madison Avenue, at East 75th Street, Upper East Side; 212-570-3676.*

Whitney Museum of American Art at Philip Morris. *120 Park Avenue, at East 42nd Street, Midtown; 212-570-3600.*

Yeshiva University Museum. *2520 Amsterdam Avenue at West 185th Street, Upper Manhattan; 212-960-5390.*

Yankee Stadium, baseball's most hallowed playing field. (New York Yankees)

■ SPORTS

Sports in Manhattan—sports in New York in general—are a serious bone of contention, ever since the Brooklyn Dodgers baseball team decamped for Los Angeles. It started a rout: the New York Giants baseball team left the Polo Grounds in Harlem for the West Coast, and football's "New York" Giants and "New York" Jets play in New Jersey.

Despite these betrayals, New York is a major sports town, a place with rabid fans and foaming-at-the-mouth columnists and commentators. Dial up WFAN (660 AM), an all-sports radio station, and a sampling of the call-in shows will reveal the depth of passion for local teams.

For one thing, there will always be the **Knicks.** The New York Knickerbockers basketball team plays in **Madison Square Garden** (Seventh Avenue and West 32nd Street; 212-465-6741) in front of highly visible VIPs and a full house of thunderous fans.

The **New York Rangers** ice hockey team, popular despite their ups and downs, also plays at the Garden (obviously, never on the same nights as the Knicks).

The Bronx Bombers, aka the **New York Yankees** (718-293-4300), continue to hold forth in that classic piece of baseball architecture, **Yankee Stadium** (West 161st Street and River Avenue, the Bronx; from Manhattan, take the 4 subway train from the East Side or the D subway from the West Side.)

The **New York Mets** (718-507-8499) play at **Shea Stadium** (Roosevelt Avenue and 126th Street, Flushing, Queens; take the 7 subway train to the Willets Point/Shea Stadium stop), beneath the thunderous flyovers from nearby La Guardia Airport.

The **U.S. Open Tennis Championships** take place in late August and early September, also under the La Guardia flight path at Flushing Meadow Park, next door to Shea Stadium. A much-heralded agreement, brokered by then-mayor David Dinkins, a major tennis buff, reroutes jets during the tournament. To get to the **U.S.T.A. National Tennis Center** (Flushing Meadow Park, Queens; 718-760-6200), take the 7 subway train to the Willets Point/Shea Stadium stop.

The most serious single sports event is probably the **New York City Marathon** (212-860-4455), run on the first Sunday in November. The course kicks off on the Staten Island side of the Verrazano-Narrows Bridge, enters Manhattan over the Queensboro Bridge, arcs briefly into the Bronx, and finishes in Central Park.

■ Major Performance Spaces

Beacon Theater. Jazz, pop, rock, hip-hop, and other acts play at this Art Deco space that opened as a vaudeville hall in 1928. *2124 Broadway, at West 74th Street, Upper West Side; 212-496-7070.*

Carnegie Hall. You don't have to practice, practice, practice (the answer to the old question, "How do you get to Carnegie Hall?") to hear a symphony here. *57th Street, at Seventh Avenue, Midtown; 212-247-7800.*

Joyce Theater. The premier space for modern dance hosts local and visiting companies. *175 Eighth Avenue, at West 19th Street, Chelsea; 212-242-0800.*

Knitting Factory. This adventurous venue books an eclectic mix of music, theater, film, and performance art. *74 Leonard Street, TriBeCa; 212-219-3006.*

Lincoln Center for the Performing Arts. Go for Verdi at the Metropolitan Opera House, *The Nutcracker* at the New York State Theater, a string quartet at Alice Tully Hall, the New York Philharmonic at Avery Fisher Hall, or an

MANHATTAN CALENDAR – 30 DAYS OF FUN

1

Tour the Statue of Liberty and Ellis Island

Wander Orchard Street, taste some treats at Economy Candy

Dinner at Sun Lok Kee in Chinatown

2

Wander through Village; check out street performers in Washington Square

Shop for shoes along Eighth Street

Mingle with the hip set at meat-packing district hot spots

3

Metropolitan Museum of Art, European Painting

Tea at the Plaza hotel's Palm Court

Window shop on Fifth Avenue

Dinner at Aquavit

4

Sip a manhattan at the Algonquin

See the Rockettes at Radio City

Dinner at Le Cirque 2000

5

Visit the observatory at the Empire State Building

Shop at Macy's

See the Knicks (or the Liberty in summer) at Madison Square Garden

6

Breakfast at H & H Bagels

American Museum of Natural History

New York City Ballet at Lincoln Center

7

Visit Teddy Roosevelt's birthplace

Stroll around Gramercy Park

Lunch at Union Square Café

Off-Broadway show

8

Browse Strand Bookstore for a few hours

Architectural tour of Madison Square Park

Evening performance at the Knitting Factory

Late-night dinner at Odeon

9

Visit Cathedral Church of St. John the Divine

Oxtail stew at Café Con Leche

Wander the Columbia University campus

Dinner at Terrace in the Sky

10

Stroll the Village

Visit Three Lives bookstore

Tea at Cornelia Street Café

Evening of jazz on Bleecker Street

11

Early morning visit to flower market, Chelsea

Visit the Whitney Museum

Dinner at the Russian Tea Room

Carnegie Hall concert

12

Stroll East Village and Tompkins Square Park

Performance at Public Theater or New York Theater Workshop

Late-night vittles at Veselka

13

Metropolitan Museum of Art, American wing

Pastrami on rye at Carnegie Deli

Broadway show

14

Visit Abyssinian Baptist Church gospel choir

Brunch at Sylvia's

Walk along the Meer in Central Park

It's show time at the Apollo

15

Walk the esplanade of the Brooklyn Bridge

View American paintings at the Brooklyn Museum of Art

Dinner at Korean barbecue in Little Korea

16

Midtown skyscraper blitz: tour Chrysler and Seagram Buildings, Lever House, Sony Building, and Trump Tower

Row a boat on the Lake in Central Park

Dinner at Jean Georges

Metropolitan Opera

17

Tour Neue Galerie

Lunch at Café Sabarsky

View period rooms at the Museum of the City of New York

Relax in the Conservatory Garden

Dinner at the Boathouse Café

18

Bus tour of Harlem

Late-afternoon drinks at Café des Artistes

New York Philharmonic performance

19

Tour St. Patrick's Cathedral

Brunch at Tavern on the Green

Stroll through Central Park to the zoo

Dinner at Hard Rock Café

20

Tour the United Nations

Lunch at the Oyster Bar, Grand Central Terminal

Shop at Bloomingdale's

Drinks at Michael's Pub

21

Wander Upper West Side

Buy mysteries at Murder, Inc.

Dinner at Ouest

22

Tour the New York Stock Exchange

Lunch at Fraunces Tavern

Drinks at South Street Seaport

Dinner in Chinatown

23

See the art at MoMA QNS

Snack on soup dumplings in Flushing's Chinatown

Wander the World's Fair site, view New York panorama

Dinner at Brasserie

24

Take the tram to Roosevelt Island and back

Tour Rockefeller Center

Watch David Letterman taping

25

American Craft Museum

Shop Fifth Avenue

Hear Bobby Short at the Carlyle

26

Visit Chelsea galleries

Art flick at Film Forum

Dinner at Florent

27

Frick Collection

Seafood dinner at Le Bernardin

Off-Off-Broadway show

28

Visit the Cloisters

Eat Cuban-Chinese in Inwood

Late night performance at Fez

29

Crash on couch; order in

30

Fly home

outdoor concert at the Damrosch Park open-air bandshell. Afterward, linger by the fountain in the center of it all. *Broadway between West 62nd and West 66th Streets, Upper West Side; 212-875-5000.*

Madison Square Garden. Concerts, circuses, dog shows, and tractor pulls. *Seventh Avenue and West 32nd Street, Garment District; 212-465-6741.*

Peter Norton Symphony Space. Two old movie houses were converted into this excellent venue for dance, music, film, theater, and lectures. *2537 Broadway, at West 95th Street; 212-864-1414.*

P.S. 122. This space inside a former city school hosts challenging dance and performance art. *150 First Avenue, at East Ninth Street; 212-477-5288.*

Radio City Music Hall. If you're in the mood for Julio Iglesias or Bette Midler, this is where they'd take Manhattan. The Rockettes perform at Christmas. *1260 Avenue of the Americas, at West 50th Street, Midtown; 212-247-4777.*

Theater at Madison Square Garden. A medium-size concert venue that's much loved by former superstars and up-and-coming talents. *Seventh Avenue and West 32nd Street, Garment District; 212-465-6741.*

■ TOURS

Big Onion Walking Tours. Architectural and cultural tours, including gastronomical challenges like the Multi-Ethnic Eating Tour. *212-439-1090.*

Central Park Rangers. The rangers' tours of Central Park are an ideal way to discover and enjoy Manhattan's greatest public space. *212-628-2345.*

Circle Line Cruises. You can cruise all or part of the way around Manhattan on these famous boats. *212-563-3200.*

Downtown Alliance. This business group sponsors a free ninety-minute Wall Street Walking Tour twice a week. *212-566-6700, ext. 5.*

Gray Line of New York. Doubledecker-bus tours of Manhattan. *212-397-2600.*

Harlem Gospel & Jazz Tours. See Harlem's major sights and listen to great music. *212-757-0425.*

Municipal Art Society. Superb schedule of bus and walking tours, concentrating on architecture and history. *212-935-3960.*

Radical Walking Tours of New York. Leftist take on the city. *718-492-0069.*

■ INFORMATION RESOURCES

For hotel and event listings, travel packages, and brochures, contact **NYC & Company** (810 Seventh Avenue, at West 52nd Street; 212-484-1222; www.nycvisit.com), run by the New York City Convention and Visitors Bureau. Another good resource is the **Times Square Information Center** (1560 Broadway, at West 46th Street; www.timessquarebid.org/visitor), which provides advice, brochures, and Internet access, and has rest rooms, a newsstand, an MTA booth where you can buy MetroCards and get transit information, and a machine that exchanges ten foreign currencies for dollars.

New York is the ultimate media town, and there are plenty of publications that can give you the skinny on what's happening on a daily or weekly basis. At present, there are three major dailies in town, although that may change according to the whims of union contracts and the depth of investors' pockets. The *New York Times* presents itself as "the paper of record," and though there are a few gaps, it generally lives up to the billing. The city's high-profile tabloids include the *Daily News* and the *New York Post.* All three major dailies have extensive listings, with the *Times* Sunday edition especially complete.

The *Amsterdam News* is Manhattan's African-American daily, and *El Diario La Prensa* is the highest-circulation Spanish-language newspaper.

The weekly publications covering New York are almost as numerous as the dailies and often are better places to check for coming events. Leading the pack is the august *New Yorker,* which covers the cultural scene in the Goings on About Town section. *New York* magazine became the model for city-oriented publications throughout the country when it was started in the late 1960s, and it also contains extensive listings. *Time Out: New York* keeps its slick eye on the latest city action, and the *New York Observer* is a salmon-sheeted weekly paper with news and gossip catering to what the politician Jerry Brown used to call "the chattering class"—the city's media elite.

The weekly *New York Blade* and *LGNY* newspapers and the *HX* and *Next* bar 'zines cover the gay community.

The Paper, a monthly, often spots trends before other publications and has good listings. But to keep current on what's happening, you need not spend a dime. The *Village Voice* covers the cultural scene and the political landscape. Its rival, the weekly *NY Press,* is lively and inclusive, if a bit shrill.

■ USEFUL WEB SITES

Dot City. The Web site of the Dorothy Parker Society of New York, with info about the author's haunts and friends; *www.dorothyparker.com*

Forgotten NY. The city's past bleeds into the present in the signs, alleys, subway stations and trains, old advertisements, and other elements documented on this captivating site; *www.forgotten-ny.com*

Metropolitan Transit Authority. Up-to-date information on New York City subways and buses; *www.mta.nyc.ny.us*

New York: A Documentary Film. Web site for the five-part, ten-hour PBS film about New York City; *www.pbs.org/wnet/new york*

New York Locator. Find the cross streets of north-south avenues; *www.ny.com/locator*

New York Metro. Lively, readable site covers arts, entertainment, shopping, and dining, and includes *New York* magazine's annual Best of New York listings; *www.newyorkmetro.com*

New York Parks and Recreation Department. Location, hours, and other information about city parks; *www.nycparks.com*

Paper Magazine. Groovy *Paper* site will keep you au courant; *www.papermag.com*

Ticketweb.com. Tickets for museums, cruises, nightclubs, and other venues and events; *www.ticketweb.com*

Theatrewire.com. Reviews, previews, and features on theater, dance, music, and performance art; *www.nytheatre-wire.com*

TKTS. Discount day-of-performance theater, dance, and music tickets; *www.tdf.org*

United Nations. All about the world organization, plus information about tours; *www.un.org*

Village Voice. Web site of New York's original alternative weekly newspaper contains articles and listings; *www.villagevoice.com*

RECOMMENDED READING

■ NONFICTION

Allen, Irving Lewis. *The City in Slang: New York Life and Popular Speech.* Oxford: Oxford University Press, 1993. Love letter to city disguised as an academic text.

Anbinder, Tyler. *Five Points: The Nineteenth-Century New York City Neighborhood That Invented Tap Dance, Stole Elections and Became the World's Most Notorious Slum.* New York: Free Press, 2001. Essential primer on Manhattan's 19th-century underbelly.

Asbury, Herbert. *The Gangs of New York: An Informal History of the Underworld.* New York: Thunder's Mouth Press, 2001. Breezy look at the boys on the street was the basis for the Martin Scorsese film *Gangs of New York.*

Bayles, W. Harrison. *Old Taverns of New York.* New York: Frank Allaben Genealogical Company, 1915. Historic anecdotes about the city's oldest pubs.

Brecher, Charles and Raymond D. Horton. *Power Failure: New York City Politics and Policy since 1960.* Oxford: Oxford University Press, 1993. A scholarly guide through the labyrinthine world of local government.

Burrows, Edwin G., and Mike Wallace. *Gotham: A History of New York City to 1898.* New York: Oxford University Press, 2000. A Pulitzer Prize–winner that's dense with information but highly readable.

Caro, Robert. *The Power Broker: Robert Moses and the Fall of New York.* New York: Viking, 1975. Moses was the man most responsible for the way New York looks and works today, and Caro is relentless in giving him his due.

Cohen, Paul E., and Augustyn, Robert T. *Manhattan in Maps: 1527-1995.* New York: Rizzoli, 1997. Watch as the city cartologically morphs through time.

Cudahy, Brian J. *Over and Back: The History of Ferryboats in New York Harbor.* New York: Fordham University Press, 1990. A loving tribute.

Diamonstein, Barbaralee. *The Landmarks of New York II.* New York: Harry Abrams, Inc., 1993. The newly updated definitive study.

Dreiser, Theodore. *The Color of a Great City.* New York: Howard Fertig, Inc., 1987. These sociological essays portray early 20th-century New York, but those describing the chasm between rich and poor could have been written yesterday.

Friedman, Josh Alan. *Tales of Times Square.* Portland: Feral House, 1993. Disturbed, disturbing, gut-wrenchingly funny bulletins from the pre-Disney era.

Gilfoyle, Timothy J. *City of Eros: New York City, Prostitution and the Commercialization of Sex, 1790–1920.* New York: W.W. Norton, 1992. The world's oldest profession, Gotham-style.

Grannick, Harry. *Underneath New York.* New York: Fordham University Press, 1991. Just what the title says. Written in 1947 and a little dated now, but not much changes underground.

Hawes, Elizabeth. *New York, New York: How the Apartment House Transformed the Life of the City.* New York: Knopf, 1993. Lively chronicle of a social upheaval, forced by spiraling real estate values.

Homberger, Eric, and Alice Hudson. *The Historical Atlas of New York City: A Visual Celebration of Nearly 400 Years of New York City's History.* New York: Henry Holt, 1998. The city's history, mapped.

Hood, Clifton. *722 Miles: The Building of the Subways and How They Transformed New York.* New York: Simon & Schuster, 1993. Academic study on the subways—curse and salvation of Manhattan.

Howe, Irving, and Kenneth Libo, eds. *How We Lived: A Documentary History of Immigrant Jews in America 1880–1930.* New York: Richard Marek Publishers, 1979. Short personal accounts and descriptions as told by Jewish immigrants of their early days in the new country.

Jackson, Kenneth T. *The Encyclopedia of New York City.* New Haven: Yale University Press, 1995. Exhaustive, exhausting, and, believe it or not, a page-turner for anyone who loves the city.

Kinkead, Gwen. *Chinatown: A Portrait of a Closed Society.* New York: Harper Collins, 1992. It may be closed to most people, but not to her. Excellent.

Lebowitz, Fran. *Metropolitan Life.* New York: Dutton/New American Library, 1988. Insights into New York style, art, and pop culture in the form of entertaining—often snippy—tales.

Lewis, David Levering. *When Harlem Was In Vogue.* Oxford: Oxford University Press, 1979. A social history of the Harlem Renaissance and the New Negro Movement.

Lewis, Michael. *Liar's Poker.* New York: Penguin Books, 1989. A look inside the psyches of stockbrokers and bond traders at Salomon Brothers, one of New York's most famous brokerage firms.

Mackay, David A. *The Building of Manhattan.* New York: Harper & Row, 1987. With perfectly rendered line drawings, a chronicle of how the borough evolved.

McNickle, Chris. *To Be Mayor of New York: Ethnic Politics in the City.* New York: Columbia University Press, 1993. Why would anyone want to be mayor? This book may not answer that question, but it tells you how mayors from O'Dwyer to Dinkins achieved the post.

Miller, Terry. *Greenwich Village and How It Got That Way.* New York: Crown, 1990. Lavish, full-color treatment of everybody's favorite neighborhood.

Mitchell, Joseph. *Up in the Old Hotel.* New York: Pantheon Books, 1992. Beautifully drawn word-portraits of city folk, as you'll hope to meet them.

Morehouse, Ward. *The Waldorf-Astoria: America's Gilded Dream.* New York: M. Evans, 1991. If any hotel deserves to have a book written about it, the Waldorf is it.

Morris, Jan. *Manhattan '45.* Oxford: Oxford University Press, 1987. A snapshot of a golden time, by a consummate travel writer.

Moscow, Henry. *The Street Book.* New York: Fordham University Press, 1978. How the streets of Manhattan came to be named.

Riis, Jacob. *How the Other Half Lives: Studies Among the Tenements of New York.* New York: Hill & Wang, 1957. When it was published in 1890, this book and its astonishing photos changed New York's treatment of its poor.

Salwen, Peter. *Upper West Side Story: A History and Guide.* New York: Abbeville Press, 1989. Well-researched study of a great residential neighborhood.

Sante, Luc. *Low Life: Lures and Snares of Old New York.* New York: Random House, 1991. Superb, rich, interpretive history, quirky and engrossing.

Schwartzman, Paul and Rob Polner. *New York Notorious.* New York: Crown, 1992. A borough-by-borough tour of the city's most infamous crime scenes.

Sleeper, Jim. *The Closest of Strangers: Liberalism and the Politics of Race in New York.* New York: Norton, 1990. Neoconservative musings, on the order of "Can't we all just get along?"

White, E. B. *Essays of E. B. White.* New York: Harper & Row, 1977. If you can only read one thing about the city, read "Here Is New York."

■ FICTION

Alford, Henry. *Municipal Bondage: One Man's Anxiety-Producing Adventures in the Big City.* New York: Random House, 1993. A highly amusing tale of woe about a wannabe entrepreneur.

Auster, Paul. *The New York Trilogy: City of Glass, Ghosts and The Locked Room.* New York: Viking, 1991. Spooky, post-postmodernist thrillers, deconstructing Manhattan.

Baldwin, James. *Go Tell It on the Mountain.* New York: Delta Books, 2000. The compelling story of a young black man growing up in Manhattan; first published in 1953.

Cohn, Nik. *The Heart of the World.* New York, Viking, 1992. A journey up Manhattan's Main Street, with stories.

Crane, Stephen. *Maggie.* New York: Modern Library, 2000. Seminal realist studies of crime and degradation a century ago in New York, and the conditions that spawned them.

Doctorow, E. L. *The Waterworks.* New York: Knopf, 1993. With this book, and with *Ragtime, World's Fair,* and *Billy Bathgate,* Doctorow has been slowly assembling a dazzling fictional chronicle of New York.

VERY SOPHISTICATED

In case you don't live in New York, the Wicker Bar is in this sort of swanky hotel, the Seton Hotel. I used to go there quite a lot, but I don't any more. I gradually cut it out. It's one of those places that are supposed to be very sophisticated and all, and the phonies are coming in the window. They used to have these two French babes, Tina and Janine, come out and play the piano and sing about three times every night. One of them played the piano—strictly lousy—and the other one sang, and most of the songs were either pretty dirty or in French....

It was pretty early when I got there. I sat down at the bar—it was pretty crowded—and had a couple of Scotch and sodas before old Luce even showed up. I stood up when I ordered them so they could see how tall I was and all and not think I was a goddam minor. Then I watched the phonies for a while. Some guy next to me was snowing hell out of the babe he was with. He kept telling her she had aristocratic hands. That killed me.

—J. D. Salinger, *The Catcher in the Rye*, 1951

Dos Passos, John. *Manhattan Transfer.* New York: Harper Bros., 1925. Jazz Age sketches of the city and its occupants.

Ellison, Ralph. *The Invisible Man.* New York: Vintage, 1995. Being black in Harlem in the 1950s, with universal applications.

Fitzgerald, F. Scott. *The Beautiful and Damned.* New York: Modern Library, 2002. The author's second novel, set just before and after World War I, depicts a glamorous Manhattan couple on a downward spiral.

Gran, Sara. *Saturn's Return to New York.* New York: Dial Press, 2001. Deft treatment of loss in Manhattan.

Hijuelos, Oscar. *Our House in the Last World.* New York: Pocket Books, 1978. Latino New York, centered on the post-World War II period. More recent years are described in Hijuelos's *The Mambo Kings Play Songs of Love* (New York: Farrar, Straus & Giroux, 1989).

Hughes, Langston. *Selected Poems of Langston Hughes.* New York: Knopf, 1929. Hughes's poetic voice sings the blues of the Jazz Age.

Hustvedt, Siri. *The Blindfold.* New York: Norton, 1992. Weird, shimmering stories of a Columbia graduate student getting swallowed up by the city.

James, Henry. *Washington Square.* New York: Modern Library, 1997. Incisive drawing-room drama of New York's patrician classes.

Janowitz, Tama. *Slaves of New York.* New York: Pocket, 1986. A collection of connected stories about a collection of disconnected people on the fringes of the '80s Manhattan cultural scene.

McInerney, Jay. *Bright Lights, Big City.* New York: Vintage, 1988. A phenomenon when published, the novel holds up as a ironic portrait of urban alienation.

Runyon, Damon. *Guys and Dolls: Three Volumes in One.* Philadelphia: Lippincott, 1929. Peopling a vast and incomparable New York of the imagination.

Salinger, J. D. *The Catcher in the Rye.* New York: Little, Brown, 1991. The classic post–World War II coming-of-age story, when a student ventures into the big city and meets only "phonies."

Schickler, David. *Kissing in Manhattan.* New York: Dial Press, 2001. Linked stories that, like some Manhattanites they portray, are only superficially superficial.

Wharton, Edith. *The House of Mirth.* New York: Bantam, 1984. Along with *The Age of Innocence* (New York: Macmillan, 1992) and other novels, Wharton's oeuvre represents a trenchant look at 19th-century Manhattan.

Wolfe, Tom. *Bonfire of the Vanities.* New York: Bantam, 1987. Marvelous fictional satire, puncturing the overinflated balloon of the '80s.

INDEX

COMPASS AMERICAN GUIDES

Alaska

American Southwest

Arizona

Boston

Chicago

Coastal California

Colorado

Florida

Georgia

Gulf South: Louisiana,
Alabama, Mississippi

Hawaii

Idaho

Kentucky

Las Vegas

Maine

Manhattan

Michigan

Minnesota

Montana

Nevada

New Hampshire

New Mexico

New Orleans

North Carolina

Oregon

Pacific Northwest

Pennsylvania

San Francisco

Santa Fe

South Carolina

South Dakota

Southern New England

Tennessee

Texas

Utah

Vermont

Virginia

Wine Country

Wisconsin

Wyoming

◼ About the Authors

Gil Reavill and Jean Zimmerman are the coauthors of *Raising Our Athletic Daughters: How Sports Can Raise Self Esteem and Save Girls' Lives.* Husband and wife as well as writing collaborators, they have published magazine articles and books, as a team and individually, on varied subjects.

◼ About the Photographers

Kelly Guenther was part of the team of *New York Times* photographers that won a Pulitzer Prize for breaking coverage of the attack on New York City on September 11, 2001. A frequent contributor to the *Times,* she has been published in *Time, Newsweek,* and *American Photo,* among other media outlets, and was on the staff of the *Minneapolis Star Tribune.* She lives in Brooklyn and works as a freelancer.

After spending a year as a foreign student at an art school in New York City, photographer Poul Hans Lange was so taken with the city that he moved there permanently from his native Denmark in 1989. He lives in Manhattan's East Village, which serves as a constant inspiration for his photography as well as his illustration and design projects. His work has appeared in numerous publications and has been shown in galleries in the United States and Europe.

ACKNOWLEDGMENTS

Compass American Guides acknowledges the following institutions and individuals for the use of their photographs, illustrations, or both: **American Museum of Natural History,** p. 261 (photo by Denis Finnin); **Jorg Brockman,** pp. 189, 190; **Brooklyn Botanic Garden,** p. 289; **Margaret Clinton Burt,** p. 232; **Café des Artistes,** p. 256, 257; **Cooper-Hewitt National Design Museum, Smithsonian Institution/Art Resource NY,** pp. 227 (photo by Matt Flynn), 244 (photo by Dave King); **Eileen Costa,** p. 290; **El Museo del Barrio,** p. 281 (photo by Eddie Bartolomei); **F.A.O. Schwarz,** p. 194; **Four Seasons Hotel,** p. 196; **Frick Collection, New York,** pp. 234–235 (photo by John Bigelow Taylor), 236 (photo by Richard di Liberto); **Matthew Girard,** p. 270; **Grand Central Oyster Bar,** pp. 174, 231. **Kelly Guenther,** pp. 8, 11, 16, 62, 63, 65, 67, 74, 77, 78, 93, 96, 105, 107, 116–117, 122, 124, 127, 132, 133, 139, 140–141, 143, 144, 145, 147, 177, 180, 184, 186, 203, 215, 220, 221, 223, 272, 274, 277, 288; **Jones Long LaSalle,** p. 173; **Poul Hans Lange,** pp. 12–13, 24, 56, 82–83, 85, 86, 87, 90, 91, 100, 108, 109, 115, 119, 122, 123, 128–129, 153, 158, 161, 163, 171, 188, 191, 198–199, 207, 212–213, 217, 252, 258, 262, 263, 283, 285; **La Guardia and Wagner Archives, La Guardia Community College, City University of New York,** p. 50; **Library of Congress, Geography and Map Division,** p. 45; **Library of Congress, Prints and Photographs Division,** pp. 19, 29, 31 (both images; top (LC-USZC4-1799), 42, 53 (Detroit Publishing Company; LC-USZC4-6821), 61 (LC-USZ62-88424), 66, 73 (LC-USZ62-8681), 99 (George Grantham Bain Collection; LC-USZ62-114764), 101, 135 (LC-USZ62-97525), 152 (LC-USZ62-97525), 157 (LC-USZ62-120926), 201, 279, 298 (Westinghouse, LC-USZ62-93231); **Lower East Side Tenement Museum,** p. 103; **Metropolitan Museum of Art,** pp. 238–239, 242; **Morgan Library,** p.155, Todd Eberle; **Museum of the City of New York, Print Archives,** pp. 21, 28 (gift of Rita and Murray Hartstein), 39, 47 (gift of Essex Sust), 246, 275 (Federal Arts Project, Changing New York); **National Academy of Design,** p. 214; **National Park Service, Statue of Liberty National Monument,** p. 40–41, 71; **New-York Historical Society,** pp. 33 (54615), 43 (31110), 104 (37363), 112 (4633), 148 (59044), 249 (31047), 250 (60883); **New York Stock Exchange,** p. 75; **New York Yankees,** p. 310; **PhotoDisc,** p. 68, 70, 252; **Plaza Hotel,** p. 193; **Solomon R. Guggenheim Foundation, New York,** p. 243 (David Heald); **Wildlife Conservation Center,** p. 287. **Michael Yamashita,** pp. 3, 89, 150, 168, 172, 182, 225, 264, 266.

Compass American Guides also wishes to thank Willard Jenkins for the original Manhattan Jazz sidebar (page 125), revised for this edition; Nina Mehta for copyediting the manuscript and Rachel Elson for proofreading it; and Chris Culwell and Grael Norton for fact-checking and additional research.